college
A PRACTICAL APPROACH
accounting

CUSTOM EDITION FOR NIAGARA COLLEGE

JEFFREY SLATER

AND

BRIAN ZWICKER

10th ED

Taken from:

College Accounting: A Practical Approach, Canadian Tenth Edition
by Jeffrey Slater and Brian Zwicker

Custom Publishing

New York   Boston   San Francisco
London   Toronto   Sydney   Tokyo   Singapore   Madrid
Mexico City   Munich   Paris   Cape Town   Hong Kong   Montreal

Cover Art: Courtesy of PhotoDisc/Getty Images.

Taken from:

College Accounting: A Practical Approach, Canadian Tenth Edition
by Jeffrey Slater and Brian Zwicker
Copyright © 2009, 2006, 2003, 2000, 1996, 1993, 1991 by Pearson Education Canada
A division of Pearson Canada Inc.
Toronto, Ontario
Canada

This special edition published in cooperation with Pearson Custom Publishing.

Printed in Canada

10 9 8 7 6 5 4 3 2 1

2009160499

BK

Pearson
Custom Publishing
is a division of

www.pearsonhighered.com

ISBN 10: 0-558-38090-5
ISBN 13: 978-0-558-38090-8

Dedicated to the memory of
Russell Maxwell Zwicker and Alma Lorraine Zwicker
B.Z.

Brief Contents

Contents

Preface

Use of computers to process accounting transactions, as well as conduct ebusiness, is taken for granted in many businesses today. Accounting students need to learn the skills that will help them succeed in business using technology. The Canadian Tenth Edition of *College Accounting: A Practical Approach* by Jeffrey Slater and Brian Zwicker helps students learn and integrate these skills by infusing the tried-and-true Slater/Zwicker system with real-world applications. Each chapter begins with a business-related vignette that helps students think about modern business activities and accounting. The Continuing Problem at the end of each chapter encourages students to apply their skills to a practical case. Throughout the book, students also read about real accounting applications in the realistic Subway scenarios that feature both local franchise operations and corporate support functions. As well, students have plenty of opportunity to learn computer accounting skills by completing carefully-crafted computer workshops using Simply Accounting® Pro and Quickbooks® Pro. The accompanying CD includes the Computer Workshops, instructions, appropriate data sets and step-by-step guides to using them.

New to This Edition

Now includes 24 chapters! In a major revamping of the book's content, the number of chapters has been increased from 16 to 24. This increase has been accomplished using two strategies:

a) Two completely new chapters have been added:

Chapter 15—Accounting for Property, Plant, Equipment, and Intangible Assets

Chapter 16—Statement of Cash Flows

b) Eight auxiliary chapters have been included on the accompanying CD:

Chapter 17—Analyzing Financial Statements

Chapter 18—Notes Receivable and Notes Payable

Chapter 19—Accounting for Merchandise Inventory

Chapter 20—Partnerships and Corporations

Chapter 21—Corporations—Bonds Payable

Chapter 22—The Voucher System

Chapter 23—Departmental Accounting

Chapter 24—Manufacturing Accounting

Chapters 17 and 20 to 24 are from the tenth U.S. edition of *College Accounting* and Chapters 18 and 19 are taken from previous editions of *College Accounting*. These new chapters should assist instructors who need to extend their students' education, while keeping the text's price under control. In general, the chapters continued from an earlier Canadian edition retain all the features instructors have come to appreciate (there are C-type problems, and even a computer workshop for Chapter 19).

Expanded Coverage of Banking Trends. This material was already the best available in Canada, but has been further upgraded to allow coverage at an enhanced level. Additional problem material has been developed and will be appreciated by any instructor who aims to provide students with plenty of practice in this vital area. In addition, the introductory part of the chapter has been completely replaced to give it a more contemporary tone. Aspects of modern banking realities in Canada are covered in greater detail

The Slater/Zwicker System. The tenth edition retains the proven pedagogy that has made *College Accounting* a classic.

Simply Accounting Pro and QuickBooks Pro Software Available! At the time of publication, the Professional versions of both these award-winning applications are offered to students free of charge by the software companies. Please check with either Sage Inc. (for Simply) or Intuit Canada Inc. (for QuickBooks) for details. You can also package this text with desired software at a small additional charge. Please speak to your local Pearson representative about this feature.

Features

Step-by-Step Guides to Computer Workshops. These detailed guides lead students through the entire process of completing each computer workshop. These guides are fully illustrated with full-colour screen grabs. This excellent feature has proven extremely popular with all students, but may be of special interest to the increasing proportion of students who approach their education through distance education courses. The detailed guide to one of the workshops in each chapter is included free to all students on the Student CD. The detailed guides for the other workshops are included on the instructor's CD and can be made available to students at the discretion of the instructor. This has been done to permit instructors to use selected workshops as examination material if that is desired.

Newly Revised Chapter Openers. Revised chapter opening vignettes introduce students to business realities and accounting. These opening scenarios are refreshing, easy to read, and interesting, and are mostly based on actual businesses in Canada. All readers should appreciate the creativity and appropriateness these short introductions provide.

Continuing Problem. A Continuing Problem runs through Chapters 1-14, asking students to apply skills to the business scenario set in the Big Picture. It is based on the Precision Computer Centre. The continuing problem is included in two of the auxiliary chapters as well (Chapters 19 and 20).

Payroll Updated. Chapters 7 and 8 have been rewritten where necessary to reflect the latest laws and taxation deduction rules in effect in Canada.

GST and HST Accounting. These taxes are a reality in Canada. The essential details of how to account for GST and HST are covered, beginning in Chapter 9. Chapters 9 and 10 have been designed to accommodate instructors who choose either to emphasize or to de-emphasize these topics.

Special Journal Coverage Continued. Canadian students will continue to have available first-class coverage of this important aspect of accounting. This decision was based on the rationale that a detailed description of special journals in manual form will greatly assist students when they first encounter the realities of computer accounting. The coverage of this worthwhile and practical material has been moved to the accompanying CD.

Subway Boxes. The real-world accounting issues facing franchise owners and corporate staff are presented in boxed features based on research of the internationally known company. Discussion questions tie the boxes to chapter concepts. The Subway boxes appear in selected Auxiliary Chapters on the CD.

Check Figures. Brief mention of key amounts, or other hints in the margins, continue to provide quick feedback for students to monitor progress in all of the A and B, and most of the C problems.

Chapter on Partnerships and Corporations. Canadian students appreciate having a chapter that covers the essentials of these two alternative forms of business activity. Based on excerpts from three chapters in the U.S. edition, yet completely rewritten for the Canadian business environment, this chapter has proven to be a popular and useful addition.

Extensive End-of-Chapter Framework. Each chapter offers extensive learning aids, including

- Discussion Questions/Classroom Demonstration Exercises
- Exercises
- Problem sets A, B, and C (D problems are supplied separately)
- Exploring E-Biz Internet exercises that put your students on the web. Now moved to the text website, based on feedback from reviewers.
- Continuing Problem: a cumulative problem that runs through Chapters 1 to 14, asking students to work through the entire business cycle for Precision Computer Centre.

- Simulations available in selected chapters. Many students will benefit from completing the extended and realistic cases that are presented at the end of chapters 5, 8, and 13.

The Slater/Zwicker Package

The text is just the starting point. Because the needs of Canadian instructors are very high on our priority list, we have taken certain other steps designed to maximize instructor effectiveness and efficiency. These steps include the provision of an Instructor's Resource Manual, Instructor's Solution Manual and Pearson TestGen, which are all available on the Instructor's Resource CD-ROM or downloadable from the Pearson online catalogue. We also offer a Study Guide with Working Papers. We have invested a great many hours into ensuring the highest quality possible, and we hope it shows in increased clarity, accuracy, and consistency. Let's look at some of the support systems included in the Slater/Zwicker package.

Instructor's Package

Instructor's Resource Manual. Newly expanded for this edition, the IRM brings together all the materials that facilitate and augment each instructor's special skills, strengths, and experience. It includes

- **Course Management Assistance.** Many schools take advantage of one of the popular course management platforms—WebCT, CourseCompass, or BlackBoard. If you need assistance with setting up courses for any of these packages, it can be quickly obtained using directions found on the IRM.

- **Type D Problems.** Like the C-type problems in the text, these problems are slightly more challenging than the A or B problems. Solutions are provided (also in the Instructor's Resource Manual) so these new problems can be used in interesting ways—such as for extra-challenging work for students, or on quizzes or examinations. The headings for most of the C-type problems in the Study Guide with Working Papers have been deliberately left off (at the request of a number of instructors). This means these forms can be used for the D-type problems as well, if that is convenient.

- **Computer Workshop Guides/Solutions.** The computer workshops have been customized for both Simply Accounting Pro and QuickBooks Pro (both applications are available free, as previously mentioned). Each student is also provided with a detailed, step-by-step guide to completing one of the workshops at the end of each chapter. In addition to the detailed guide supplied on the student CD, the instructor CD contains a detailed guide for the other workshop at the end of selected chapters. This allows instructors to better control this important feature and help ensure they are used appropriately— i.e., not as a substitute for learning. Naturally, a solution data set is provided for each of the computer workshops. This provides all instructors with a starting point for providing feedback to students who complete them.

- **Class Quizzes.** These short exercises or review questions are designed to reinforce aspects of the chapter coverage.

- **Class Activities.** The whole class can take part in these activities in order to review and reinforce key points.

- **Lesson Outlines.** Chapter material is designed for a variety of classroom situations. There is probably a style that closely fits most educational institutions' scheduling preferences.

- **Typical Student Misconceptions.** This identification of common errors gathered from almost 50 years of accounting teaching experience may be valuable—especially to instructors just beginning their careers.

- **Teaching Tips.** Valuable suggestions help students remember and assimilate the material.

- **Business-world Notes.** These cover what actually happens in accounting in the real world and take students beyond the textbook

- **Lecture Notes.** While not intended to replace an appropriate lesson plan, these notes may be very useful as a check that nothing critical is overlooked.

Instructor's Solutions Manual. This manual provides answers to discussion questions and solutions to exercises, problems, practice problems, and classroom demonstration exercises. The manual also offers guidance in the discussion of ethical issues.

In the front of the Solutions Manual is a grid of all problems showing level of difficulty and estimated time needed for completion.

To ensure accurate solutions, each page of the Solutions Manual was carefully reviewed by Laurence P. Hanchard, C.A. His exacting review will be appreciated by all instructors using this package.

Pearson TestGen. The Pearson TestGen is a computerized version of the Test Item File. It enables instructors to view and edit the existing questions, add questions, generate tests, and print the tests in a variety of formats. Powerful search and sort functions make it easy to locate questions and arrange them in any order desired. TestGen also enables instructors to administer tests on a local area network, have the tests graded electronically, and have the results prepared in electronic or printed reports. The TestGen is compatible with PC or Macintosh systems.

For Students

Study Guide with Working Papers. This publication has undergone all necessary revisions and enhancements. It contains forms for the quiz at the end of each learning unit in the chapter, for all exercises, for the problems (A, B, and C) at the end of each chapter, and for the practice-set problems that follow Chapters 5, 8, and 13. In addition, all worksheets are treated as foldouts—an appreciated enhancement by all accounts. At the end of each, there is a summary practice test designed to prepare students for in-class exams. It consists of fill-in-the-blank questions, a matching question, and true/false questions. As with the previous editions, the Study Guide with Working Papers is a completely Canadian publication. Many changes have been made to help ensure that each student's experience is as effective and efficient as possible.

Special Text Website with Internet Exercises and Simply Accounting Pro and QuickBooks Pro Data Sets. Our exciting website includes Internet Exercises for every chapter. It also features the data sets for the computer workshops in the text, and these will be updated each year as new versions of the software are released. A syllabus builder for instructors is also available. See **www.pearsoned.ca/text/slater** and explore.

Student Resource CD-ROM. Accompanying every copy of this text is a copy of the Student CD, which includes

- **Accounting Cycle Tutorial (ACT).** This new feature gives students online practice and a review of the accounting cycle. The tutorial is directed specifically at the first five chapters.

- **Expanded Computer Workshops.** Continuing with this edition is the inclusion of updated computer accounting workshops in Chapters 3-6, 8-10, 13 & 15. These workshops are available in two different formats: Simply Accounting Pro and QuickBooks Pro. These two accounting software packages represent the best available in Canada, and are the most popular, based on total sales.

- **Auxiliary Chapters 17-24**
  Offered in PDF format, these auxiliary chapters will assist instructors who need to extend their students' education, while keeping the text's price under control.

- **Appendices A & B**
  Appendix A offers additional information on Special Journals and Credit Card Sales, while Appendix B offers a clear ovierview of the steps in a computerized accounting system.

- **Appendices to accompany Chapters 9, 10 and 12: Extensive Perpetual Coverage Inventory**
  The special appendix that accompanies Chapter 9 uses the general journal approach to teach entries for a merchandise company using perpetual inventory while the appendix for Chapter 10 shows how all the special journals in Chapters 9 and 10 would look in a perpetual system. The related appendix for Chapter 12 shows how a worksheet for a merchandise company would look in a perpetual inventory system. Auxiliary Chapter 19 extends this coverage in a very complete way, where the bulk of the material is directed to perpetual inventory issues. A very realistic computer workshop is made available in this chapter for those who would benefit from this added challenge.

The Accountant's Toolbox. Pearson Education Canada is proud to present The Accountant's Toolbox, a portal to the best accounting websites on the internet. Whether you are a student or an instructor, it will give you access to the latest information from the world of accounting.

Using The Accountant's Toolbox drop-down menu on Pearson Education Canada's AccountingCentral home page, you can link to dozens of websites grouped into the following broad categories: International, Careers, Firms, Resources, Tax, Software, and Humour. You can access The Accountant's Toolbox by visiting **www.pearsoned.ca/accounting**.

Be sure to visit The Accountant's Toolbox when you need accounting information on the Internet. And don't forget to check it out frequently for new features and updates!

Acknowledgments

The task of publishing a Canadian edition of any textbook is a challenging venture. In this case it helped to be working from an outstanding original and with an outstanding team.

Thanks are certainly due to the many helpful folks at Pearson Education Canada, including Senior Acquisitions Editor Samantha Scully, Assistant Editor Mary Wong, Production Editor Mary Ann Field and Production Coordinator Andrea Falkenberg. And special thanks to copy editor Rodney Rawlings for his diligence and hard work.

Thanks are also due to the following reviewers who provided valuable criticism and suggestions during the development of the manuscript: Maureen Antonio (Saskatchewan Institute of Applied Science and Technology, Wascana campus), Alice Beddoe (Fanshawe College), Grace Credico (Lethbridge Community College), Augusta Ford (College of the North Atlantic), Fran Maksymiw (Saskatchewan Institute of Applied Science and Technology, Palliser campus), and Muriel Towriss (Saskatchewan Institute of Applied Science and Technology, Palliser campus).

The *Study Guide with Working Papers* and the *Solutions Manual* were created by Pat Tuttle, whose skills with the software used are substantial. Pat cheerfully took on several other tasks as well, and in general made the whole process run quite smoothly.

My final thanks go to Laurie Hanchard who, once again, not only carried out his assigned duties of reviewing the text, the Study Guide with Working Papers, and the Solutions Manual with remarkable care and attention, but also took it as a personal goal to add substantial value to the overall package. The text—indeed, all aspects of this project—is much improved because of Laurie's caring and thoughtful review.

Despite the best efforts of so many talented people, it is inevitable that a few errors will persist. I accept responsibility for them and would appreciate your help in identifying them so that they can be totally eliminated in future printings.

Brian Zwicker
Edmonton, Alberta
e-mail me at: brian@bzwicker.ca

Testimonial

As requested, I have read the first pass pages of *College Accounting*, Canadian Tenth Edition, by Slater and Zwicker, Chapters 1-16. I have also read the pages of the *Study Guide with Working Papers* and the *Solutions Manual for College Accounting*. I checked the arithmetic and logic in all three books with respect to the worked examples and exhibits in the proofed copies. I also ensured that the references to these examples and exhibits within the text were accurate.

Laurence P. Hanchard, C.A.

1 Accounting Concepts and Procedures

An Introduction

THE BIG PICTURE

In the summer of 2000, Nortel—one of Canada's leading companies, which sells products related to the new electronic economy—saw its share price fall from more than $200 to less than $40. Nortel's shares were listed on the Toronto and New York stock exchanges, and many investors saw their investment in this company plunge in value.

What went wrong? A huge number of articles have tried to explain this dramatic fall in share price. In the end, everyone had to agree that the fall happened because the people who buy such stocks had determined that the high prices paid up to the first half of 2000 were much too inflated according to a realistic assessment of the company's prospects.

What factors help in deciding how much a share is worth? In simple terms, stock exchanges help buyers and sellers do business with each other. Prices of shares are not set by these exchanges—they just provide a marketplace where sales can occur in an organized way. The prices for Nortel shares, as for all shares trading on stock exchanges, are set by market forces. The price you get if you sell is determined by the price another person is willing to pay.

Stock exchanges exist in most countries. They are a vital part of those economies, because business activity is an essential element in society. Many things influence the prices investors are willing to pay for any given share: who heads up the company, the economic forecast for the industry, recent significant events like mergers or amalgamations, and so on. But by anyone's measurement system, the most influential factor affecting share prices is the accounting reports the company prepares and sends to its shareholders (and others).

Accounting has been called the language of business, and with excellent reason. There is a need in the business world for a reliable means of communicating financial events in a clear and precise way. Accounting meets the criteria for such a communication system and today exists as a profession, the members of which earn their livelihood preparing, distributing, auditing, and interpreting such financial reports.

But the need for accurate and reliable accounting reports and information is not restricted to companies like Nortel, whose shares are listed on major exchanges. All businesses (and many other entities like churches, associations, etc.) rely on accounting reports to help them manage their affairs and meet their goals. This book is for anyone who wants to know how the basics of accounting work. It is practical and useful, and will serve well the needs of those who wish to learn the basics.

Shares in Nortel hit a low of $0.69 in 2002 before gradually climbing back to $2.40 by December 2006. With so many Canadians owning Nortel shares as part of their pension plans or mutual funds, it remains a much-watched stock. Where will the price go in the future? If you know the answer to that question, please let me know, because like most people I am interested in making a few million dollars.

During the past few years, you could pick up almost any newspaper and read stories about financial scandals. In the United States, the events related to WorldCom and Enron are good examples, while here in Canada, Nortel Networks Corporation has created headlines. Were these companies "cooking the books"? With jail sentences of up to 25 years for some of the corporate officers convicted of unlawful activities, the answer is clearly—yes! In the United States, a federal statute called the **Sarbanes-Oxley Act** was passed into law to help prevent future attempts to defraud the public. In Canada, the Ontario Securities Commission has created National Policies (Numbers 58-102—which gave birth to the Canadian Public Accountability Board—and 58-201) that cover much the same thing. Both countries are attempting to increase the focus on internal controls, the role and responsibility of auditors, and increased penalties for business fraud in order to improve the accuracy and reliability of published accounting reports.

> Many corporate executives feel that Sarbanes-Oxley is too strict and costly to implement. In Canada, our new legislation is seen as less objectionable—possibly because our laws did not require as much of a change as in the United States.

Accounting is the language of business; it provides information to managers, owners, investors, governmental agencies, and others inside and outside the organization. Accounting provides answers and insights to questions like these:

◆ Should I invest in Amazon.com?

◆ Is Subway's cash balance sufficient?

◆ Will Internet companies show a good return in the future?

◆ Can Air Canada pay its debt obligations?

◆ What percentage of IBM's marketing budget is for e-business? How does this compare with the competition? What is the overall financial condition of IBM?

Smaller businesses also need answers to their financial questions:

◆ Did business increase enough over the last year to warrant hiring a new assistant?

◆ Should we spend more money to design, produce, and send out new brochures in an effort to create more business?

◆ What role should the Internet play in our business?

> The Internet is creating many new opportunities and challenges for all forms of business organizations.

Accounting is as important to individuals as it is to businesses; it answers questions like:

◆ Should I take out a loan for a new car or wait until I can afford to pay cash?

◆ Would my money work better in a chartered bank or in a credit union savings plan?

Accounting is the process that analyzes, records, classifies, summarizes, reports, and interprets financial information for decision-makers—whether individuals, small businesses, large corporations, or governmental agencies—in a timely fashion. It is important that students understand the "whys" of the accounting process. Just knowing the mechanics is not enough.

TABLE 1-1 Types of Business Organization

	Sole Proprietorship	Partnership	Corporation
Ownership	Business owned by one person	Business owned by more than one person	Business owned by shareholders
Formation	Easy to form	Easy to form	More difficult to form
Liability	Owner could lose personal assets to meet obligations of business	Partners could lose personal assets to meet obligations of partnership	Limited personal risk; shareholders' loss is usually limited to their investment in the company
Closing	Ends with death of owner or closing of business	Ends with death of a partner or exit of a partner	Can continue indefinitely

CATEGORIES OF BUSINESS ORGANIZATION

There are three main categories of business organization: (1) sole proprietorship, (2) partnership, and (3) corporation. Let's define each of them and look at their advantages and disadvantages. This information also appears in Table 1-1, and is more extensively discussed in one of the auxiliary chapters now appearing on the CD that accompanies this text.

Sole Proprietorship

A **sole proprietorship** is a business that has one owner. That person is both the owner and the manager of the business. One advantage of a sole proprietorship is that the owner makes all the decisions for the business. One disadvantage is that if the business cannot pay its obligations, the business owner must pay them. This means that the owner could lose some personal assets (e.g., house or savings).

Sole proprietorships are easy to form. They end if the business closes or when the owner dies.

Partnership

A **partnership** is a form of business ownership that has at least two owners (partners). Each partner acts as an owner of the company. This is an advantage because the partners can share the decision-making and the risks of the business. A disadvantage is that, as in a sole proprietorship, the partners' personal assets could be lost if the partnership cannot meet its obligations.

Partnerships are easy to form. They end when a partner dies or leaves the partnership.

Corporation

eBay is an example of a corporation.

A **corporation**, such as Canadian Tire, is a business owned by shareholders. The corporation may have only a few shareholders or it may have many shareholders. The shareholders are not personally liable for the corporation's debts, and they usually do not have input into the business decisions.

Corporations are more difficult to form than sole proprietorships or partnerships. Corporations can exist indefinitely.

CLASSIFYING ORGANIZATIONS BY ACTIVITY

Whether we are looking at a sole proprietorship, a partnership, or a corporation, the business can be classified by what the business does to earn money. Companies are categorized as service, merchandising, or manufacturing businesses (see Table 1-2 for examples of each type).

TABLE 1-2	Examples of Service, Merchandising, and Manufacturing Businesses	
Service Businesses	**Merchandising Businesses**	**Manufacturing Businesses**
eBay	Sears	Mattel
Jane's Painting Co.	Eddie Bauer	General Motors
Dr. Wheeler, M.D.	The Bay	Intel
H&R Block	Amazon.com	Bombardier

CAREERS IN ACCOUNTING

There are many career opportunities in accounting. They vary according to the amount of education and experience required. You should note that while a lot of routine accounting work is now done using computers, this has not lessened the need for all kinds of accounting personnel.

Accounting Clerks: Accounting clerks perform most of a business's record-keeping functions. Sometimes, accounting clerks perform specific functions and are given a title that relates to these functions. *Payroll clerk* and *accounts payable clerk* are examples of such titles. Accounting clerks may perform their work manually or by computer.

Accounting clerks generally are required to have completed at least a one-semester accounting course, and have some computer skills.

Bookkeepers: Bookkeepers are sometimes called "general bookkeepers" or "full-charge bookkeepers." That is because they do general accounting work, perform some summarizing and analyzing of accounting information, and supervise the accounting clerks. In some companies, they also may help managers and owners interpret accounting information. The size of the company determines the bookkeeper's responsibility.

Usually, bookkeepers need one or two years of accounting training and experience as an accounting clerk. Some computer knowledge is necessary too.

Accountants: Accountants plan, summarize, analyze, report, and interpret accounting information. Other responsibilities include assisting the owners and managers of the business in making financial decisions, and supervising other accounting personnel.

Generally, accountants need a college diploma in accounting. They also may need additional professional credentials.

Accountants fall into three general classifications: public accountants, private accountants, and non-profit accountants. (The opportunities in these categories are discussed in the following sections for each classification.)

A local cab company is a good example of a **service company** because it provides a service. The first part of this book focuses on service businesses.

Stores like Sears and Eddie Bauer sell products. They are called merchandising companies. **Merchandising companies** can either make and sell their own products or sell products that are made by other suppliers. Companies like Intel and General Motors that only make products and sell to wholesalers are called **manufacturing companies.**

Definition of Accounting

Accounting (also called the **accounting process**) is a system that measures the activities of a business in financial terms. It provides reports and financial statements that show how the various transactions the business undertook (e.g., buying and selling goods) affected the business. It does this by performing the following functions:

- **Analyzing:** Looking at what happened and how the business was affected
- **Recording:** Putting the information into the accounting system
- **Classifying:** Grouping all of the same activities (e.g., all purchases) together
- **Summarizing:** Creating totals by category and/or date, which are used in the next two functions
- **Reporting:** Issuing the reports that tell the results of the previous functions
- **Interpreting:** Examining the reports to determine how the various pieces of information they contain relate to each other

The system communicates the reports and financial statements to people who are interested in the information, such as the business's decision-makers, investors, creditors, governmental agencies (e.g., Canada Revenue Agency), and so on.

As you can see, a lot of people use these reports. A set of procedures and guidelines exists to make sure that everyone prepares and interprets the reports the same way.

Canadian accountants rely on a set of **generally accepted accounting principles** (abbreviated as GAAP) to guide them in the process of preparing financial reports for business entities. To study these in detail usually takes a complete course, so don't expect them to make perfect sense to you at this time. The most notable of these are described briefly below.

Business Entity Principle: This is a straightforward rule, which requires that the financial affairs of a business (or other entity such as a church, mosque, or service club—but we will refer to a business hereafter in this brief summary) be kept separate from the affairs of its owner (or members). The business entity can take many legal forms, but it is essential to know the identity of the entity for which the reports are prepared.

Historical Cost Principle: All financial events of a business are recorded at their actual transaction value (or historical cost) expressed in dollars. Accountants are strict about this matter, and it is very rare to encounter a situation that is not covered by this principle. One important consequence is that the value of assets, once recorded, is never changed.

The Realization/Recognition Principle: Accountants need to agree on a time when revenue is recognized. In most businesses, the process of earning revenue is continuous, so it is not always easy to say exactly when revenue has been earned. Despite the theoretical difficulties, for most businesses the revenue recognition point is considered to be when a sale takes place, as evidenced by an invoice being prepared and sent (delivered) to the customer, or client.

Going-Concern Assumption: Accountants always assume a business entity is going to continue to operate into the foreseeable future unless there is believable evidence that this is not valid (a petition for bankruptcy is one example). The implication is that assets continue to be valued at historical cost instead of some other possibility such as liquidation value.

Matching Principle: Once a business decides on a rule about recognizing revenue, it then must *match* against that revenue the expenses incurred to earn it. This matching process is usually quite clear. For example, if a computer store sells a new computer, it must deduct as expenses the various costs associated with the sale— (i.e., the wholesale cost of the computer plus any sales commissions). For some other expenses the matching may be determined by the passage of time. Insurance expense is typically written off over the number of months the policy is in force. In a few cases, the matching of expenses is unclear and accountants refer to other conventions—advertising expense is a good example. The value of an advertising campaign may extend into the future to some extent, but most accountants are reluctant to record this value as an asset because it is so difficult to measure. They prefer instead to say that advertising is an expense of a given period.

Conservatism: When in doubt, accountants take the position that it is better to be pessimistic about computing the current year's net income. In the example above, for instance, accountants usually write off advertising expenditures as expenses rather than try to determine an asset value at period-end. Conservatism is not a substitute for an attempt to be accurate; however, it is the principle that compels an accountant to pick the least beneficial alternative if two or more equally probable events may happen.

Fiscal Year-End: Accountants prepare financial statements for a given entity at least yearly. The fiscal year need not be the same as the calendar year, and statements may be prepared more often than once a year. However, for both legal (the Income Tax Act) and historical reasons, each entity has a fiscal year-end.

Materiality: All bookkeeping records are maintained in dollars and cents of course and typically balanced to the penny. This does not mean, however, that accountants go to extraordinary lengths to ensure absolute accuracy. Whether calculating amortization, setting up prepaid office supplies, or determining an accrued liability, accountants rarely insist on computations that are accurate to the nearest penny. Naturally, the borderline between a material item and one that is not material varies depending on the size of the reporting entity. A local community league, for instance, may be concerned with an error of only $100 in computing its prepaid insurance figure, while a large multinational business may be only mildly interested in a $500,000 fluctuation in reported revenue. Because of materiality, it is unusual for two accountants to produce the same set of financial statements for a given entity. However, major differences should be rare.

Consistency: An accountant is able to choose from such a large number of possible alternatives in preparing financial statements that any given year could be "customized" by selecting the particular set of options, which would give the desired results (within wide limits, of course). So that there is needed comparability from year to year, accountants follow a simple rule: no changes in the chosen set of accounting alternatives are permitted from year to year. In other words, you can select a unique set of rules for your business, but you are then stuck with them for a long time. Changes can be made for a good reason, but the results of the new rules must be disclosed in the year of change.

In more advanced courses, each of these principles can be studied for many weeks, and there are even some others not included here (see one of the chapters on the CD that comes with this text for a discussion of inventory cost flow assumptions, for example). The study of accounting can be a lengthy and complex process, but don't worry—our goals in this textbook are not so challenging as to require a detailed understanding of GAAP. However, knowing that GAAP exists and having an elementary appreciation of the sorts of things covered is a desired outcome for all introductory accounting students.

Types of Accountants

Public Accountants: Public accountants provide services to clients for a fee. They may work alone or work for an accounting firm. Two professional accounting bodies are chiefly concerned with public accounting in Canada: the Certified General Accountants Association and the Canadian Institute of Chartered Accountants. (All professional groups have provincial identities as well.) Membership is restricted to those who have passed a challenging set of qualifying examinations and who have served a period of training in various accounting positions. These professional accountants perform many accounting tasks, but they also provide advice on taxation, perform audits, and consult on many aspects of business operations.

Private Accountants (Managerial Accountants): The main difference between public accountants and private accountants is that most private accountants work for a single business. A business may employ one accountant or it may have many.

Private accountants who pass an examination prepared by the Society of Management Accountants of Canada will become Certified Management Accountants (CMAs). Those who pass the exam given by the Institute of Internal Auditors can become Certified Internal Auditors (CIAs).

There are many opportunities in private accounting. Private accountants may manage the accounting system, prepare reports and financial statements, prepare budgets, or determine certain costs (e.g., the cost of producing a new product). Some large firms have their own tax accountants and internal auditors.

Non-profit (Governmental) Accountants: Non-profit accounting is used by governmental agencies and non-profit agencies such as religious organizations, hospitals, and charitable organizations. These entities use accountants to prepare budgets and to keep records.

It is important to know that some non-profit agencies do make money. These agencies can keep their non-profit classifications if they keep the profit in the agency. Also, accounting procedures are very similar to procedures for profit-seeking businesses.

Difference Between Bookkeeping and Accounting

On October 28, 2004, ZDNet News reported that Nortel Networks, which had been embroiled in an accounting scandal since earlier that year, had again delayed restating financial results for the first half of 2004, and all of 2003. This story was widely reported by the world's financial press, and followed the efforts of Nortel as it tried to clean up several years' worth of flawed financial reports.*

Confusion often arises concerning the difference between bookkeeping and accounting. **Bookkeeping** is the recording (record-keeping) function of the accounting process; a bookkeeper enters accounting information in the company's books. An accountant takes that information and prepares the financial reports that are used to analyze the company's financial position. **Accounting** involves many complex activities. Often, it includes the preparation of tax and financial reports, budgeting, and analyses of financial information.

Today, computers are used for routine bookkeeping operations that used to take weeks or months to complete. This text explains how the advantages of the computer can be applied to a manual accounting system by using hands-on knowledge of how accounting works. Basic accounting knowledge is needed even though computers can help with routine tasks.

---

*Any student who wants to follow this story can do a Google search on *Nortel restating financial statements*. This will bring up thousands of references to the plight of Nortel as it deals with this unwelcome and serious business problem.

ASSETS, LIABILITIES, AND EQUITIES

Let's begin our study of accounting concepts and procedures by looking at a small business: Catherine Hall's law practice. Catherine decided to open her practice at the end of August 2010. She consulted her accountant Todd Amark before she made her decision. Todd told her some important things before she made this decision. First, he told her the new business would be considered a separate **business entity** whose finances had to be kept separate and distinct from Catherine's personal finances. The accountant went on to say that all transactions can be analyzed using the basic accounting equation: Assets = Liabilities + Owner's Equity.

Catherine had never heard of the basic accounting equation. She listened carefully as Todd explained the terms used in the equation and how the equation works.

Assets

Cash, land, supplies, office equipment, buildings, and other properties of value *owned* by a firm are called **assets.**

Equities

The rights or financial claims to the assets are called **equities**. Equities belong to those who supply the assets. If you are the only person to supply assets to the firm, you have the sole right or financial claim to them. For example, if you supply the law firm with $5,000 in cash and $4,000 in office equipment, your equity in the firm is $9,000.

Relationship Between Assets and Equities

The relationship between assets and equities is:

| **Assets** | **=** | **Equities** |
| (Total value of items *owned* by a business) | | (Total claims *against* the assets) |

The total dollar value of the assets of the law firm will be equal to the total dollar value of the financial claims to those assets; that is, equal to the total dollar value of the equities.

The total dollar value is broken down on the left-hand side of the equation to show the specific items of value owned by the business and on the right-hand side to show the types of claims against the assets owned.

Liabilities

A firm may have to borrow money to buy more assets; when this occurs, it means the firm is *buying assets on account* (buy now, pay later). Suppose Catherine's law firm purchases a desk for $400 on account from Joe's Stationery, and the store is willing to wait 10 days for payment. The law firm has created a **liability**: an obligation to pay that comes due in the future. Joe's Stationery is called the **creditor**. This liability—the amount owed to Joe's Stationery—gives the store the right, or the financial claim, to $400 of the law firm's assets. When Joe's Stationery is paid, the store's rights to the assets of the law firm will end since the obligation has been paid off.

Basic Accounting Equation

To better understand the various claims to a business's assets, accountants divide equities into two parts. The claims of creditors—outside persons or businesses—are labelled *liabilities*. The claims of the business's owner are labelled **owner's equity**. Let's see how the accounting equation looks now. It can be rewritten as follows:

Assets = **Equities**

1. Liabilities: rights of creditors
2. Owner's equity: rights of owner

Assets = Liabilities + Owner's Equity

The total value of all the assets of a firm equals the combined total value of the financial claims of the creditors (liabilities) and the claims of the owner (owner's equity). This is known as the **basic accounting equation**. The basic accounting equation provides a basis for understanding the conventional accounting system of a business. The equation is used to record business transactions in a logical and orderly way that shows their impact on the company's assets, liabilities, and owner's equity.

Importance of Creditors

Another way of presenting the basic accounting equation is:

Assets − Liabilities = Owner's Equity

This form of the equation stresses the importance of creditors. The owner's rights to the business's assets are determined after the rights of the creditors are subtracted. In other words, creditors have first claim on assets. If a firm has no liabilities—and therefore no creditors—the owner has the total rights to assets. Another term for the owner's current investment, or equity, in the business's assets is **capital.**

As Catherine Hall's law firm engages in business transactions (paying bills, serving clients, and so on), changes will take place in the assets, liabilities, and owner's equity (capital). Let's analyze some of these transactions.

> The term *cash* in accounting includes currency and cheques on hand and bank accounts also. In this textbook, *cash account* will usually mean the balance in the company's bank account.

| **Transaction A:** | **Aug. 26: Catherine invests $7,000 in cash and $800 worth of office equipment into the business.** |

On August 26, Catherine withdraws $7,000 from her personal bank account and deposits the money in the law firm's newly opened bank account. She also invests $800 worth of office equipment in the business. She plans to be open for business on September 1. With the help of her accountant, Catherine begins to prepare the accounting records for the business. We put this information into the basic accounting equation as follows:

> In our analyses, assume that any number without a sign in front of it is a + amount.

ASSETS		= LIABILITIES	+ OWNER'S EQUITY
Cash	+ Office Equipment	=	C. Hall, Capital
$7,000	+ $800		$7,800
	$7,800	= $7,800	

> *Note:* Capital is part of owner's equity; it is not an asset.

Note that the total value of the assets, cash, and office equipment—$7,800—is equal to the combined total value of liabilities (none, so far) and owner's equity ($7,800). Remember, Catherine Hall has supplied all the cash and office equipment, so she has the sole financial claim to the assets. Note that the heading "C. Hall, Capital" is written under the owner's equity heading. The $7,800 is Catherine's investment, or equity, in the firm's assets.

| **Transaction B:** | **Aug. 27: Law practice buys office equipment for cash, $900.** |

From the initial investment of $7,000 cash, the law firm buys $900 worth of office equipment (such as a desk). **Equipment** lasts a long time, while **supplies** (such as pens) tend to be used up relatively quickly.

	ASSETS		=	LIABILITIES	+ OWNER'S EQUITY
	Cash	+ Office Equipment	=		C. Hall, Capital
BEGINNING BALANCE	$7,000	+ $ 800	=		$7,800
TRANSACTION	−900	+ 900			
ENDING BALANCE	6,100	+ $1,700	=		$7,800

$$\$7,800 \; = \; \$7,800$$

Shift in Assets

As a result of the last transaction, the law office has less cash but has increased its amount of office equipment. This is called a **shift in assets**—the makeup of the assets has changed, but the total of the assets remains the same.

Suppose you go food shopping at the supermarket with $100 and spend $60. Now you have two assets, food and money. The composition of the assets has been *shifted*—you have more food and less money than you did—but the *total* of the assets has not increased or decreased. The total value of the food, $60, plus the cash, $40, is still $100. When you borrow money from the bank, on the other hand, you have an increase in cash (an asset) and an increase in liabilities; overall there is an increase in assets, not just a shift.

An accounting equation can remain in balance even if only one side is affected. The key point to remember is that the left-hand-side total of assets must always equal the right-hand-side total of liabilities and owner's equity.

Transaction C: **Aug. 30: Business buys additional office equipment on account, $400.**

The law firm purchases an additional $400 worth of chairs and desks from Wilmington Company. Instead of demanding cash right away, Wilmington agrees to deliver the equipment and to allow up to 60 days for the law practice to pay the invoice (bill).

This liability, or obligation to pay in the future, has some interesting effects on the basic accounting equation. Wilmington Company has accepted as payment a partial claim against the assets of the law practice. This claim exists until the law firm pays the bill. This unwritten promise to pay the creditor is a liability called **accounts payable.**

	ASSETS		=	LIABILITIES	+ OWNER'S EQUITY
	Cash	+ Office Equipment	= Accounts Payable		C. Hall, Capital
BEGINNING BALANCE	$6,100	+ $1,700	=		$7,800
TRANSACTION		+400	= +$400		
ENDING BALANCE	$6,100	+ $2,100	= $ 400		$7,800

$$\$8,200 \; = \; \$8,200$$

When this information is analyzed, we can see that the law practice has increased what it owes (accounts payable) as well as what it owns (office equipment) by $400. The law practice gains $400 in an asset but has an obligation to pay Wilmington Company at a future date.

The owner's equity remains unchanged. This transaction results in an increase of total assets from $7,800 to $8,200.

Finally, note that after each transaction, the basic accounting equation remains in balance.

LEARNING UNIT 1-1 REVIEW

AT THIS POINT you should be able to:

- ◆ List the functions of accounting. (pp. 2, 4–5)
- ◆ Define and explain the differences between sole proprietorships, partnerships, and corporations. (p. 3)
- ◆ Compare and contrast bookkeeping and accounting. (p. 7)
- ◆ Explain the role of the computer as an accounting tool. (p. 7)
- ◆ State the purpose of the accounting equation. (p. 8)
- ◆ Explain the difference between liabilities and owner's equity. (p. 9)
- ◆ Define capital. (p. 9)
- ◆ Explain the difference between a shift in assets and an increase in assets. (p. 10)

To test your understanding of this material, complete Self-Review Quiz 1-1. The blank forms you need are in the *Study Guide with Working Papers* for Chapter 1. The solution to the quiz follows the quiz here in the text. If you have difficulty doing the problems, review Learning Unit 1-1 and the solution to the quiz. You might also check the text's website for helpful student aids. Your instructor will provide details.

Keep in mind that learning accounting is like learning to type—the more you practise, the better you become. You will not be an expert in one day. Be patient. It will all come together.

Self-Review Quiz 1-1

(The blank forms you need are on page 1-1 of the *Study Guide with Working Papers*.)

Record the following transactions in the basic accounting equation:

1. Gracie Ryan invests $17,000 to begin a real estate office.

2. The real estate office buys $600 worth of computer equipment for cash.

3. The real estate office buys $500 worth of additional computer equipment on account.

Solution to Self-Review Quiz 1-1

	Cash +	Computer Equipment	=	Accounts Payable	+	Gracie Ryan, Capital
1.	+$17,000					+$17,000
BALANCE	17,000		=			17,000
2.	−600	+$600				
BALANCE	16,400 +	600	=			17,000
3.		500		+$500		
ENDING BALANCE	$16,400	+$ 1,100	=	$500	+	$17,000

$$\$17,500 = \$17,500$$

| | ASSETS | = | LIABILITIES | + | OWNER'S EQUITY |

Quiz Tip
<PARA>Note that transaction 2 is a shift in assets while transaction 3 is an increase in assets. Keep asking yourself what did the business get and who supplied it to the business. Remember, capital is not cash. Cash is an asset, while capital is part of owner's

Learning Unit 1-2
The Balance Sheet

> The balance sheet shows the company's financial position as of a particular date. (In our example, that date is at the end of August.)

In the first learning unit, the transactions for Catherine Hall's law office were recorded in the accounting equation. The transactions we recorded occurred before the law firm opened for business. A report, called a **balance sheet** or **statement of financial position**, can show the position of the company before it started operating. The balance sheet is a formal report that presents the information from the ending balances of both sides of the accounting equation. Think of the balance sheet as a snapshot of the business's financial position as of a particular date.

Let's look at the balance sheet of Catherine Hall's law practice for August 31, 2010, shown in Figure 1-1. The figures in the balance sheet come from the ending balances of the accounting equation for the law practice as shown in Learning Unit 1-1.

Note in Figure 1-1 that the assets owned by the law practice appear on the left-hand side and that liabilities and owner's equity appear on the right-hand side. Both sides equal $8,200. This *balance* between left and right gives the balance sheet its name. In later chapters, we will be looking at other ways to set up a balance sheet.

POINTS TO REMEMBER IN PREPARING A BALANCE SHEET
The Heading

> Do you remember the three elements that make up a balance sheet? They are assets, liabilities, and owner's equity.

The heading of the balance sheet provides the following information:

- The company name: Catherine Hall, Barrister and Solicitor
- The name of the report: Balance Sheet
- The date for which the report is prepared: August 31, 2010

Figure 1-1
The Balance Sheet

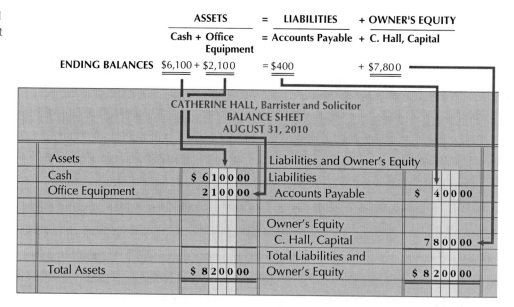

Use of the Dollar Sign

Note that the dollar sign is not repeated every time a figure appears. As shown in the balance sheet for Catherine Hall's law practice, it is usually placed to the left of each column's top figure and to the left of the column's total.

Distinguishing the Total

CATHERINE HALL, Barrister and Solicitor BALANCE SHEET AUGUST 31, 2010		A single line means the numbers above it have been added or subtracted.
Assets		
Cash	$ 6 1 0 0 00	
Office Equipment	2 1 0 0 00	
Total Assets	$ 8 2 0 0 00	A double line indicates a total.

When adding numbers down a column, use a single line before the total and a double line beneath it. A single line means that the numbers above it have been added or subtracted. A double line indicates a total. It is important to align the numbers in the column; many errors occur because these figures are not lined up. These rules are the same for all accounting reports.

This balance sheet gives Catherine the information she needs to see the law firm's financial position before it opens for business. This information does not tell her, however, whether the firm will make a profit.

LEARNING UNIT 1-2 REVIEW

AT THIS POINT you should be able to:

◆ Define and state the purpose of a balance sheet. (p. 12)
◆ Identify and define the elements making up a balance sheet. (p. 12)
◆ Show the relationship between the accounting equation and the balance sheet. (p. 12)
◆ Prepare a balance sheet in proper form from information provided. (p. 12)
◆ Place dollar signs correctly in a formal report. (p. 13)

Self-Review Quiz 1-2

(The blank forms you need are on page 1-2 of the *Study Guide with Working Papers.*)

The date is November 30, 2010. Use the following information to prepare in proper form a balance sheet for Janning Company:

Accounts Payable	$30,000
Cash	8,000
A. Janning, Capital	9,000
Office Equipment	31,000

Quiz Tip

The heading of a balance sheet answers the questions *Who, What,* and *When.* November 30, 2010 is the particular date.

Solution to Self-Review Quiz 1-2

Assets		Liabilities and Owner's Equity		Capital does not mean cash. The capital amount is the owner's current investment of assets in the business.
		JANNING COMPANY **BALANCE SHEET** **NOVEMBER 30, 2010**		
Cash	$ 8 0 0 0 00	Liabilities		
Office Equipment	31 0 0 0 00	Accounts Payable	$ 30 0 0 0 00	
		Owner's Equity		
		A. Janning, Capital	9 0 0 0 00	
		Total Liabilities and		
Total Assets	$ 39 0 0 0 00	Owner's Equity	$ 39 0 0 0 00	

Learning Unit 1-3

The Accounting Equation Expanded: Revenue, Expenses, and Withdrawals

As soon as Catherine Hall's office opened, she began performing legal services for her clients and earning revenue for the business. At the same time, as a part of doing business, she incurred various expenses, such as rent. See Figure 1-2 for an example of how these activities affect owner's equity.

When Catherine asked her accountant how these transactions fitted into the accounting equation, he began by defining some terms.

KEY TERMS IN THE ACCOUNTING EQUATION

> When revenue is earned, it is recorded as an increase in owner's equity and an increase in assets.

Revenue   A service company earns **revenue** when it provides services to its clients. Catherine's law firm earned revenue when she provided legal services to her clients for legal fees. When revenue is earned, owner's equity is increased. In effect, revenue is a subdivision of owner's equity.

Assets are increased. The increase is in the form of cash if the client pays right away. If the client promises to pay in the future, the increase is called **accounts receivable**. When revenue is earned, the transaction is recorded as an increase in revenue and an increase in assets (either as cash and/or as accounts receivable, depending on whether it was paid right away or will be paid in the future).

Figure 1-2
Owner's Equity

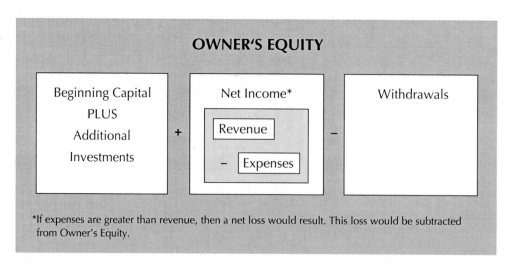

*If expenses are greater than revenue, then a net loss would result. This loss would be subtracted from Owner's Equity.

Expenses   A business's **expenses** are the costs the company incurs in carrying on operations in its effort to create revenue. Expenses are also a subdivision of owner's equity; when expenses are incurred, they *decrease* owner's equity. Expenses can be paid for in cash or they can be charged.

Net Income/Net Loss   When revenue totals more than expenses, **net income** is the result; when expenses total more than revenue, **net loss** is the result.

Withdrawals   At some point, Catherine Hall may need to withdraw cash or other assets from the business to pay living or other personal expenses that do not relate to the business. We will record these transactions in an account called **withdrawals**. Sometimes this account is called the *owner's drawing account*. The withdrawals account is a subdivision of owner's equity that records personal expenses not related to the business. Withdrawals decrease owner's equity.

It is important to remember the difference between expenses and withdrawals. Expenses relate to business operations; withdrawals are the result of personal needs outside the normal operations of the business.

Now let's analyze the September transactions for Catherine Hall's law firm using an **expanded accounting equation** that includes withdrawals, revenues, and expenses.

EXPANDED ACCOUNTING EQUATION

Transaction D: **Sept. 1–30: Provided legal services for cash, $3,000.**

Transactions A, B, and C were discussed earlier when the law office was being formed in August. See Learning Unit 1-1.

In the law firm's first month of operation, a total of $3,000 in cash was received for legal services performed. In the accounting equation, the asset Cash is increased by $3,000. Revenue is also increased by $3,000, resulting in an increase in owner's equity.

	ASSETS			= LIABILITIES	+		OWNER'S EQUITY		
	Cash	+ Accts. Rec.	+ Office Equip.	=	Accts. Pay.	+ C. Hall, Capital	− C. Hall, Withdr.	+ Revenue	− Expenses
BAL. FWD.	$6,100		+$ 2,100 =		$ 400	+$7,800			
TRANS.	+3,000							+ $3,000	
END. BAL.	$9,100		+$ 2,100 =		$ 400	+$7,800		+ $3,000	
			$11,200 =		$11,200				

A revenue column was added to the basic accounting equation. Amounts are recorded in the revenue column when they are earned. They are also recorded in the assets columns, under Cash and/or under Accounts Receivable. Do not think of revenue as an asset. It is part of owner's equity. It is the revenue that creates an inward flow of cash and accounts receivable.

Transaction E: **Sept. 1–30: Provided legal services on account, $4,000.**

	ASSETS			= LIABILITIES	+		OWNER'S EQUITY		
	Cash	+ Accts. Rec.	+ Office Equip.	=	Accts. Pay.	+ C. Hall, Capital	− C. Hall, Withdr.	+ Revenue	− Expenses
BAL. FWD.	$9,100		+ $ 2,100 =		$ 400	+ $7,800		+ $3,000	
TRANS.		+$4,000						+4,000	
END. BAL.	$9,100 +	$4,000	+ $ 2,100 =		$ 400	+ $7,800		+ $7,000	
			$15,200 =		$ 15,200				

Catherine's law practice performed legal work on account for $4,000. Her firm did not receive the cash for these earned legal fees; it accepted an unwritten promise from these clients that payment would be made in the future.

During September, some of Catherine's clients who had received services and promised to pay in the future decided to reduce what they owed the practice by $700 when their bills came due. This is shown as follows on the expanded accounting equation.

Transaction F: Sept. 1–30: Received $700 cash as partial payment of previous services performed on account.

	ASSETS			= LIABILITIES +		OWNER'S EQUITY			
	Cash	+ Accts. Rec.	+ Office Equip.	= Accts. Pay.	+ C. Hall, Capital	− C. Hall, Withdr.	+ Revenue	− Expenses
BAL. FWD.	$9,100	+ $4,000	+ $2,100	= $ 400	+ $7,800		+ $7,000	
TRANS.	+700	−700						
END. BAL.	$9,800	+ $3,300	+ $2,100	= $ 400	+ $7,800		+ $7,000	
		$15,200		= $15,200				

The law firm increased the asset Cash by $700 and decreased another asset, Accounts Receivable, by $700. The *total* of assets does not change. The right-hand side of the expanded accounting equation has not been touched because the total on the left-hand side of the equation has not changed. The revenue was recorded when it was earned, and the *same revenue cannot be recorded twice*. This transaction analyzes the situation *after* the revenue has been previously earned and recorded. Transaction F shows a shift in assets—increased cash and reduced accounts receivable.

Transaction G: Sept. 1–30: Paid salaries expense, $600.

	ASSETS			= LIABILITIES +		OWNER'S EQUITY			
	Cash	+ Accts. Rec.	+ Office Equip.	= Accts. Pay.	+ C. Hall, Capital	− C. Hall, Withdr.	+ Revenue	− Expenses
BAL. FWD.	$9,800	+ $3,300	+ $ 2,100	= $ 400	+ $7,800		+ $7,000	
TRANS.	−600							+$600
END. BAL.	$9,200	+ $3,300	+ $ 2,100	= $ 400	+ $7,800		+ $7,000	−$600
		$14,600		= $14,600				

> While her law firm cannot pay Catherine a salary, it can legally pay a salary (or wages) to any employee. This $600 was not paid to Catherine.

As expenses increase, they decrease owner's equity. This incurred expense of $600 reduces the cash by $600. Although the expense was paid, the total of our expenses to date has *increased* by $600. Keep in mind that owner's equity decreases as expenses increase, so the accounting equation remains in balance.

Transaction H: Sept. 1–30: Paid rent expense, $700.

	ASSETS		=	LIABILITIES +		OWNER'S EQUITY		
Cash	+ Accts. Rec.	+ Office Equip.	=	Accts. Pay.	+ C. Hall, Capital	− C. Hall, Withdr.	+ Revenue	− Expenses
BAL. FWD. $9,200	+ $3,300	+ $2,100	=	$400	+$7,800		+ $7,000	− $ 600
TRANS. −700								+700
END. BAL. $8,500	+ $3,300	+ $2,100	=	$400	+$7,800		+ $7,000	− $1,300
		$13,900	=	$13,900				

During September, the practice incurred rent expenses of $700. This rent was not paid in advance; it was paid when it came due. The payment of rent reduces the asset Cash by $700 and increases the expenses of the firm, resulting in a decrease in owner's equity. The firm's expenses are now $1,300.

Transaction I: Sept. 1–30: Incurred advertising expenses of $300, to be paid next month.

	ASSETS		=	LIABILITIES +		OWNER'S EQUITY		
Cash	+ Accts. Rec.	+ Office Equip.	=	Accts. Pay.	+ C. Hall, Capital	− C. Hall, Withdr.	+ Revenue	− Expenses
BAL. FWD. $8,500	+ $3,300	+ $2,100	=	$400	+$7,800		+ $7,000	− $1,300
TRANS.				+300				+300
END. BAL. $8,500	+ $3,300	+ $2,100	=	$700	+$7,800		+ $7,000	− $1,600
		$13,900	=	$13,900				

Catherine ran an ad in the local newspaper and incurred an expense of $300. This increase in expenses caused a corresponding decrease in owner's equity. Since Catherine has not paid the newspaper for the advertising yet, her firm owes $300. Thus the firm's liabilities (Accounts Payable) increase by $300. Eventually, when the bill comes in and is paid, both Cash and Accounts Payable will be decreased.

Transaction J: Sept. 1–30: Catherine withdrew $200 for personal use.

	ASSETS		=	LIABILITIES +		OWNER'S EQUITY		
Cash	+ Accts. Rec.	+ Office Equip.	=	Accts. Pay.	+ C. Hall, Capital	− C. Hall, Withdr.	+ Revenue	− Expenses
BAL. FWD. $8,500	+ $3,300	+ $ 2,100	=	$700	+ $7,800		+ $7,000	− $1,600
TRANS. −200						+$200		
END. BAL. $8,300	+ $3,300	+ $ 2,100	=	$700	+ $7,800	− $200	+ $7,000	− $1,600
		$13,700	=	$13,700				

By taking $200 for personal use, Catherine has *increased* her withdrawals from the business by $200 and decreased the asset Cash by $200. Note that, as withdrawals increase, the owner's equity will *decrease*. Keep in mind that a withdrawal is *not* a business expense. It is a subdivision of owner's equity that records money or other assets an owner withdraws from the business for *personal* use.

Subdivision of Owner's Equity

Take a moment to review the subdivisions of owner's equity:

◆ As capital increases, owner's equity increases (see transaction A).
◆ As withdrawals increase, owner's equity decreases (see transaction J).
◆ As revenue increases, owner's equity increases (see transaction D).
◆ As expenses increase, owner's equity decreases (see transaction G).

Catherine Hall's Expanded Accounting Equation

The following is a summary of the expanded accounting equation for Catherine Hall's law firm. The + or − sign in front of a transaction indicates whether the account is increased or decreased by that transaction.

Catherine Hall
Barrister and Solicitor
Expanded Accounting Equation: A Summary

	Cash	+	Accts. Rec.	+	Office Equip.	=	Accts. Pay.	+	C. Hall, Capital	−	C. Hall, Withdr.	+	Revenue	−	Expenses
A.	$7,000			+	$800	=			+$7,800						
BALANCE	7,000			+	800	=			7,800						
B.	−900				+900										
BALANCE	6,100			+	1,700	=			7,800						
C.					+400		+$400								
BALANCE	6,100			+	2,100	=	400	+	7,800						
D.	+3,000												+$3,000		
BALANCE	9,100			+	2,100	=	400	+	7,800			+	3,000		
E.			+$4,000										+4,000		
BALANCE	9,100	+	4,000	+	2,100	=	400	+	7,800			+	7,000		
F.	+700		−700												
BALANCE	9,800	+	3,300	+	2,100	=	400	+	7,800			+	7,000		
G.	−600														+$600
BALANCE	9,200	+	3,300	+	2,100	=	400	+	7,800			+	7,000	−	600
H.	−700														+700
BALANCE	8,500	+	3,300	+	2,100	=	400	+	7,800			+	7,000	−	1,300
I.							+300								+300
BALANCE	8,500	+	3,300	+	2,100	=	700	+	7,800			+	7,000	−	1,600
J.	−200										+$200				
END. BAL.	$8,300	+	$3,300	+	$2,100	=	$700	+	$7,800	−	$200	+	$7,000	−	$1,600

$13,700 = $13,700

LEARNING UNIT 1-3 REVIEW

AT THIS POINT you should be able to:

◆ Define and explain the difference between revenue and expenses. (pp. 14–15)
◆ Define and explain the difference between net income and net loss. (p. 15)
◆ Explain the subdivision of owner's equity. (pp. 16–18)
◆ Explain the effects of withdrawals, revenue, and expenses on owner's equity. (pp. 16–17)
◆ Record transactions in an expanded accounting equation and balance the basic accounting equation as a means of checking the accuracy of your calculations. (p. 18)

(The blank forms you need are on page 1-2 of the *Study Guide with Working Papers*.)

Record the following transactions in the expanded accounting equation for the Bing Company. Note that all titles have a beginning balance.

1. Received cash revenue, $4,000.
2. Billed customers for services rendered, $6,000.
3. Received a bill for telephone expenses (to be paid next month), $125.
4. Bob Bing withdrew cash for personal use, $500.
5. Received $1,000 from customers in partial payment for services performed in transaction 2.

Quiz Tip

Think of expenses and withdrawals as *increasing*. As they increase, they will reduce the owner's rights. For example, in transaction 4, withdrawals increased by $500, resulting in total withdrawals increasing from $800 to $1,300. This represents a decrease in owner's equity.

Solution to Self-Review Quiz 1-3

	ASSETS			=	LIABILITIES +		OWNER'S EQUITY			
	Cash	+ Accts. Rec.	+ Cleaning Equip.	=	Accts. Pay.	+ B. Bing, Capital	− B. Bing, Withdr.	+ Revenue	− Expenses	
BEG. BAL.	$ 9,000	+ $ 2,500	+ $6,500	=	$1,000	+ $11,800	− $ 800	+ $ 8,000	− $2,000	
1.	+4,000							+4,000		
BALANCE	13,000	+ 2,500	+ 6,500	=	1,000	+ 11,800	− 800	+ 12,000	− 2,000	
2.		+6,000						+6,000		
BALANCE	13,000	+ 8,500	+ 6,500	=	1,000	+ 11,800	− 800	+ 18,000	− 2,000	
3.					+125				+125	
BALANCE	13,000	+ 8,500	+ 6,500	=	1,125	+ 11,800	− 800	+ 18,000	− 2,125	
4.	−500						+500			
BALANCE	12,500	+ 8,500	+ 6,500	=	1,125	+ 11,800	− 1,300	+ 18,000	− 2,125	
5.	+1,000	−1,000								
END. BAL.	$13,500	+ $ 7,500	+ $6,500	=	$1,125	+ $11,800	− $ 1,300	+ $18,000	− $2,125	
	$27,500			=		$27,500				

Learning Unit 1-4

Preparing Financial Reports

Catherine Hall would like to be able to find out whether her firm is making a profit, so she asks her accountant whether he can measure the firm's financial performance on a monthly basis. Her accountant replies that there are a number of financial reports that he can prepare, such as the income statement, which shows how well the law firm has performed over a specific period of time. The accountant can use the information in the income statement to prepare other reports.

THE INCOME STATEMENT

The income statement is prepared from data found in the revenue and expense columns of the expanded accounting equation.

An **income statement** is an accounting report that shows business results in terms of revenue and expenses. If revenues are greater than expenses, the report shows net income. If expenses are greater than revenues, the report shows net loss. An income statement can cover any number of months up to 12. It does not usually cover more than one year. The report shows the result of all revenues and expenses throughout the entire period and not just as of a specific date. The income statement for Catherine Hall's law firm is shown in Figure 1-3.

Figure 1-3
The Income Statement

CATHERINE HALL, Barrister and Solicitor
INCOME STATEMENT
FOR MONTH ENDED SEPTEMBER 30, 2010

Revenue:		
Legal Fees		$ 7 0 0 0 00
Operating Expenses:		
Salaries Expense	$ 6 0 0 00	
Rent Expense	7 0 0 00	
Advertising Expense	3 0 0 00	
Total Operating Expenses		1 6 0 0 00
Net Income		$ 5 4 0 0 00

Note that withdrawals are not shown in the Income Statement. They are not an expense.

Points to Remember in Preparing an Income Statement

Heading The heading of an income statement tells the same three things as all other accounting reports: the company's name, the name of the report, and the period of time the report covers (or the date prepared).

The Set-Up As you can see on the income statement, the inside column of numbers ($600, $700, and $300) is used to subtotal all expenses ($1,600) before subtracting them from revenue ($7,000 − $1,600 = $5,400).

Operating expenses may be listed in alphabetical order, in order of largest amounts to smallest, or in a set order established by the accountant.

Locate the dollar signs used in the Income Statement. They are shown at the top of each column and in the total.

THE STATEMENT OF OWNER'S EQUITY

As we said, the income statement is a business report that shows business results in terms of revenue and expenses. However, how does net income or net loss affect owner's equity? To find that out, we have to look at another category of report, the statement of owner's equity.

The **statement of owner's equity** shows for a certain period of time what changes occurred in Catherine Hall, Capital. The statement of owner's equity is shown in Figure 1-4.

The capital of Catherine Hall can be

Increased by:	Owner Investment
	Net Income (Revenue greater than Expenses)
Decreased by:	Owner Withdrawals
	Net Loss (Expenses greater than Revenue)

If this statement of owner's equity is omitted, the information will be included in the owner's equity section of the balance sheet.

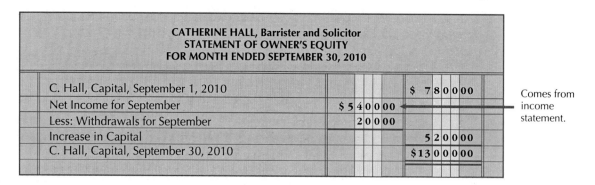

CATHERINE HALL, Barrister and Solicitor
STATEMENT OF OWNER'S EQUITY
FOR MONTH ENDED SEPTEMBER 30, 2010

C. Hall, Capital, September 1, 2010		$ 7 8 0 0 00
Net Income for September	$ 5 4 0 0 00	
Less: Withdrawals for September	2 0 0 00	
Increase in Capital		5 2 0 0 00
C. Hall, Capital, September 30, 2010		$13 0 0 0 00

Comes from income statement.

Figure 1-4   Statement of Owner's Equity

Remember, a withdrawal is *not* a business expense and thus is not involved in the calculation of net income or net loss on the income statement. It appears on the statement of owner's equity. The statement of owner's equity summarizes the effects of all the subdivisions of owner's equity (revenue, expenses, withdrawals) on beginning capital. The ending capital figure ($13,000) will be the beginning figure in the next statement of owner's equity.

Suppose that Catherine's law firm had operated at a loss in the month of September. Instead of net income, there was a net loss and an additional investment of $700 was made on September 15. This is how the statement would look if this had happened.

This statement is for illustration only, and is not directly related to the set of transactions shown earlier.

CATHERINE HALL, Barrister and Solicitor
STATEMENT OF OWNER'S EQUITY
FOR MONTH ENDED SEPTEMBER 30, 2010

C. Hall, Capital, September 1, 2010		$7 800 00
Additional Investment, September 15, 2010		700 00
		$8 500 00
Less: Net Loss for September	$ 400 00	
Withdrawals for September	200 00	
Decrease in Capital		600 00
C. Hall, Capital, September 30, 2010		$7 900 00

THE BALANCE SHEET

Now let's look at how to prepare a balance sheet from the expanded accounting equation (see Figure 1-5). As you can see, the asset accounts (Cash, Accounts Receivable, and Office Equipment) appear on the left side of the balance sheet. Accounts Payable and C. Hall, Capital, appear on the right side. Notice that the $13,000 of capital can be calculated within the accounting equation or read from the statement of owner's equity.

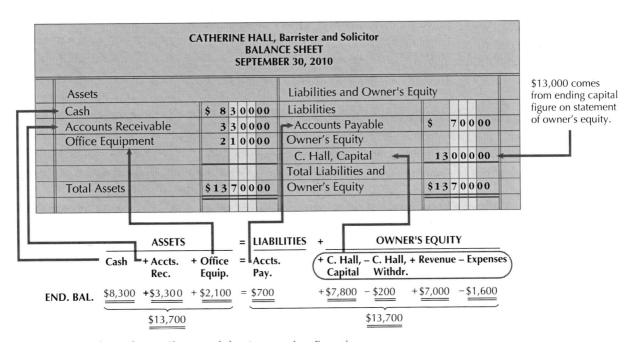

Figure 1-5   The Balance Sheet and the Accounting Equation

MAIN ELEMENTS OF THE INCOME STATEMENT, THE STATEMENT OF OWNER'S EQUITY, AND THE BALANCE SHEET

In this chapter, we have discussed three financial reports: the income statement, the statement of owner's equity, and the balance sheet. (There is a fourth report, called the cash flow statement, that is covered in Chapter 16 of this textbook.) Let us review the elements of the expanded accounting equation that go into each report and the usual order in which the reports are prepared. Figure 1-5 presents a diagram of the accounting equation and the balance sheet. Table 1-3 summarizes what information goes on each report.

- The income statement is prepared first; it includes revenues and expenses and shows net income or net loss. This net income or net loss is used to update the next report, the statement of owner's equity.

- The statement of owner's equity is prepared second; it includes beginning capital and any additional investments, the net income or net loss shown on the income statement, withdrawals, and the total, which is the **ending capital.**

- The balance sheet is prepared last; it includes the final balances of each of the elements listed in the accounting equation under Assets and Liabilities. The balance in Capital comes from the statement of owner's equity.

TABLE 1-3 What Goes on Each Financial Report

	Income Statement	Statement of Owner's Equity	Balance Sheet
Assets			X
Liabilities			X
Capital (beginning)		X	
Additional Investments		X	
Capital (ending)		X	X
Withdrawals		X	
Revenues	X		
Expenses	X		
Net Income (Loss)	X	X	

LEARNING UNIT 1-4 REVIEW

AT THIS POINT you should be able to:

- Define and state the purpose of the income statement, the statement of owner's equity, and the balance sheet. (pp. 19–21)
- Discuss why the income statement should be prepared first. (p. 22)
- Compare and contrast these three financial reports. (p. 22)
- Calculate a new figure for capital on the statement of owner's equity and balance sheet. (p. 21)
- Show what happens on a statement of owner's equity if there is a net loss. (p. 21)

Self-Review Quiz 1-4

(The blank forms you need are on pages 1-3 and 1-4 of the *Study Guide with Working Papers.*)

From the following balances for Rusty Realty, prepare:

1. Income statement for month ended November 30, 2011
2. Statement of owner's equity for the month ended November 30, 2011
3. Balance sheet as of November 30, 2011

Cash	$40,000	R. Rusty, Withdrawals	1,000
Accounts Receivable	13,700	Commissions Earned	15,000
Office Furniture	14,900	Rent Expense	2,000
Accounts Payable	9,000	Advertising Expense	1,500
R. Rusty, Capital,		Salaries Expense	900
November 1, 2011	$50,000		

Solution to Self-Review Quiz 1-4

RUSTY REALTY
INCOME STATEMENT
FOR MONTH ENDED NOVEMBER 30, 2011

Revenue:		
Commissions Earned		$15 000 00
Operating Expenses:		
Rent Expense	$2 000 00	
Advertising Expense	1 500 00	
Salaries Expense	9 00 00	
Total Operating Expenses		4 400 00
Net Income		$10 600 00

Subtotal Columns

RUSTY REALTY
STATEMENT OF OWNER'S EQUITY
FOR MONTH ENDED NOVEMBER 30, 2011

R. Rusty, Capital, November 1, 2011		$50 000 00
Net Income for November	$10 600 00	
Less: Withdrawals for November	1 000 00	
Increase in Capital		9 600 00
R. Rusty, Capital, November 30, 2011		$59 600 00

RUSTY REALTY
BALANCE SHEET
NOVEMBER 30, 2011

Assets		Liabilities and Owner's Equity	
Cash	$40 000 00	Liabilities	
Accounts Receivable	13 700 00	Accounts Payable	$ 9 000 00
Office Furniture	14 900 00		
		Owner's Equity	
		R. Rusty, Capital	59 600 00
		Total Liabilities and	
Total Assets	$68 600 00	Owner's Equity	$68 600 00

"Hey, Stan the man!" a loud voice boomed. "I never thought I'd see you making sandwiches!" Stan Hernandez stopped layering lettuce in a foot-long submarine sandwich and grinned at his old college buddy, Ron.

"Neither did I. But then again," said Stan, "I never thought I'd own a profitable business either." That night, catching up on their lives over dinner, Stan told Ron how he became the proud owner of a Subway sandwich restaurant. "After working like crazy at Xellent Media for five years and *finally* making it to marketing manager, then wham . . . I got laid off," said Stan. "That very day I was having my lunch at the local Subway as usual, when . . . "

"Hmmm, wait a minute! I did notice you've lost quite a bit of weight," Ron interrupted and began to hum the bars of Subway's latest ad featuring Clay Henry, yet another hefty male who lost weight on a diet of Subway sandwiches.

"Right!" Stan quipped, "Not only was I laid off, but I was 'downsizing!' *Anyway*, I was eating a Dijon horseradish melt when I opened up an *Entrepreneur* magazine someone had left on the table—right to the headline 'Subway Named #1 Franchise in All Categories for 11th Time in 15 Years.' "

To make a foot-long submarine sandwich story short, Stan realized his long-time dream of being his own boss by owning a business with a proven product and highly successful business model. When you look at Stan's restaurant, you are really seeing two businesses. While Stan is the sole proprietor of his business, he operates under an agreement with Subway head office. Subway supplies the business know-how and support (like training at Subway University, national advertising, and gourmet bread recipes). Stan supplies capital (his $12,500 investment) and his food preparation, management, and elbow grease. Subway and Stan operate interdependent businesses, and both rely on accounting information for their success.

Subway, in business since 1965, has grown dramatically over the years and now has over 18,000 locations in 73 countries. It has even

SUBWAY
A FRESH START

surpassed McDonald's in the number of locations in the United States and Canada. To manage this enormous service business requires very careful control of each of its stores.

At a Subway regional office, Mariah Washington, a field consultant for Stan's territory, monitors Stan's restaurant closely. In addition to making monthly visits to check whether Stan is complying with Subway's model in everything from décor to uniforms to food quality and safety, she also looks closely at Stan's weekly sales and inventory reports. When Stan's sales go up, Subway's do too, because each Subway franchisee, like Stan, pays Subway, the franchiser, a percentage of sales in the form of royalties.

Why does headquarters require accounting reports? Accounting reports give the information both Stan and the company need to make business decisions in a number of vital areas. For example:

◆ Before Stan could buy his Subway restaurant, the company needed to know how much cash Stan had, the value of his assets, and the amount of his liabilities (such as credit card debt). Stan prepared a personal balance sheet to give them this information.

◆ Stan must have the right amount of supplies on hand. If he has too few, he can't make the sandwiches. If he has too much for the amount he expects to sell, items like sandwich meats and bread dough may spoil. The inventory report tells Mariah what supplies are on hand. In combination with the sales report, it also alerts Mariah to potential red flags. If Stan is reporting that he is using far too much bread dough for the number of sandwiches he is selling, then there is a problem.

◆ Although Subway does not require its restaurant owners to report operating costs and profit information, Subway gives them the option and most franchisees choose to report. Information on profitability helps Mariah and Stan make decisions like whether and when to remodel or buy new equipment.

So that its restaurant owners can make business decisions in a timely manner, Subway requires them to submit the weekly sales and inventory report to headquarters electronically every Thursday by 2 p.m. Stan has his latest report in mind as he makes a move to pay the bill for his dinner with Ron. "We had a great week. Let me get this," he says. "Thanks, Stan the Man. I'm going to keep in touch because I may just be ready for a business opportunity of my own!"

DISCUSSION QUESTIONS

1. What makes Stan a sole proprietor?
2. Why are Stan and Subway interdependent businesses?
3. Why did Stan have to share his personal balance sheet with Subway? Do you think most interdependent businesses do this?
4. What does Subway learn from Stan's weekly sales and inventory reports?

DEMONSTRATION PROBLEM WITH SOLUTION TIPS

(The blank forms you need are on pages 1-5 and 1-6 of the *Study Guide with Working Papers*.)

Michael Brown opened his law office on June 1, 2009. During the first month of operations, Michael conducted the following transactions:

1. Invested $6,000 in cash in the law practice.
2. Paid $600 for office equipment purchased.
3. Purchased additional office equipment on account, $1,000.
4. Performed legal services for clients, receiving cash, $2,000.
5. Paid salaries, $800.
6. Performed legal services for clients on account, $1,000.
7. Paid rent, $1,200.
8. Withdrew $500 from his law practice for personal use.
9. Received $500 from customers in partial payment for legal services performed, transaction 6.

Assignment

a. Record these transactions in the expanded accounting equation.
b. Prepare the financial statements at June 30 for Michael Brown, Barrister and Solicitor.

Solution to Comprehensive Demonstration Problem

	Cash		+ Accts. Rec.		+ Office Equip.	=	Accts. Pay.		+ M. Brown, Capital		− M. Brown, Withdr.		+ Revenue		− Expenses
ASSETS						**= LIABILITIES +**			**OWNER'S EQUITY**						
1.	+ $6,000								+ $6,000						
BAL.	6,000					=			6,000						
2.	− 600				+ $ 600										
BAL.	5,400				+ 600	=			6,000						
3.					+ 1,000	+	$1,000								
BAL.	5,400				+ 1,600	=	1,000		+ 6,000						
4.	+ 2,000												+	$2,000	
BAL.	7,400				+ 1,600	=	1,000		+ 6,000				+	2,000	
5.	− 800														+ $800
BAL.	6,600				+ 1,600	=	1,000		+ 6,000				+	2,000	− 800
6.		+	$1,000										+	1,000	
BAL.	6,600	+	1,000	+	1,600	=	1,000		+ 6,000				+	3,000	− 800
7.	− 1,200														+ 1,200
BAL.	5,400	+	1,000	+	1,600	=	1,000		+ 6,000				+	3,000	− 2,000
8.	− 500										+	$500			
BAL.	4,900	+	1,000	+	1,600	=	1,000		+ 6,000		−	500	+	3,000	− 2,000
9.	+ 500	−	500												
END. BAL.	$5,400	+	$ 500	+	$1,600	=	$1,000		+ $6,000		−	$500	+	$3,000	− $2,000
					$7,500	=	$7,500								

Solution Tips to Expanded Accounting Equation

- **Transaction 1:** The business increased its cash by $6,000. Owner's equity (Capital) increased when Michael supplied the cash to the business.
- **Transaction 2:** A shift in assets when the equipment was purchased. The business lowered its cash by $600, and a new column—Office Equipment—was introduced for the $600 worth of equipment that was bought. The amount of capital was not altered because the owner did not supply any new funds.
- **Transaction 3:** When creditors supplied $1,000 worth of additional equipment, the business's Accounts Payable showed the debt. The business had increased what it *owed* the creditors.
- **Transaction 4:** Legal Fees, a revenue account and a subdivision of owner's equity, was increased when the law firm provided a service. The service provided an inward flow of $2,000 cash, an asset. Remember, legal fees are *not* an asset. As legal fees increase, owner's equity increases.
- **Transaction 5:** The salary paid by Michael showed as an $800 increase in expenses and a corresponding decrease in cash.
- **Transaction 6:** Michael did the work and earned the $1,000. That $1,000 was recorded as revenue. This time the legal fees created an inward flow of assets, called Accounts Receivable, of $1,000. Remember, legal fees are *not* an asset. They are a subdivision of owner's equity.
- **Transaction 7:** The $1,200 rent expense reduced owner's equity as well as cash.
- **Transaction 8:** Withdrawals are for personal use. Here, business cash decreased by $500 while Michael's Withdrawals account increased $500. Withdrawals decrease the owner's equity.
- **Transaction 9:** This transaction did not reflect new revenue in the form of legal fees. It was only a shift in assets: more cash and reduced accounts receivable.

b. Financial Statements

Michael Brown, Barrister and Solicitor
Income Statement
for the Month Ended June 30, 2009

Revenue:		
Legal Fees		$3,000
Operating Expenses:		
Salaries Expense	$ 800	
Rent Expense	1,200	
Total Operating Expenses		2,000
Net Income		$1,000

Michael Brown, Barrister and Solicitor
Statement of Owner's Equity
for the Month Ended June 30, 2009

Michael Brown, Capital, June 1, 2009		$6,000
Net Income for June	$1,000	
Less: Withdrawals for June	500	
Increase in Capital		500
Michael Brown, Capital, June 30, 2009		$6,500

Michael Brown, Barrister and Solicitor
Balance Sheet
June 30, 2009

Assets		*Liabilities and Owner's Equity*	
Cash	$5,400	Liabilities	
Accounts Receivable	500	Accounts Payable	$1,000
Office Equipment	1,600	Owner's Equity	
		M. Brown, Capital	6,500
Total Assets	$7,500	Total Liabilities and Owner's Equity	$7,500

Solution Tips to Financial Statements

◆ **Income statement:** This statement lists only revenues and expenses for a specified period of time. Inside column is for subtotalling. Withdrawals are not listed here.

◆ **Statement of owner's equity:** The statement of owner's equity takes the net income figure of $1,000 and adds it to beginning capital less any withdrawals. This new capital figure of $6,500 will go on the balance sheet. This report shows changes in capital for a specified period of time.

◆ **Balance sheet:** The $5,400, $500, $1,600, and $1,000 came from the totals of the expanded accounting equation. The capital figure of $6,500 came from the statement of owner's equity. This balance sheet reports assets, liabilities, and a new figure for capital at a specific date.

SUMMARY OF KEY POINTS

Learning Unit 1-1

1. The functions of accounting involve analyzing, recording, classifying, summarizing, reporting, and interpreting financial information.
2. A sole proprietorship is a business owned by one person. A partnership is a business owned by two or more persons. A corporation is a business owned by shareholders.
3. Bookkeeping is the recording part of accounting.
4. The computer is a tool to use in the accounting process.
5. Assets = Liabilities + Owner's Equity is the basic accounting equation that helps in analyzing business transactions.
6. Liabilities represent amounts owed to creditors, while capital represents what is invested by the owner.
7. Capital does not mean cash. Capital is the owner's current investment. The owner could have invested equipment that was purchased before the new business was started.
8. In a shift of assets, the composition of assets changes, but the total value of assets does not change. For example, if a bill is paid by a customer, the firm increases cash (an asset) but decreases accounts receivable (an asset), so there is no overall increase in assets; total assets remain the same. When you borrow money from a bank, you have an increase in cash (an asset) and an increase in liabilities; overall there is an increase in assets, not just a shift.

Learning Unit 1-2

1. The balance sheet is a report written as of a particular date. It lists the assets, liabilities, and owner's equity of a business. The heading of the balance sheet answers the questions *Who, What,* and *When* (as of a specific date).

2. The balance sheet is a formal report of a financial position.

Learning Unit 1-3

1. Revenue generates an inward flow of assets. Expenses generate an outward flow of assets or a potential outward flow. Revenue and expenses are subdivisions of owner's equity. Revenue is not an asset.

2. When revenue totals more than expenses, net income is the result; when expenses total more than revenue, net loss is the result.

3. Owner's equity can be subdivided into four elements: capital, withdrawals, revenue, and expenses.

4. Withdrawals decrease owner's equity; revenue increases owner's equity; expenses decrease owner's equity. A withdrawal is not a business expense; it is for personal use.

Learning Unit 1-4

1. The income statement is a report written for a specific period of time that lists earned revenue and expenses incurred to produce the earned revenue. The net income or net loss will be used in the statement of owner's equity.

2. The statement of owner's equity reveals the causes of a change in capital. This report lists additional investments in the company, net income (or net loss), and withdrawals. The ending figure for capital will be used on the balance sheet.

3. The balance sheet uses the ending balances of assets and liabilities from the accounting equation and the capital from the statement of owner's equity.

4. The income statement should be prepared first because the information on it relating to net income or net loss is used to prepare the statement of owner's equity, which in turn provides information about capital for the balance sheet. In this way, one builds upon the previous information and it begins with the income statement.

KEY TERMS

Accounting A system that measures a business's activities in financial terms, provides written reports and financial statements about those activities, and communicates these reports to decision-makers and others (p. 5)

Accounting process See *Accounting* (p. 5)

Accounts payable Amounts owed to creditors that result from the purchase of goods or services on account; a liability (p. 10)

Accounts receivable Amounts to be paid by customers resulting from sales of goods and/or services on credit; an asset (p. 14)

Assets Properties (resources) of value owned by a business (cash, supplies, equipment, land, and so on) (p. 8)

Balance sheet A report, as of a particular date, that shows the amount of assets owned by a business as well as the amount of claims (liabilities and owner's equity) against these assets (p. 12)

Basic accounting equation Assets = Liabilities + Owner's Equity (p. 9)

Bookkeeping The recording function of the accounting process (p. 7)

Business entity In accounting, it is assumed that a business is separate and distinct from the personal assets of the owner. Each unit or entity requires separate accounting functions. (p. 8)

Capital The owner's investment of equity in the company (p. 9)

Corporation A type of business organization that is owned by shareholders.

Usually, shareholders are not personally liable for the corporation's debts. (p. 3)

Creditor   Someone who has a claim to assets (p. 8)

Ending capital   Beginning Capital + Additional Investments + Net Income − Withdrawals = Ending Capital. *Or:* Beginning Capital + Additional Investments − Net Loss − Withdrawals = Ending Capital (p. 22)

Equipment   Assets acquired to be used in business activities, usually with an expected life of from two to ten years (p. 10)

Equities   The financial claim of creditors (liabilities) and owners (owner's equity) who supply the assets and expenses to a firm (p. 8)

Expanded accounting equation   Assets = Liabilities + Capital − Withdrawals + Revenue − Expenses (p. 15)

Expense   Cost incurred in running a business by consuming goods or services in producing revenue; a subdivision of owner's equity. When expenses increase, there is a decrease in owner's equity. (p. 15)

Generally accepted accounting principles (GAAP)   The procedures and guidelines that must be followed during the accounting process (p. 5)

Income statement   An accounting report that details the performance of a firm (revenue minus expenses) for a specific period of time (p. 19)

Liability   An obligation that comes due in the future. A liability increases the financial rights or claims of creditors to assets (p. 8)

Manufacturing companies   Businesses that make a product and sell it to their customers; they may also make and sell their own products (p. 5)

Merchandising companies   Businesses that buy a product from a manufacturing company, distributor, or wholesaler to sell to their customers (p. 5)

Net income   When revenue totals more than expenses, the result is net income. (p. 15)

Net loss   When expenses total more than revenue, the result is net loss. (p. 15)

Owner's equity   Rights or financial claims to the assets of a business by the owner (in the accounting equation, assets minus liabilities) (p. 9)

Partnership   A form of business organization that has at least two owners. The partners are usually personally liable for the partnership's debts. (p. 3)

Revenue   An amount earned by performing services for customers or selling goods to customers. Revenue increases cash and/or accounts receivable. It is a subdivision of owner's equity—as revenue increases, owner's equity increases. (p. 14)

Sarbanes-Oxley Act   Legislation passed in the United States that attempts to prevent false or misleading financial statements by public companies (p. 2)

Service company   Business that provides a service (p. 4)

Shift in assets   A shift that occurs when the composition of the assets has changed, but the total of the assets remains the same (p. 10)

Sole proprietorship   A business that has one owner. The owner is personally liable for paying the business's debts. (p. 3)

Statement of financial position   Another name for a balance sheet (p. 12)

Statement of owner's equity   A financial report that reveals the change in capital. The ending figure for capital is then placed on the balance sheet. (p. 20)

Supplies   One type of asset acquired by a firm. A supply item is temporarily treated as an asset until it is consumed, when it is transferred to expense.

Sometimes if it is not a significant amount it is treated as an expense when purchased—both treatments are possible. (p. 10)

Withdrawals A subdivision of owner's equity that records money or other assets an owner withdraws from a business for personal use (p. 15)

BLUEPRINT OF FINANCIAL REPORTS

❶ Income Statement

Measuring performance

Revenue		XXX	
Less: Operating expenses:			
Expense 1	XXX		
Expense 2	XX		
Expense 3	XX	XXX	
Net Income		XXX	

❷ Statement of Owner's Equity

Calculating new figure for Capital

Beginning Capital		XXX	
Additional Investments		XXX	
Total Investments		XXX	
Net Income (or Loss)	XXX		
Less: Withdrawals	XXX		
Change in Capital		XXX	
Ending Capital		XXX	

❸ Balance Sheet

Showing where we now stand

	Assets		Liabilities and Owner's Equity	
		XXX	Liabilities	XXX
		XXX	Owner's Equity	
		XXX	Ending Capital	XXX
			Total Liabilities +	
	Total Assets	XXX	Owner's Equity	XXX

QUESTIONS, CLASSROOM DEMONSTRATION EXERCISES, EXERCISES, AND PROBLEMS

Discussion Questions and Critical Thinking/Ethical Case

1. What are the functions of accounting?
2. Define, compare, and contrast sole proprietorships, partnerships, and corporations.
3. How are businesses classified?
4. What is the relationship of bookkeeping to accounting?
5. List the three elements of the basic accounting equation.
6. Define capital.

7. The total of the left-hand side of the accounting equation must equal the total of the right-hand side. True or false? Please explain.

8. A balance sheet tells a company where it is going and how well it will perform. True or false? Please explain.

9. Revenue is an asset. True or false? Please explain.

10. Into what categories is owner's equity subdivided?

11. A withdrawal is a business expense. True or false? Please explain.

12. As expenses increase, they cause owner's equity to increase. Defend or reject.

13. What does an income statement show?

14. The statement of owner's equity calculates only ending withdrawals. True or false? Please explain.

15. Paul Kloss, accountant for Lowe & Co., travelled to Vancouver on company business. His total expenses came to $350. Paul felt that since the trip extended over the weekend, he could pad his expense account with an additional $100 of expenses. After all, weekends represent his own time, not the company's. What would you do? Write your specific recommendations to Paul.

Classroom Demonstration Exercises

(The blank forms you need are on page 1-7 of the *Study Guide with Working Papers*.)

Set A

Classifying Accounts

1. Classify each of the following items as an asset (A), liability (L), or part of owner's equity (OE).

   a. Sony Flat-Screen Television _____
   b. J. Ling, Capital _____
   c. Accounts Payable _____
   d. Cash _____
   e. Supplies on Hand _____
   f. Kodak Digital Camera _____

The Accounting Equation

2. Complete:

   a. _____: rights of the creditors.
   b. _____ are the total value of items owned by a business.
   c. _____ _____ is an unwritten promise to pay the creditor.

Shift Versus Increase in Assets

3. Identify which transaction below results in a shift in assets (S) and which transaction causes an increase in assets (I).

   a. Jay's Internet Cafe bought computer equipment on account _____.
   b. Eastern Tile Co. bought office equipment for cash _____.

The Balance Sheet

4. From the following, calculate what would be the total of assets on the balance sheet.

Lee Winn, Capital	$14,000
Computer Equipment	2,000
Accounts Payable	5,000
Cash	17,000

The Accounting Equation Expanded

5. Identify with a ✓ which of the following are subdivisions of owner's equity.

a. Vehicles _____   e. Accounts Receivable _____
b. J. Penny, Capital _____   f. Advertising Expense _____
c. Accounts Payable _____   g. Taxi Fees Earned _____
d. J. Penny, Withdrawals _____   h. Computer Equipment _____

Identifying Assets

6. Identify with a ✓ which of the following are *not* assets.

a. DVD Player _____
b. Accounts Receivable _____
c. Accounts Payable _____
d. Grooming Fees Earned _____

The Accounting Equation Expanded

7. Which of the following statements are false?

a. _____ Revenue provides only outward flows of cash.
b. _____ Revenue is a subdivision of assets.
c. _____ Revenue provides an inward flow of cash and/or accounts receivable.
d. _____ Expenses are part of total assets.

Preparing Financial Statements

8. Indicate whether the following items would appear on the income statement (IS), statement of owner's equity (OE), or balance sheet (BS).

a. _____ Tutoring Fees Earned
b. _____ Office Equipment
c. _____ Accounts Receivable
d. _____ Supplies on Hand
e. _____ Legal Fees Earned
f. _____ Advertising Expense
g. _____ J. Earl, Capital (Beginning)
h. _____ Accounts Payable

Preparing Financial Statements

9. Indicate next to each statement whether it refers to the income statement (IS), statement of owner's equity (OE), or balance sheet (BS).

a. _____ Withdrawals found on it
b. _____ Lists total of all assets
c. _____ Statement that is prepared last
d. _____ Statement listing net income

Set B

Classifying Accounts

1. Classify each of the following items as an asset (A), liability (L), or part of owner's equity (OE).

   a. Panasonic DVD Recorder _____
   b. Accounts Payable _____
   c. P. Jean, Capital _____
   d. Supplies on Hand _____
   e. Cash _____
   f. Canon Digital Camera _____

The Accounting Equation

2. Complete:

   a. A(n) _____ _____ _____ results when the total of the assets remains the same, but the makeup of the assets has changed.
   b. Assets – _____ = Owner's Equity.
   c. Capital does not mean _____.

Shift Versus Increase in Assets

3. Identify which transaction below results in a shift in assets (S) and which transaction causes an increase in assets (I).

   a. Ace Jewellery bought computer equipment for cash _____.
   b. Jake's Appliances bought office equipment on account _____.

The Balance Sheet

4. From the following, calculate what would be the total of assets on the balance sheet.

H. Sung, Capital	$11,000
Desktop Publishing Equipment	1,000
Accounts Payable	2,000
Cash	12,000

The Accounting Equation Expanded

5. Identify with a ✓ which of the following are subdivisions of owner's equity.

   a. Land _____   e. Accounts Payable _____
   b. M. Kaminsky, Capital _____   f. Rent Expense _____
   c. Accounts Receivable _____   g. Office Equipment _____
   d. M. Kaminsky, Withdrawals _____   h. Hair Salon Fees Earned _____

Identifying Assets

6. Identify with a ✓ which of the following are *not* assets.

   a. Fax Machines _____
   b. Accounts Payable _____
   c. Legal Fees Earned _____
   d. Accounts Receivable _____

The Accounting Equation Expanded

7. Which of the following statements are false?

a. _____ Revenue is an asset.

b. _____ Revenue is a subdivision of owner's equity.

c. _____ Revenue provides an inward flow of cash and/or accounts receivable.

d. _____ Withdrawals are part of total assets.

Preparing Financial Statements

8. Indicate whether the following items would appear on the income statement (IS), statement of owner's equity (OE), or balance sheet (BS).

a. _____ B. Clo, Withdrawals

b. _____ Supplies on Hand

c. _____ Accounts Payable

d. _____ Computer Equipment

e. _____ Commission Fees Earned

f. _____ Salaries Expense

g. _____ B. Clo, Capital (Beginning)

h. _____ Accounts Receivable

Preparing Financial Statements

9. Indicate next to each statement whether it refers to the income statement (IS), statement of owner's equity (OE), or balance sheet (BS).

a. _____ Calculate new figure for Capital

b. _____ Prepared as of a particular date

c. _____ Statement that is prepared first

d. _____ Report listing revenues and expenses

Exercises

(The forms you need are on pages 1-8 and 1-9 of the *Study Guide with Working Papers*.)

The accounting equation

1-1. Complete the following table:

Assets	=	Liabilities	+	Owner's Equity
a. $16,000	=	?	+	$2,000
b. ?	=	$6,000	+	$9,000
c. $10,000	=	$4,000	+	?

Recording transactions in the accounting equation

1-2. Record the following transactions in the basic accounting equation:

Assets = Liabilities + Owner's Equity

Treat each transaction separately.

a. Ralph invests $8,000 in his company.

b. The company buys equipment for cash, $600.

c. The company buys equipment on account, $900.

1-3. From the following, prepare a balance sheet for Jingle's Cleaners at the end of November 2010: Cash, $30,000; Cleaning Equipment, $8,000; Accounts Payable, $9,000; J. Jingle, Capital.

1-4. Record the following transactions in the expanded accounting equation. The running balance may be omitted for simplicity.

ASSETS			=	LIABILITIES	+	OWNER'S EQUITY			
Cash + Accounts Receivable	+ Computer Equipment		=	Accounts Payable	+ B. Bell, Capital	− B. Bell, Withdrawals		+ Revenue	− Expenses

a. B. Bell invested $60,000 in Bell's Computer company.

b. Bought computer equipment on account, $7,000.

c. Paid personal telephone bill from company bank account, $200.

d. Received cash for services rendered, $14,000.

e. Billed customers for services rendered for the month, $30,000.

f. Paid current rent expense, $4,000.

g. Paid supplies expense, $1,500.

1-5. From the following account balances for June 2010, prepare in proper form **a.** an income statement, **b.** a statement of owner's equity, and **c.** a balance sheet for French Realty.

Cash	$3,310	S. French, Withdrawals	40
Accounts Receivable	1,490	Professional Fees	2,900
Office Equipment	6,700	Salaries Expense	500
Accounts Payable	2,000	Utilities Expense	360
S. French, Capital, June 1, 2010	8,000	Rent Expense	500

Group A Problems

(The forms you need are on pages 1-10 to 1-16 of the *Study Guide with Working Papers*.) (c) B/S Pg 21 c6.

1A-1. Betty Sullivan, who lives in Winnipeg, decided to open Betty's Dog Grooming Centre. Betty completed the following transactions:

a. Invested $19,000 cash from her personal bank account into the business.

b. Bought equipment for cash, $3,000.

c. Bought additional equipment on account, $2,000.

d. Paid $300 cash to reduce what was owed from the transaction in **(c)**.

Based on the above information, record these transactions in the basic accounting equation.

1A-2. Roger Clay is the accountant for Blue's Internet Service of Halifax. His task is to construct a balance sheet from the following information, as of September 30, 2011, in proper form. Could you help him?

Building	$40,000	Cash	12,000
Accounts Payable	20,000	Equipment	16,000
R. Clay, Capital	48,000		

1A-3. At the end of November, Rick Fox of Corner Brook decided to open his own desktop publishing business. Analyze the following transactions he completed by recording their effects in the expanded accounting equation.

a. Invested $12,000 in his desktop publishing business.

b. Bought new office equipment on account, $4,000.

c. Received cash for desktop publishing services rendered, $500.

d. Performed desktop publishing services on account, $2,100.

e. Paid part-time secretary's salary, $650.

f. Paid office supplies expense for the month, $210.

g. Rent expense for office due but not yet paid, $900.

h. Rick Fox withdrew cash for personal use, $400.

1A-4. Jane West, owner of West's Stencilling Service in Grande Prairie, has requested that you prepare from the following balances (a) an income statement for June 2011, (b) a statement of owner's equity for June, and (c) a balance sheet as of June 30, 2011.

Cash	$2,300	Stencilling Fees	3,000
Accounts Receivable	400	Advertising Expense	110
Equipment	685	Repair Expense	25
Accounts Payable	310	Travel Expense	250
J. West, Capital, June 1, 2011	1,200	Supplies Expense	190
J. West, Withdrawals	300	Rent Expense	250

1A-5. Jill Martin of Regina opened Martin's Catering Service. As her accountant, analyze the transactions listed below and present in proper form:

1. The analysis of the transactions by utilizing the expanded accounting equation

2. A balance sheet showing the position of the firm before opening on November 1, 2010

3. An income statement for the month of November

4. A statement of owner's equity for November

5. A balance sheet as of November 30, 2010

2010

Oct. 25 Jill Martin invested $8,000 in the catering business from her personal savings account.

26 Bought equipment for cash from Munroe Co., $900.

27 Bought additional equipment on account from Ryan Co., $1,800.

29 Paid $1,000 to Ryan Co. as partial payment of the October 27 transaction.

(You should now prepare your balance sheet as of October 31, 2010.)

Nov. 1 Catered a graduation and immediately collected cash, $2,900.

4 Paid salaries of employees, $720.

8 Prepared desserts for customers on account, $300.

11 Received $100 cash as partial payment of November 8 transaction.

15 Paid telephone bill, $75.

16 Jill paid her home electricity bill from the company's bank account, $90.

17 Catered a wedding and received cash, $1,800.

25 Bought additional equipment on account, $400.

29 Rent expense due but not yet paid, $600

30 Paid supplies expense, $400.

CONTINUING PROBLEM

The following problem will continue from one chapter to the next, carrying the balances forward from month to month. Each chapter will focus on the learning experience of the chapter and add additional information as the business grows. The necessary forms are provided on pages 1-26 to 1-28 of the *Study Guide with Working Papers*.

Assignment

1. Set up an expanded accounting equation spreadsheet using the following accounts:

Assets	Liabilities	Owner's Equity
Cash	Accounts Payable	T. Freedman, Capital
Supplies		T. Freedman, Withdrawals
Computer Shop		Service Revenue
Equipment		Expenses (notate type)
Office Equipment		

2. Analyze and record each transaction in the expanded accounting equation.

3. Prepare the financial statements for Precision Computer Centre for the period ending July 31.

Tony Freedman decided to begin his own computer service business on July 2, 2010. He named the business the Precision Computer Centre. During the first month, Tony conducted the following business transactions:

(a) Invested $4,500 of his savings into the business.

(b) Paid $1,200 (cheque No. 201) for a computer from Multi Systems, Inc.

(c) Paid $600 (cheque No. 202) for office equipment from Office Furniture, Inc.

(d) Set up a new account with Office Depot and purchased $250 in office supplies on credit.

(e) Paid July rent, $400 (cheque No. 203).

(f) Repaired a system for a customer; collected $250.

(g) Collected $200 for system upgrade labour charge from a customer.

(h) Electric bill due but unpaid, $85.

(i) Received $1,200 for services performed on Taylor Golf computers.

(j) Tony withdrew $100 (cheque No. 204) to take his wife Carol out in celebration of opening the new business. *Note:* The business is too small to worry about GST (or HST).

Debits and Credits

Analyzing and Recording Business Transactions

THE BIG PICTURE

What would you sacrifice to see your dreams come true? Would you invest every penny of your savings, sleep under your desk, and eat a constant diet of canned beans and Kraft Dinner?

Albertans Evan and Shane Chrapko and their former business partner Valerian Pappes know what it's like to sacrifice to make their dream a success. While it took only 19 months to take the DocSpace Company, a Toronto-based technology startup, to a value of more than $800 million, the personal and financial sacrifices began years earlier. The trio gave up many comforts to make their business succeed: their office furniture was salvaged, home was a futon under the desk, and dinner was student fare.

Their commitment led to one of the fastest and greatest successes in Canadian e-business history. In March 2000, less than two years after DocSpace was founded, the company was purchased by Critical Path, a California dot-com, for a whopping C$811 million.

The three entrepreneurs were fortunate to sell at the height of dot-com madness, benefiting from an inflated technology market. But their success had more to do with sound business principles than with merely being in the right place at the right time.

The partners decided early to operate as a business—protecting the technology with patent applications and keeping a close eye on the bottom line. They resisted throwing money around and gathered a strong workforce, many who received some or all of their compensation in the form of shares rather than cash. While their would-be competitors were offering products for free, DocSpace established reasonable market prices and sought out paying customers.

The strategy worked. By the time Critical Path made its offer, the partners had considered and declined three offers that would have made them—and many loyal employees—millionaires. However, with a clear idea of the value of their technology, the young Canadians held out until they received a bid that represented the value of their creation.

In this chapter, you learn the steps that go into generating a financial statement. When you analyze a business transaction you decide not only which accounts change in value, but also whether they increase or decrease. You'll see how to use a *T Account* to write the value of a transaction as a debit or credit in a standard format and total the account at any time. You'll use the ending balances on every T account to prepare a *trial balance*, a test of the equality of debits and credits in all your accounts. You can then use the account balances to generate financial statements that you can compare month to month. By comparing financial statements, you can estimate how the financials will look in the future.

This chapter won't teach you how to turn your ideas and dreams into a multimillion-dollar company. However, if $811 million ever happens your way, at least you'll know how to record the transaction in the proper T account!

◆ **Setting up and organizing a chart of accounts (p. 47)**
◆ **Recording transactions in T accounts according to the rules of debit and credit (p. 48)**
◆ **Preparing a trial balance (p. 57)**
◆ **Preparing financial statements from a trial balance (pp. 57–58)**

In Chapter 1, we used the expanded accounting equation to document the financial transactions performed by Catherine Hall's law firm. Remember how long it was: the cash column had a long list of pluses and minuses, and there was no quick system of recording and summarizing the increases and decreases of cash or other items. Can you imagine the problem Canadian Tire or Tim Hortons would have if they used the expanded accounting equation to track the thousands of business transactions they do each day?

Let's look at the problem a little more closely. Every business transaction is recorded in the accounting equation under a specific **account**. There are different accounts for each of the subdivisions of the accounting equation—there are asset accounts, liability accounts, expense accounts, revenue accounts, and so on. What is needed is a way to record the increases and decreases in specific account *categories* and yet keep them together in one place. The answer is the **standard account** form (see Figure 2-1). A standard account is a formal account that includes columns for date, explanation, posting reference, debit, and credit. Each account has a separate form and all transactions affecting that account are recorded on the form. All the business's account forms (which often are referred to as *ledger accounts*) are then placed in a **ledger**. Each page of the ledger contains one account. The ledger may be in the form of a bound or a loose-leaf book. If computers are used, the ledger may be part of a computer printout. For simplicity's sake, in this chapter, we will use the **T account** form, which got its name because it looks like the letter T. Generally, T accounts are used for classroom demonstration purposes.

Figure 2-1
The Standard Account Form

The standard account form is the source of the T account's shape.

Account Title								Account No.
Date	Item	PR	Debit	Date	Item	PR	Credit	

Learning Unit 2-1
The T Account

Each T account contains three basic parts:

1 **Title of Account**	
2 **Left side**	**Right side** 3

All T accounts have this structure. In accounting, the left side of any T account is called the **debit** side.

At this point, for you, the word *debit* in accounting means a position, the left side of an account. Don't think of it as good (+) or bad (−).

Left side	
Dr. (debit)	

Amounts entered on the left side of any account are said to be *debited* to an account. The word *debit* is from the Latin *debere*; the abbreviation for debit is Dr.

The right side of any T account is called the **credit** side.

	Right side
	Cr. (credit)

Amounts entered on the right side of any account are said to be *credited* to an account. The word *credit* is from the Latin *credere*; the abbreviation for credit is Cr.

At this point, do not associate the definitions of debit and credit with the words *increase* and *decrease*. Think of debit or credit as only indicating a *position* (left side or right side) of a T account.

BALANCING AN ACCOUNT

No matter which individual account is being balanced, the procedure used to balance it will be the same.

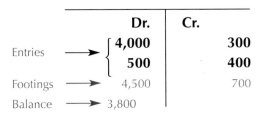

	Dr.	Cr.
Entries	4,000	300
	500	400
Footings	4,500	700
Balance	3,800	

In the "real" world, the T account would also include the date of the transaction. The date would appear to the left of the entry.

Note that on the debit (left) side, the amounts add up to $4,500. On the credit (right) side, the amounts add up $700. The $4,500 and the $700 written in small type are called **footings**. Footings help in calculating the new (or ending) balance. The **ending balance** ($3,800) is placed on the debit or left side, since the total of the debit side is greater than that of the credit side.

	Dr.		Cr.
4/2	4,000	4/3	300
4/20	500	4/25	400
Footings	4,500		700
Balance	3,800		

Remember, the ending balance does not tell us anything about increase or decrease. It tells us only that we have an ending balance of $3,800 on the debit side.

LEARNING UNIT 2-1 REVIEW

AT THIS POINT you should be able to:

◆ Define ledger. (p. 44)
◆ State the purpose of a T account. (p. 44)
◆ Identify the three parts of a T account. (pp. 44–45)
◆ Define debit. (p. 45)
◆ Define credit. (p. 45)
◆ Explain footings and calculate the balance of an account. (p. 45)

Self-Review Quiz 2-1

(The blank forms you need are on page 2-1 of the *Study Guide with Working Papers.*)

Respond True or False to the following:

1.

Dr.	Cr.
3,000	200
200	600

The balance of the account is $2,400 Cr.

2. A credit always means increase.
3. A debit is the left side of any account.
4. A ledger can be prepared manually or by computer.
5. Footings replace the need for debits and credits.

Quiz Tip

Dr. + Dr. ⟶ Add to get Dr. balance.

Cr. + Cr. ⟶ Add to get Cr. balance.

Dr. – Cr. ⟶ Subtract to get balance for the larger side.

Solutions to Self-Review Quiz 2-1

1. False   2. False   3. True   4. True   5. False

Learning Unit 2-2

Recording Business Transactions: Debits and Credits

Can you get a queen in checkers? Is there a fourth down in the CFL? In a baseball game, does a runner rounding first base skip second base and run over the pitcher's mound to get to third? No—most of us don't do such things because we follow the rules of the game. Usually we learn the rules first and reflect on the reasons for them afterward. The same is true in accounting.

Instead of first trying to understand all the rules of debit and credit and how they were developed in accounting, it will be easier to learn the rules by "playing the game."

T ACCOUNT ENTRIES FOR ACCOUNTING IN THE ACCOUNTING EQUATION

Have patience. Learning the rules of debit and credit is like learning to play any game—the more you play, the easier it becomes. Table 2-1 shows the rules for the side on which you enter an increase or a decrease for each of the separate accounts in the accounting equation. For example, an increase is entered on the debit side in the asset account but on the credit side for a liability account.

TABLE 2-1   Rules of Debit and Credit

Account Category	Increase (Normal Balance)	Decrease
Assets	Debit	Credit
Liabilities	Credit	Debit
Owner's Equity:		
Capital	Credit	Debit
Withdrawals	Debit	Credit
Revenue	Credit	Debit
Expenses	Debit	Credit

It might be easier to visualize these rules of debit and credit if we look at them in the T account form, using + to show increase and − to show decrease.

ASSETS	=	LIABILITIES	+	OWNER'S EQUITY				
				Capital	− **Withdrawals**	+ **Revenue**	− **Expenses**	
Dr. | Cr.		Dr. | Cr.		Dr. | Cr.	Dr. | Cr.	Dr. | Cr.	Dr. | Cr.	
+ | −		− | +		− | +	+ | −	− | +	+ | −	

Rules for Assets Work in the Opposite Direction to Those for Liabilities

When you look at the equation, you can see that the rules for assets work in the opposite direction to those for liabilities. That is, for assets, the increases appear on the debit side and the decreases are shown on the credit side; the opposite is true for liabilities. As for owner's equity, the rules for withdrawals and expenses, which *decrease* owner's equity, work in the opposite direction to the rules for capital and revenue, which *increase* owner's equity.

Assets	+ **Withdrawals**	+ **Expenses**	= **Liabilities**	+ **Capital**	+ **Revenue**
Dr. | Cr.	Dr. | Cr.	Dr. | Cr.	Dr. | Cr.	Dr. | Cr.	Dr. | Cr.
+ | −	+ | −	+ | −	− | +	− | +	− | +

This setup may help you understand that the rules for withdrawals and expenses are just the opposite of the rules for capital and revenue.

A **normal balance of an account** is the side that increases by the rules of debit and credit. For example, the balance of cash is a debit balance because an asset is increased by a debit. We will discuss normal balances further in Chapter 3.

Normal Balance	
Dr.	Cr.
Assets	Liabilities
Expenses	Capital
Withdrawals	Revenue

Balancing the Equation

It is important to remember that any amount(s) entered on the debit side of a T account or accounts also must be on the credit side of another T account or accounts. This ensures that the total amount added to the debit side will equal the total amount added to the credit side, thereby keeping the accounting equation in balance.

Chart of Accounts

Our job is to analyze Catherine Hall's business transactions—the transactions we looked at in Chapter 1—using a system of accounts guided by the rules of debits and credits that will summarize increases and decreases of individual accounts in the ledger. The goal is to prepare an income statement, statement of owner's equity, and balance sheet for Catherine Hall. Sound familiar? If this system works, the rules of debits and credits and the use of accounts will give us the same answers as in Chapter 1 but with greater ease.

Balance Sheet Accounts	
Assets	**Liabilities**
111 Cash	211 Accounts Payable
112 Accounts Receivable	
121 Office Equipment	**Owner's Equity**
	311 Catherine Hall, Capital
	312 Catherine Hall, Withdrawals

Income Statement Accounts	
Revenue	**Expenses**
411 Legal Fees	511 Salaries Expense
	512 Rent Expense
	513 Advertising Expense

Balance Sheet Accounts

Catherine's accountant developed what is called a **chart of accounts**. The chart of accounts is a numbered list of all of the business's accounts. It allows accounts to be located quickly. In Catherine's business, for example, 100s are assets, 200s are liabilities, and so on. As you can see in Table 2-2, each separate asset and liability has its own number. Note that the chart may be expanded as the business grows.

THE ACCOUNTING ANALYSIS: FIVE STEPS

We will analyze the transactions in Catherine Hall's law firm using a teaching device called a *transaction analysis chart*. (Keep in mind that the transaction analysis chart is not a part of any formal accounting system.) There are five steps in analyzing each business transaction:

Step 1: Determine which accounts are affected. Example: cash, accounts payable, rent expense. A transaction always affects at least two accounts.

Step 2: Determine which categories the accounts belong to—assets, liabilities, capital, withdrawals, revenue, or expenses. Example: Cash is an asset.

Step 3: Determine whether the accounts increase or decrease. Example: If you receive cash, that account is increasing.

Step 4: What do the rules of debits and credits say (Table 2-1)?

Step 5: What does the T account look like? Place amounts in the accounts on either the left or right side depending on the rules in Table 2-1.

This is how the five-step analysis looks in chart form:

1 Accounts Affected	2 Category	3 ↓ or ↑ (decrease) (increase)	4 Rules of Dr. and Cr.	5 Appearance of T Accounts

Let us emphasize a major point: *Do not try to debit or credit an account until you have gone through the first four steps of the transaction analysis.*

Sidebar (left margin):

Large companies may have four digits assigned to each title, and sometimes up to 24 digits (e.g., Exxon).

Steps to analyze and record transactions. Steps 1 and 2 will come from the chart of accounts. Remember the rules of debit and credit tell us only on which side to place information. Whether the debit or credit represents increases or decreases depends on the account category:

- Assets, Expenses, and Withdrawals, which are increased with a debit

- Liabilities, Owner's Equity, and Revenue, which are increased with a credit

Think of a business transaction as an exchange—you get something and you give up or part with something.

APPLYING THE TRANSACTION ANALYSIS TO CATHERINE HALL'S LAW PRACTICE

Transaction A: Aug. 26: Catherine Hall invests $7,000 cash and $800 worth of office equipment in the business.

1 Accounts Affected	2 Category	3 ↓ ↑	4 Rules of Dr. and Cr.	5 Appearance of T Accounts
Cash	Asset	↑	Dr.	**Cash 111** (A) 7,000
Office Equipment	Asset	↑	Dr.	**Office Equipment 121** (A) 800
C. Hall, Capital	Owner's Equity	↑	Cr.	**C. Hall, Capital 311** 7,800 (A)

Note again that every transaction affects at least two T accounts, and the total amount added to the debit side(s) must equal the total amount added to the credit side(s) of the T accounts for each transaction.

Analysis of Transaction A

Step 1: Which accounts are affected? The law firm receives cash and office equipment, so three accounts are involved: cash, office equipment, and C. Hall, Capital. These account titles come from the chart of accounts.

Step 2: Which categories do these accounts belong to? Cash and office equipment are assets; C. Hall, Capital, is owner's equity.

Step 3: Are the accounts increasing or decreasing? The cash and office equipment, both assets, are increasing in the business. The rights or claims of C. Hall, Capital, are also increasing since Catherine invested money and office equipment in the business.

Step 4: What do the rules say? According to the rules of debit and credit, an increase in assets (cash and office equipment) is a debit. An increase in capital is a credit. Note that the total dollar amount of debits will equal the total dollar amount of credits when the T accounts are updated in column 5.

Step 5: What does the T account look like? The amount for cash and office equipment is entered on the debit side. The amount for C. Hall, Capital, goes on the credit side.

A transaction that involves more than one credit or more than one debit is called a **compound entry**. This first transaction of Catherine Hall's law firm is a compound entry; it involves a debit of $7,000 to Cash and a debit of $800 to Office Equipment (as well as a credit of $7,800 to C. Hall, Capital).

There is a name for this double-entry analysis of transactions, where two or more accounts are affected and the total of debits equals the total of credits. It is called **double-entry bookkeeping**. This double-entry system helps in checking the recording of business transactions.

As we continue, the explanations will be brief, but do not forget to apply the five steps in analyzing and recording each business transaction.

Transaction B: Aug. 27: Law practice bought office equipment for cash, $900.

1 Accounts Affected	2 Category	3 ↓　↑	4 Rules of Dr. and Cr.	5 T Account Update
Office Equipment	Asset	↑	Dr.	**Office Equipment 121** (A)　800 (B)　900
Cash	Asset	↓	Cr.	**Cash 111** (A) 7,000　│　900 (B)

Analysis of Transaction B

Step 1: The law firm paid cash for the office equipment it received. The accounts involved in the transaction are Cash and Office Equipment.

Step 2: The accounts belong to these categories: Office Equipment is an asset account; Cash is an asset account.

Step 3: The asset account Office Equipment is increasing. The asset account Cash is decreasing—it is being reduced in order to buy the office equipment.

Step 4: An increase in the asset account Office Equipment is a debit; a decrease in the asset account Cash is a credit.

Step 5: When the amounts are placed in the T accounts, the amount for office equipment goes on the debit side and the amount for cash on the credit side.

Transaction C: Aug. 30: Bought more office equipment on account, $400.

1 Accounts Affected	2 Category	3 ↓　↑	4 Rules of Dr. and Cr.	5 T Account Update
Office Equipment	Asset	↑	Dr.	**Office Equipment 121** (A) 800 (B) 900 (C) 400 │
Accounts Payable	Liability	↑	Cr.	**Accounts Payable 211** │　400 (C)

Analysis of Transaction C

Step 1: The law firm receives office equipment by promising to pay in the future. An obligation or liability account, Accounts Payable, is created.

Step 2: Office Equipment is an asset. Accounts Payable is a liability.

Step 3: The asset account Office Equipment is increasing; the liability account Accounts Payable is increasing because the law firm is increasing what it owes.

Step 4: An increase in the asset account, Office Equipment, is a debit. An increase in the liability account, Accounts Payable, is a credit.

Step 5: Enter the amount for office equipment on the debit side of the T account. The amount for accounts payable goes on the credit side.

Transaction D: Sept. 1–30: Provided legal services for cash, $3,000.

---

1 Accounts Affected	2 Category	3 ↓ ↑	4 Rules of Dr. and Cr.	5 T Account Update
Cash	Asset	↑	Dr.	**Cash 111** (A) 7,000 | 900 (B) (D) 3,000 |
Legal Fees	Revenue	↑	Cr.	**Legal Fees 411** | 3,000 (D)

Analysis of Transaction D

Step 1: The firm has earned revenue from legal services and receives $3,000 in cash.

Step 2: Cash is an asset account. Legal fees are revenue.

Step 3: Cash, an asset account, is increasing. Legal fees, or revenue, is also increasing.

Step 4: An increase in cash, an asset, is debited. An increase in legal fees, or revenue, is credited.

Step 5: Enter the amount for cash on the debit side of the T account. Enter the amount for legal fees on the credit side.

Transaction E: Sept. 1–30: Provided legal services on account, $4,000.

---

1 Accounts Affected	2 Category	3 ↓ ↑	4 Rules of Dr. and Cr.	5 T Account Update
Accounts Receivable	Asset	↑	Dr.	**Accounts Receivable 112** (E) 4,000 |
Legal Fees	Revenue	↑	Cr.	**Legal Fees 411** | 3,000 (D) | 4,000 (E)

Analysis of Transaction E

Step 1: The law practice has earned revenue but has not yet received payment (cash). The amounts owed by these clients are called *accounts receivable*. Revenue is earned at the time the legal services are provided, whether payment is received then or will be received sometime in the future.

Step 2: Accounts Receivable is an asset account. Legal Fees is a revenue account.

Step 3: The Accounts Receivable account is increasing because the law practice has increased the amount owed to it for legal fees that have been earned but not paid. The Legal Fees account, or revenue, is increasing.

Step 4: An increase in the asset account, Accounts Receivable, is a debit. An increase in revenue is a credit.

Step 5: Enter the amount for Accounts Receivable on the debit side of the T account. The amount for Legal Fees goes on the credit side.

Transaction F: Sept. 1–30: Received $700 cash from clients for services rendered previously on account.

1 Accounts Affected	2 Category	3 ↓ ↑	4 Rules of Dr. and Cr.	5 T Account Update
Cash	Asset	↑	Dr.	**Cash 111** (A) 7,000 | 900 (B) (D) 3,000 (F) 700
Accounts Receivable	Asset	↓	Cr.	**Accounts Receivable 112** (E) 4,000 | 700 (F)

Analysis of Transaction F

Step 1: The law firm collects $700 in cash from previous revenue earned. Since the revenue is recorded at the time it is earned and not when the payment is made, in this transaction, we are concerned only with the payment, which affects the Cash and Accounts Receivable accounts.

Step 2: Cash is an asset account. Accounts Receivable is an asset account.

Step 3: Since clients are paying what is owed, cash (asset) is increasing and the amount owed (accounts receivable) is decreasing (the total amount owed by clients to Catherine Hall is going down). This transaction results in a shift in assets, more cash for less accounts receivable.

Step 4: An increase in the Cash account, an asset, is a debit. A decrease in the Accounts Receivable account, an asset, is a credit.

Step 5: Enter the amount for Cash on the debit side of the T account. The amount for Accounts Receivable goes on the credit side.

Transaction G: Sept. 1–30: Paid salaries expense, $600.

1 Accounts Affected	2 Category	3 ↓ ↑	4 Rules of Dr. and Cr.	5 T Account Update
Salaries Expense	Expense	↑	Dr.	**Salaries Expense 511** (G) 600 |
Cash	Asset	↓	Cr.	**Cash 111** (A) 7,000 | 900 (B) (D) 3,000 | 600 (G) (F) 700

Analysis of Transaction G

Step 1: The law firm pays $600 worth of salaries expense by cash.

Step 2: Salaries Expense is an expense account. Cash is an asset account.

Step 3: The salaries expense of the law firm is increasing, which results in a decrease in cash available.

Step 4: An increase in Salaries Expense, an expense account, is a debit. A decrease in Cash, an asset account, is a credit.

Step 5: Enter the amount for Salaries Expense on the debit side of the T account. The amount for Cash goes on the credit side.

Transaction H: Sept. 1–30: Paid rent expense, $700.

1 Accounts Affected	2 Category	3 ↓ ↑	4 Rules of Dr. and Cr.	5 T Account Update
Rent Expense	Expense	↑	Dr.	**Rent Expense 512** (H) 700 │
Cash	Asset	↓	Cr.	**Cash 111** (A) 7,000 │ 900 (B) (D) 3,000 │ 600 (G) (F) 700 │ 700 (H)

Analysis of Transaction H

Step 1: The law firm's rent expenses are paid in cash.

Step 2: Rent is an expense. Cash is an asset.

Step 3: The rent expense increases the expenses, and the payment for the rent expense decreases the cash.

Step 4: An increase in Rent Expense, an expense account, is a debit. A decrease in Cash, an asset account, is a credit.

Step 5: Enter the amount for Rent Expense on the debit side of the T account. Place the amount for Cash on the credit side.

Transaction I: Sept. 1–30: Received a bill for advertising expense
(to be paid next month), $300.

1 Accounts Affected	2 Category	3 ↓ ↑	4 Rules of Dr. and Cr.	5 T Account Update
Advertising Expense	Expense	↑	Dr.	**Advertising Expense 513** (I) 300 │
Accounts Payable	Liability	↑	Cr.	**Accounts Payable 211** │ 400 (C) │ 300 (I)

Analysis of Transaction I

Step 1: The advertising bill has come in and payment is due but has not yet been made. Therefore, the accounts involved here are Advertising Expense and Accounts Payable; the expense has created a liability.

Step 2: Advertising Expense is an expense account. Accounts Payable is a liability account.

Step 3: Both the expense and the liability are increasing.

Step 4: An increase in an expense is a debit. An increase in a liability is a credit.

Step 5: Enter the amount for the Advertising Expense account on the debit side of the T account. Enter the amount for the Accounts Payable account on the credit side.

Transaction J: Sept. 1–30: Hall withdrew cash for personal use, $200.

1 Accounts Affected	2 Category	3 ↓ ↑	4 Rules of Dr. and Cr.	5 T Account Update
C. Hall, Withdrawals	Owner's Equity (Withdrawals)*	↑	Dr.	C. Hall, Withdrawals 312 (J) 200 |
Cash	Asset	↓	Cr.	Cash 111 (A) 7,000 | 900 (B) (D) 3,000 | 600 (G) (F) 700 | 700 (H) | 200 (J)

*Withdrawals are actually a subcategory of Owner's Equity and act as a contra account—that is, as the Withdrawals account increases the Owner's Equity account decreases.

Analysis of Transaction J

> Withdrawals are always increased by debits.

Step 1: Catherine Hall withdraws cash from the business for *personal* use. This withdrawal is not a business expense.

Step 2: This transaction affects the Withdrawals and Cash accounts.

Step 3: Catherine has increased what she has withdrawn from the business for personal use. The business cash has been decreased.

Step 4: An increase in withdrawals is a debit. A decrease in cash is a credit. (*Remember:* Withdrawals go on the statement of owner's equity; expenses go on the income statement.)

Step 5: Enter the amount for C. Hall, Withdrawals, on the debit side of the T account. The amount for Cash goes on the credit side.

SUMMARY OF TRANSACTIONS FOR CATHERINE HALL

ASSETS	=	LIABILITIES	+	CAPITAL	−	WITHDRAWALS	+	REVENUE	−	EXPENSES
Cash 111	=	**Accounts Payable 211**	+	**C. Hall, Capital 311**	−	**C. Hall, Withdrawals 312**	+	**Legal Fees 411**	−	**Salaries Expense 511**
(A) 7,000 | 900 (B)		400 (C)		| 7,800 (A)		(J) 200 |		| 3,000 (D)		(G) 600 |
(D) 3,000 | 600 (G)		300 (I)						| 4,000 (E)		
(F) 700 | 700 (H)										
| 200 (J)										

Accounts Receivable 112

(E) 4,000 | 700 (F)

Rent — Expense 512

(H) 700 |

Office Equipment 121

(A) 800 |
(B) 900 |
(C) 400 |

Advertising — Expense 513

(I) 300 |

LEARNING UNIT 2-2 REVIEW

AT THIS POINT you should be able to:

- State the rules of debit and credit. (p. 47)
- List the five steps of a transaction analysis. (p. 48)
- Show how to fill out a transaction analysis chart. (p. 49)
- Explain double-entry bookkeeping. (p. 49)

Self-Review Quiz 2-2

(The blank forms you need are on pages 2-1 and 2-2 of the *Study Guide with Working Papers.*)

O'Malley Company uses the following accounts from its chart of accounts: Cash (111), Accounts Receivable (112), Equipment (121), Accounts Payable (211), Bill O'Malley, Capital (311), Bill O'Malley, Withdrawals (312), Professional Fees (411), Utilities Expense (511), and Salaries Expense (512).

Record the following transactions in transaction analysis charts.

A. Bill O'Malley invested $1,000 cash and equipment worth $700 from his personal assets into the business.

B. Billed clients for services rendered, $12,000.

C. Utilities bill due but as yet unpaid, $150.

D. Bill O'Malley withdrew cash for personal use, $120.

E. Paid salaries expense, $250.

Solution to Self-Review Quiz 2-2

Quiz Tip

Column 1 titles must come from the chart of accounts. The order doesn't matter as long as the total of all debits equals the total of all credits.

A.

1 Accounts Affected	2 Category	3 ↓ ↑	4 Rules of Dr. and Cr.	5 T Account Update
Cash	Asset	↑	Dr.	**Cash 111** (A) 1,000 |
Equipment	Asset	↑	Dr.	**Equipment 121** (A) 700 |
Bill O'Malley, Capital	Capital	↑	Cr.	**Bill O'Malley, Capital 311** | 1,700 (A)

B.

1 Accounts Affected	2 Category	3 ↓ ↑	4 Rules of Dr. and Cr.	5 T Account Update
Accounts Receivable	Asset	↑	Dr.	**Accounts Receivable 112** (B) 12,000 |
Professional Fees	Revenue	↑	Cr.	**Professional Fees 411** | 12,000 (B)

C.

1 Accounts Affected	2 Category	3 ↓ ↑	4 Rules of Dr. and Cr.	5 T Account Update
Utilities Expense	Expense	↑	Dr.	**Utilities Expense 511** (C) 150 |
Accounts Payable	Liability	↑	Cr.	**Accounts Payable 211** | 150 (C)

D.

1 Accounts Affected	2 Category	3 ↓ ↑	4 Rules of Dr. and Cr.	5 T Account Update
Bill O'Malley, Withdrawals	Owner's Equity (Withdrawals)	↑	Dr.	**Bill O'Malley, Withdrawals 312** (D) 120 |
Cash	Asset	↓	Cr.	**Cash 111** (A) **1,000** | 120 (D)

E.

1 Accounts Affected	2 Category	3 ↓	↑	4 Rules of Dr. and Cr.	5 T Account Update
Salaries Expense	Expense		↑	Dr.	**Salaries Expense 512** (E) 250 |
Cash	Asset	↓		Cr.	**Cash 111** (A) 1,000 | 120 (D) | 250 (E)

> Think of expenses as always increasing.

Learning Unit 2-3
The Trial Balance and Preparation of Financial Statements

Let us look at all the transactions we have discussed for Catherine Hall's business, arranged by T account and recorded using the rules of debit and credit.

ASSETS	=	LIABILITIES	+	CAPITAL	−	WITHDRAWALS	+	REVENUE	−	EXPENSES

Cash 111 = **Accounts Payable 211** + **C. Hall, Capital 311** − **C. Hall, Withdrawals 312** + **Legal Fees 411** − **Salaries Expense 511**

Cash 111		Accounts Payable 211	C. Hall, Capital 311	C. Hall, Withdrawals 312	Legal Fees 411	Salaries Expense 511
(A) 7,000	900 (B)	400 (C)	7,800 (A)	(J) 200	3,000 (D)	(G) 600
(D) 3,000	600 (G)	300 (I)			4,000 (E)	
(F) 700	700 (H)	700			7,000	
	200 (J)					
10,700	2,400	←—Footings				
8,300←		—Ending Balance				

Accounts Receivable 112   **Office Equipment 121**

Accounts Receivable 112		Office Equipment 121		Advertising Expense 513	Rent Expense 512
(E) 4,000	700 (F)	(A) 800		(I) 300	(H) 700
3,300		(B) 900			
		(C) 400			
		2,100			

This grouping of accounts is much easier to use than the expanded accounting equation because all of the transactions that affect a particular account are in one place.

As we saw in Learning Unit 2-2, when all the transactions are recorded in the accounts, the total of all the debits should be equal to the total of all the credits. (If they are not equal, the accountant must go back and find the error by checking the numbers and adding every column again.)

THE TRIAL BALANCE

> Footings are used to indicate or obtain the balance of any T account. They are not needed if there is only one entry in the account.

Footings are used to indicate or obtain the balance of any T account that has more than one entry. If all entries in the account are on one side, the total *is* the footing. If there are entries on both sides of the account, the balance is obtained by subtracting the smaller total (footing) from the larger. For example, look at the Cash account above. The footing for the debit side is $10,700 and the footing for

Figure 2-2
Trial Balance for
Catherine Hall's Law Firm

CATHERINE HALL, Barrister and Solicitor TRIAL BALANCE SEPTEMBER 30, 2010	Dr.	Cr.
Cash	8 3 0 0 00	
Accounts Receivable	3 3 0 0 00	
Office Equipment	2 1 0 0 00	
Accounts Payable		7 0 0 00
C. Hall, Capital		7 8 0 0 00
C. Hall, Withdrawals	2 0 0 00	
Legal Fees		7 0 0 0 00
Salaries Expense	6 0 0 00	
Rent Expense	7 0 0 00	
Advertising Expense	3 0 0 00	
Totals	15 5 0 0 00	15 5 0 0 00

Since this is not a formal report, there is no need to use dollar signs; however, the single and double lines under subtotals and final totals are still used for clarity.

the credit side is $2,400. Since the debit side is larger, we subtract $2,400 from $10,700 to arrive at an *ending balance* of $8,300. Now look at the Rent Expense account. There is no need for a footing because there is only one entry. The amount itself is the ending balance. When the ending balance has been found for every account, we should be able to show that the total of all debits equals the total of all credits.

As mentioned earlier, the ending balance of cash, $8,300, is a *normal balance* because it is on the side that increases the asset account.

The ending balances are used to prepare a **trial balance**. The trial balance is not a financial report, although it is used to prepare financial reports. The trial balance lists all of the accounts with their balances in the same order as they appear in the chart of accounts. It proves the accuracy of the ledger.

In the ideal situation, businesses would take a trial balance every day. The large number of transactions most businesses conduct each day makes this impractical. Instead, trial balances are prepared periodically.

Keep in mind that the figure for capital might not be the beginning figure if any additional investment has taken place during the period. You can tell this by looking at the capital account in the ledger.

Only the ending balance of each account is listed.

A more detailed discussion of the trial balance will be provided in the next chapter. For now, notice the heading, how the accounts are listed, the debits in the left column, the credits in the right, and the fact that the total of debits is equal to the total of credits.

A trial balance for Catherine Hall's firm's accounts is shown in Figure 2-2.

PREPARING FINANCIAL STATEMENTS

The trial balance is used to prepare the financial statements. The diagram in Figure 2-3 shows how financial statements can be prepared from a trial balance. Financial statements do not have debit or credit columns. The left column in the income statement and the statement of owner's equity is used only to subtotal numbers. If there were more than one liability, we would have two columns on the right-hand side of the balance sheet, one to subtotal the liabilities (inside column) and the total of the liabilities in the right column.

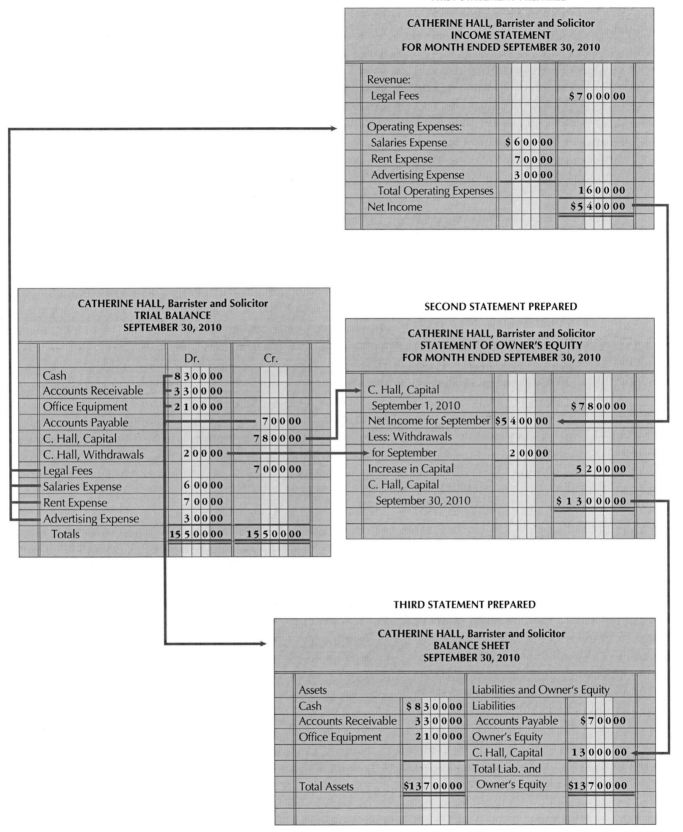

CATHERINE HALL, Barrister and Solicitor
INCOME STATEMENT
FOR MONTH ENDED SEPTEMBER 30, 2010

Revenue:		
Legal Fees		$7 0 0 00
Operating Expenses:		
Salaries Expense	$6 0 0 00	
Rent Expense	7 0 0 00	
Advertising Expense	3 0 0 00	
Total Operating Expenses		1 6 0 0 00
Net Income		$5 4 0 0 00

CATHERINE HALL, Barrister and Solicitor
TRIAL BALANCE
SEPTEMBER 30, 2010

	Dr.	Cr.
Cash	8 3 0 0 00	
Accounts Receivable	3 3 0 0 00	
Office Equipment	2 1 0 0 00	
Accounts Payable		7 0 0 00
C. Hall, Capital		7 8 0 0 00
C. Hall, Withdrawals	2 0 0 00	
Legal Fees		7 0 0 0 00
Salaries Expense	6 0 0 00	
Rent Expense	7 0 0 00	
Advertising Expense	3 0 0 00	
Totals	15 5 0 0 00	15 5 0 0 00

CATHERINE HALL, Barrister and Solicitor
STATEMENT OF OWNER'S EQUITY
FOR MONTH ENDED SEPTEMBER 30, 2010

C. Hall, Capital		
September 1, 2010		$7 8 0 0 00
Net Income for September	$5 4 0 0 00	
Less: Withdrawals		
for September	2 0 0 00	
Increase in Capital		5 2 0 0 00
C. Hall, Capital		
September 30, 2010		$1 3 0 0 0 00

CATHERINE HALL, Barrister and Solicitor
BALANCE SHEET
SEPTEMBER 30, 2010

Assets		Liabilities and Owner's Equity	
Cash	$8 3 0 0 00	Liabilities	
Accounts Receivable	3 3 0 0 00	Accounts Payable	$7 0 0 00
Office Equipment	2 1 0 0 00	Owner's Equity	
		C. Hall, Capital	13 0 0 0 00
		Total Liab. and	
Total Assets	$13 7 0 0 00	Owner's Equity	$13 7 0 0 00

Figure 2-3 Steps in Preparing Financial Statements from a Trial Balance

AT THIS POINT you should be able to:

- Explain the role of footings. (p. 57)
- Prepare a trial balance from a set of accounts. (p. 57)
- Prepare financial statements from a trial balance. (p. 58)

Self-Review Quiz 2-3

(The blank forms you need are on pages 2-2 to 2-4 of the *Study Guide with Working Papers*.)

As the bookkeeper of Pam's Hair Salon, you are to prepare from the following accounts on June 30, 2011: (1) a trial balance as of June 30; (2) an income statement for the month ended June 30; (3) a statement of owner's equity for the month ended June 30; and (4) a balance sheet as of June 30, 2011.

Cash 111		Accounts Payable 211		Salon Fees 411
4,500	300	300	700	3,500
2,000	100		400	1,000
1,000	1,200			4,500
300	1,300			
	2,600			
7,800	5,500			
2,300				

Accounts Receivable 121		Pam Jay, Capital 311	Rent Expense 511
1,000	300	4,000*	1,200
700			

Salon Equipment 131	Pam Jay, Withdrawals 321	Salon Supplies Expense 521
700	100	1,300

Salaries Expense 531

2,600

*No additional investments.

Solution to Self-Review Quiz 2-3

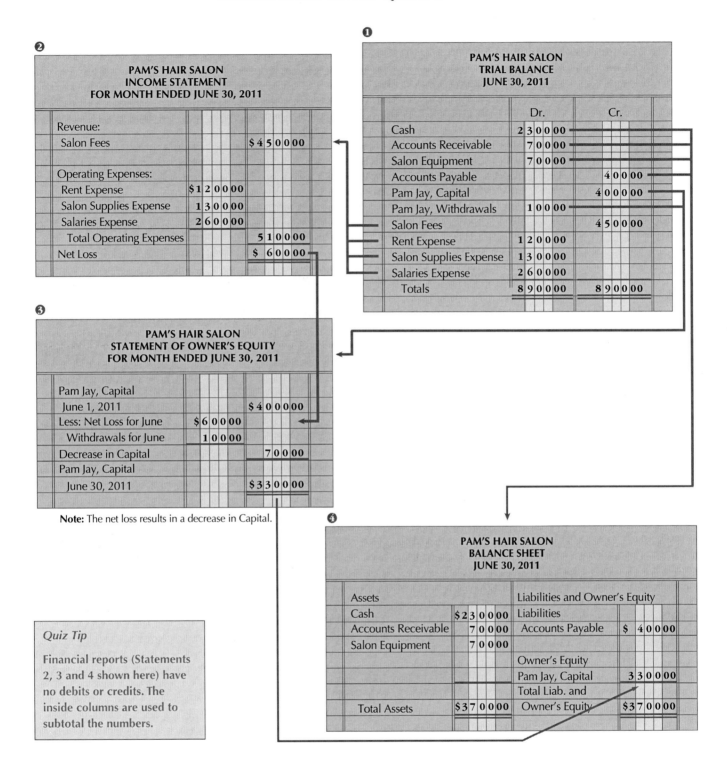

❷

PAM'S HAIR SALON
INCOME STATEMENT
FOR MONTH ENDED JUNE 30, 2011

Revenue:			
Salon Fees			$45000 00
Operating Expenses:			
Rent Expense	$120000		
Salon Supplies Expense	130000		
Salaries Expense	260000		
Total Operating Expenses		510000	
Net Loss		$60000	

❶

PAM'S HAIR SALON
TRIAL BALANCE
JUNE 30, 2011

	Dr.	Cr.
Cash	230000	
Accounts Receivable	70000	
Salon Equipment	70000	
Accounts Payable		40000
Pam Jay, Capital		400000
Pam Jay, Withdrawals	10000	
Salon Fees		450000
Rent Expense	120000	
Salon Supplies Expense	130000	
Salaries Expense	260000	
Totals	890000	890000

❸

PAM'S HAIR SALON
STATEMENT OF OWNER'S EQUITY
FOR MONTH ENDED JUNE 30, 2011

Pam Jay, Capital			
June 1, 2011		$400000	
Less: Net Loss for June	$60000		
Withdrawals for June	10000		
Decrease in Capital		70000	
Pam Jay, Capital			
June 30, 2011		$330000	

Note: The net loss results in a decrease in Capital.

❹

PAM'S HAIR SALON
BALANCE SHEET
JUNE 30, 2011

Assets		Liabilities and Owner's Equity	
Cash	$230000	Liabilities	
Accounts Receivable	70000	Accounts Payable	$40000
Salon Equipment	70000		
		Owner's Equity	
		Pam Jay, Capital	330000
		Total Liab. and	
Total Assets	$370000	Owner's Equity	$370000

Quiz Tip

Financial reports (Statements 2, 3 and 4 shown here) have no debits or credits. The inside columns are used to subtotal the numbers.

When Stan took the big leap from being an employee to a Subway owner, the thing that terrified him most was not the part about managing people—that was one of his strengths as a marketing manager. Why, at Xellent Media, 40 sales reps reported to him! No, Stan was terrified of having to manage the accounts. Subway restaurant owners have so many accounts to deal with—food costs, payroll, rent, utilities, supplies, advertising, promotion, and, biggest of all, cash. It's critical for them to keep debits and credits straight. If not, both they and Subway could lose a lot of money, quickly.

While Stan got some intense training in accounting and bookkeeping at Subway University, he still felt shaky about doing his own books. When he confided his fears to Mariah Washington, his field consultant, she suggested he hire an accountant. "You need to play to your strengths," said Mariah, "more and more owners are using accountants, and almost all owners of multiple franchises do. In fact, some accountants actually specialize in handling Subway accounts for these multi-restaurant owners."

Even though Stan decided to hire his cousin, Lila, to do his accounting, he still needs to feed her the right data so she can calculate his T accounts. Like many small business owners, Stan enters data

SUBWAY

DEBITS ON THE LEFT

into an accounting software program such as QuickBooks® or Simply Accounting®, which he then uploads to his accountant who edits it and reviews it for accuracy. Several times in the beginning, Stan mistakenly debited both cash and supplies when he paid for orders of paper cups, bread dough, and other supplies.

Lila urged Stan to review the rules for recording debits and credits. She even told him to practise for a while using a paper ledger. "On the computer, debits and credits are not as visible as they are with your paper system. Since you only enter the payables, the computer does the other side of the balance sheet. So you have to bone up on debits and credits to ensure that your QuickBooks® data are correct."

DISCUSSION QUESTIONS

1. Why is the cash account so important in Stan's business?
2. Why do you think that most owners of the larger shops use accountants to do their books instead of doing the books themselves?
3. Is the difference between debits and credits important to Subway restaurant owners who don't do their own books?

Chapter Review

DEMONSTRATION PROBLEM

(The blank forms you need are on pages 2-5 to 2-7 of the *Study Guide with Working Papers.*)

The chart of accounts of Mel's Delivery Service includes the following: Cash, 111; Accounts Receivable, 112; Office Equipment, 121; Delivery Trucks, 122; Accounts Payable, 211; Mel Free, Capital, 311; Mel Free, Withdrawals, 312; Delivery Fees Earned, 411; Advertising Expense, 511; Gas Expense, 512; Salaries Expense, 513; and Telephone Expense, 514. The following transactions occurred for Mel's Delivery Service during the month of July 2010:

Transaction A: Mel invested $10,000 in the business from his personal savings account.

Transaction B: Bought delivery trucks on account, $17,000.

Transaction C: Received but did not yet pay advertising bill, $700.

Transaction D: Bought office equipment for cash, $1,200.

Transaction E: Received cash for delivery services rendered, $15,000.

Transaction F: Paid salaries expense, $3,000.

Transaction G: Paid gas expense for company trucks, $1,250.

Transaction H: Billed customers for delivery services rendered, $4,000.

Transaction I: Paid telephone bill, $300.

Transaction J: Received $3,000 as partial payment of transaction H.

Transaction K: Mel paid home telephone bill from the company bank account, $150.

As Mel's newly employed accountant, you must do the following:

1. Set up T accounts in a ledger.
2. Record transactions in the T accounts. (Place the letter of the transaction next to the entry.)
3. Foot the T accounts where appropriate.
4. Prepare a trial balance at the end of July.
5. Prepare from the trial balance, in proper form, (a) an income statement for the month of July, (b) a statement of owner's equity, and (c) a balance sheet as of July 31, 2010.

Solution to Demonstration Problem

1, 2, 3.   **GENERAL LEDGER**

Cash 111				Accounts Payable 211			Advertising Expense 511	
(A) 10,000	1,200	(D)			17,000 (B)		(C) 700	
(E) 15,000	3,000	(F)			700 (C)			
(J) 3,000	1,250	(G)			*17,700*			
	300	(I)						
	150	(K)						
28,000	*5,900*							
22,100								

Accounts Receivable 112	
(H) 4,000	3,000 (J)
1,000	

Mel Free, Capital 311	
	10,000 (A)

Gas Expense 512	
(G) 1,250	

Office Equipment 121	
(D) 1,200	

Mel Free, Withdrawals 312	
(K) 150	

Salaries Expense 513	
(F) 3,000	

Delivery Trucks 122	
(B) 17,000	

Delivery Fees Earned 411	
	15,000 (E)
	4,000 (H)
	19,000

Telephone Expense 514	
(I) 300	

Solution Tips to Recording Transactions

A.	Cash	A	↑	Dr.
	Mel Free, Capital	OE	↑	Cr.

F.	Salaries Expense	Exp.	↑	Dr.
	Cash	A	↓	Cr.

B.	Delivery Trucks	A	↑	Dr.
	Accounts Payable	L	↑	Cr.

G.	Gas Expense	Exp.	↑	Dr.
	Cash	A	↓	Cr.

C.	Advertising Expense	Exp.	↑	Dr.
	Accounts Payable	L	↑	Cr.

H.	Accts. Receivable	A	↑	Dr.
	Del. Fees Earned	Rev.	↑	Cr.

D.	Office Equipment	A	↑	Dr.
	Cash	A	↓	Cr.

I.	Tel. Expense	Exp.	↑	Dr.
	Cash	A	↓	Cr.

E.	Cash	A	↑	Dr.
	Del. Fees Earned	Rev.	↑	Cr.

J.	Cash	A	↑	Dr.
	Accts. Receivable	A	↓	Cr.

K.	Mel Free, Withdr.	OE	↑	Dr.
	Cash	A	↓	Cr.

Solution Tips to Footings

3. Footings:

Cash	Add left side $28,000.
	Add right side $5,900.
	Take difference $22,100 and place on side that is larger.
Accounts Payable	Add $17,000 + $700 and leave on same side. Total is $17,700.

Solution Tips to Preparation of a Trial Balance

4. Trial balance is a list of the ledger's ending balances. The list is in the same order as the chart of accounts. Each title has only one amount listed, either as a debit or credit balance.

Mel's Delivery Service
Trial Balance
July 31, 2010

	Dr.	Cr.
Cash	22,100	
Accounts Receivable	1,000	
Office Equipment	1,200	
Delivery Trucks	17,000	
Accounts Payable		17,700
Mel Free, Capital		10,000
Mel Free, Withdrawals	150	
Delivery Fees Earned		19,000
Advertising Expense	700	
Gas Expense	1,250	
Salaries Expense	3,000	
Telephone Expense	300	
Totals	46,700	46,700

5. (a)

Mel's Delivery Service
Income Statement
July 31, 2010

Revenue:		
Delivery Fees Earned		$19,000
Operating Expenses:		
Advertising Expense	$ 700	
Gas Expense	1,250	
Salaries Expense	3,000	
Telephone Expense	300	
Total Operating Expenses		5,250
Net Income		$13,750

(b)

Mel's Delivery Service
Statement of Owner's Equity
for Month Ended July 31, 2010

Mel Free, Capital, July 1, 2010		$10,000
Net Income for July	$13,750	
Less: Withdrawals for July	150	
Increase in Capital		13,600
Mel Free, Capital, July 31, 2010		$23,600

(c)

Mel's Delivery Service
Balance Sheet
July 31, 2010

Assets		Liabilities and Owner's Equity	
Cash	$22,100	Liabilities	
Accounts Receivable	1,000	Accounts Payable	$17,700
Office Equipment	1,200		
Delivery Trucks	17,000	Owner's Equity	
		Mel Free, Capital	23,600
		Total Liabilities and	
Total Assets	**$41,300**	**Owner's Equity**	**$41,300**

Solution Tips for Preparing Financial Statements from a Trial Balance

			Trial Balance	
			Dr.	**Cr.**
Balance Sheet	{	Assets	X	
		Liabilities		X
Statement of Equity	{	Capital		X
		Withdrawals	X	
Income Statement	{	Revenues		X
		Expenses	X	
			XX	XX

Net income on the income statement of $13,750 goes on the statement of owner's equity.

Ending capital of $23,600 on the statement of owner's equity goes on the balance sheet as the new figure for capital.

Note: There are no debits or credits on financial statements. The inside column is used for subtotalling.

SUMMARY OF KEY POINTS

Learning Unit 2-1

1. A T account is a simplified version of a standard account.
2. A ledger is a group of accounts.
3. A debit is the left-hand position (side) of an account and a credit is the right-hand position (side) of an account.
4. A footing is the total of one side of an account. The ending balance is the difference between the footings on the left and right sides.

Learning Unit 2-2

1. A chart of accounts for a company lists the account titles and their numbers.
2. The transaction analysis chart is a teaching device, not to be confused with standard accounting procedures.
3. A compound entry is a transaction involving more than one debit or credit.

1. In double-entry bookkeeping, the recording of each business transaction affects two or more accounts, and the total of debits equals the total of credits.

2. A trial balance is a list of the ending balances of all accounts, listed in the same order as on the chart of accounts.

3. Any additional investments during the period will result in having a figure for capital in the trial balance different from the beginning figure for capital in the statement of owner's equity.

4. There are *no* debit or credit columns on the three financial statements.

KEY TERMS

Account An accounting device used in bookkeeping to record increases and decreases of business transactions relating to individual assets, liabilities, capital, withdrawals, revenue, and expenses. (p. 44)

Chart of accounts A numbering system of accounts that lists the account titles and account numbers to be used by a company (p. 48)

Compound entry A transaction involving more than one debit or credit (p. 49)

Credit The right-hand side of any account. A number entered on the right side of any account is said to be credited to an account. (p. 45)

Debit The left-hand side of any account. A number entered on the left side of any account is said to be debited to an account. (p. 45)

Double-entry bookkeeping An accounting system in which the recording of each transaction affects two or more accounts, and the total of the debits is equal to the total of the credits (p. 49)

Ending balance The difference between footings in a T account (p. 45)

Footings The totals of the two sides of a T account (p. 45)

Ledger A group of accounts that records data from business transactions (p. 44)

Normal balance of an account The side of an account that increases by the rules of debit and credit (p. 47)

Standard account A formal account that includes columns for date, explanation, posting reference, debit, and credit (p. 44)

T account A skeleton version of a standard account, used for demonstration purposes (p. 44)

Trial balance A list of the ending balances of all the accounts in a ledger. The total of the debits should equal the total of the credits. (p. 58)

BLUEPRINT FOR PREPARING FINANCIAL STATEMENTS FROM A TRIAL BALANCE

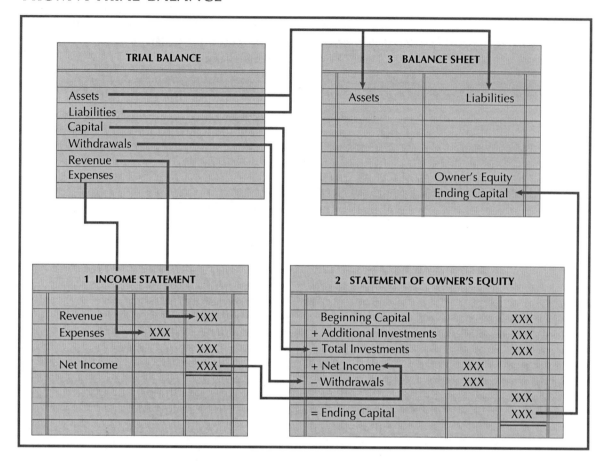

QUESTIONS, CLASSROOM DEMONSTRATION EXERCISES, EXERCISES, AND PROBLEMS

Discussion Questions and Critical Thinking/Ethical Case

1. Define a ledger.
2. Why is the left-hand side of an account called a debit?
3. Footings are used in balancing all accounts. True or false? Please explain.
4. What is the end product of the accounting process?
5. What do we mean when we say that a transaction analysis chart is a teaching device?
6. What are the five steps of the transaction analysis chart?
7. Explain the concept of double-entry bookkeeping.
8. A trial balance is a formal report. True or false? Please explain.
9. Why are there no debit or credit columns on financial reports?
10. Compare the financial statements prepared from the expanded accounting equation with those prepared from a trial balance.
11. Audrey Flet, the bookkeeper of ALN Co., was scheduled to leave on a three-week vacation at 5:00 on Friday. She couldn't get the company's trial balance to balance. At 4:30, she decided to put in fictitious figures to make it balance. Audrey told herself she would fix it when she got back from her vacation. Was Audrey right or wrong to do this? Why?

(The blank forms you need are on page 2-8 in the *Study Guide with Working Papers.*)

Set A

The T Account

1. For the following, foot and balance each account.

Cash 110					J. Jones, Capital 311		
7/6	8,000	600	4/7			9,000	2/9
9/12	3,000					2,000	3/12
						6,000	5/16

Transaction Analysis

2. Complete the following:

Account	Category	↑	↓	Normal Balance
A. Advertising Expense	Asset	Dr.	Cr.	Dr.
B. Fees Earned				
C. Accounts Receivable				
D. J. Jones, Capital				
E. J. Jones, Withdrawals				
F. Prepaid Advertising				
G. Rent Expense				

Transaction Analysis

3. Record the following transaction in the transaction analysis chart: Provided bookkeeping services for $2,500, receiving $600 cash with the remainder to be paid next month.

Accounts Affected	Category	↓	↑	Rules of Dr. and Cr.	T Accounts

Trial Balance

4. Rearrange the following titles in the order in which they would appear in a trial balance:

J. Joy, Withdrawals	Hair Salon Fees Earned
Accounts Receivable	Utility Expense
Cash	Salary Expense
J. Joy, Capital	Advertising Expense
Office Equipment	Accounts Payable

Trial Balance/Financial Statements

5. For the following trial balance, identify the statement in the following list in which each title will appear:

- ◆ Income Statement (IS)
- ◆ Statement of Owner's Equity (OE)
- ◆ Balance Sheet (BS)

Bernie Co.
Trial Balance
November 20, 2009

		Dr.	Cr.
A. _____	Cash	500	
B. _____	Accounts Receivable	200	
C. _____	Computer Equipment	600	
D. _____	Accounts Payable		900
E. _____	L. Bernard, Capital		240
F. _____	L. Bernard, Withdrawals	250	
G. _____	Legal Fees Earned		1,000
H. _____	Director's Fees Earned		500
I. _____	Wage Expense	300	
J. _____	Supplies Expense	700	
K. _____	Internet Advertising Expense	90	
	TOTALS	2,640	2,640

Set B

The T Account

1. For the following, foot and balance each account.

Cash 110				C. Clark, Capital 311			
6/9	4,000	500	4/8			7,000	3/7
7/14	8,000					3,000	3/9
						6,000	4/12

Transaction Analysis

2. Complete the following:

Account	Category	↑	↓	Normal Balance
A. Digital Cameras	Asset	Dr.	Cr.	Dr.
B. Prepaid Rent				
C. Accounts Payable				
D. A. Sung, Capital				
E. A. Sung, Withdrawals				
F. Legal Fees Earned				
G. Salary Expense				

Transaction Analysis

3. Record the following transaction in the transaction analysis chart: Provided legal services for $4,000, receiving $3,000 cash with the remainder to be paid next month.

Accounts Affected	Category	↓ ↑	Rules of Dr. and Cr.	T Accounts

Trial Balance

4. Rearrange the following titles in the order in which they would appear in a trial balance:

Salaries Expense   Legal Fees Earned
Accounts Receivable   D. Cope, Withdrawals
Accounts Payable   Rent Expense
D. Cope, Capital   Advertising Expense
Computer Equipment   Cash

Trial Balance/Financial Statements

5. For the following trial balance, identify the statement in the following list in which each title will appear:

  ◆ Income Statement (IS)
  ◆ Statement of Owner's Equity (OE)
  ◆ Balance Sheet (BS)

Logan Co.
Trial Balance
September 30, 2009

			Dr.	Cr.
A.	_____	Cash	390	
B.	_____	Supplies	100	
C.	_____	Office Equipment	200	
D.	_____	Accounts Payable		100
E.	_____	D. Logan, Capital		450
F.	_____	D. Logan, Withdrawals	160	
G.	_____	Hair Salon Fees		290
H.	_____	Cosmetic Sales		300
I.	_____	Salaries Expense	130	
J.	_____	Rent Expense	120	
K.	_____	Advertising Expense	40	
		TOTALS	1,140	1,140

Exercises

(The blank forms you need are on pages 2-9 and 2-10 in the *Study Guide with Working Papers.*)

Preparing a chart of accounts

2-1. From the following account titles, prepare a chart of accounts using the same numbering system as used in this chapter.

Sony Flat-Screen Television	Legal Fees
Salary Expense	B. Bryan, Capital
Accounts Payable	Cash
Accounts Receivable	Advertising Expense
Repair Expense	B. Bryan, Withdrawals

Preparing a transaction analysis chart

2-2. Record the following transaction in the transaction analysis chart: Allison Ritter bought a new piece of office equipment for $18,000, paying $2,000 down and agreeing to pay the balance in 30 days.

2-3. Complete the following table. For each account listed on the left, indicate the category to which it belongs, whether increases and decreases in the account are marked on the debit or credit side, and in which financial report the account appears. A sample is provided.

Accounts Affected	Category	↑	↓	Appears on Which Financial Report
Supplies	Asset	Dr.	Cr.	Balance Sheet
Legal Fees Earned				
P. Rey, Withdrawals				
Accounts Payable				
Salaries Expense				
Auto				

Rules of debits and credits

2-4. Given the following accounts, complete the table by inserting the appropriate number next to each individual transaction to indicate which account is debited and which account is credited.

1. Cash
2. Accounts Receivable
3. Equipment
4. Accounts Payable
5. B. Baker, Capital

6. B. Baker, Withdrawals
7. Plumbing Fees Earned
8. Salaries Expense
9. Advertising Expense
10. Supplies Expense

Transaction	Rules Dr.	Cr.
A. Paid salaries expense.	8	1
B. Bob paid personal utilities bill from company bank account.		
C. Advertising bill was received but not yet paid.		
D. Received cash from plumbing fees.		
E. Paid supplies expense.		
F. Bob invested additional equipment in the business.		
G. Billed customers for plumbing services rendered.		
H. Received one-half the balance from transaction G.		
I. Bought equipment on account.		

Preparing financial statements

2-5. From the following trial balance of Hall's Cleaners, prepare the following:
   ◆ Income statement
   ◆ Statement of owner's equity
   ◆ Balance sheet

HALL'S CLEANERS TRIAL BALANCE JULY 31, 2012		
	Dr.	Cr.
Cash	5 5 0 00	
Equipment	6 9 2 00	
Accounts Payable		4 5 5 00
J. Hall, Capital		8 0 0 00
J. Hall, Withdrawals	1 9 8 00	
Cleaning Fees		4 5 8 00
Salaries Expense	1 6 0 00	
Utilities Expense	1 1 3 00	
Totals	1 7 1 3 00	1 7 1 3 00

Group A Problems

(The forms you need are on pages 2-11 to 2-16 of the *Study Guide with Working Papers*.)

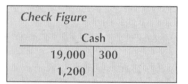

Using a transaction analysis chart

Check Figure

Cash

19,000	300
1,200	

2A-1. The following transactions occurred in the opening and operation of MayBell's Shuttle Service of Charlottetown:

a. MayBell Lee opened the shuttle service by investing $19,000 from her personal savings account.
b. Purchased used shuttle van on account, $7,000.
c. Rent expense was due but unpaid, $700.
d. Received cash for services rendered, $1,200.
e. Billed a client on account, $75.
f. MayBell withdrew cash for her personal use, $300.

Complete the transaction analysis chart in the *Study Guide with Working Papers*. The chart of accounts includes Cash; Accounts Receivable; Shuttle Van; Accounts Payable; MayBell Lee, Capital; MayBell Lee, Withdrawals; Fees Earned; and Rent Expense.

Recording transactions in ledger accounts

Check Figure

Cash

(a)	18,000	75	(d)
(c)	800	600	(e)
		900	(g)

2A-2. Jill Jay opened a consulting company in Fairview and the following transactions resulted:

a. Jill invested $18,000 in the consulting business.
b. Bought office equipment on account, $3,000.
c. Received cash for consulting work that it completed for a client, $800.
d. Jill paid a personal bill from the company bank account, $75.
e. Paid advertising expense for the month, $600.
f. Rent expense for the month was due but not yet paid, $1,200.
g. Paid $900 as partial payment of what was owed from the transaction in **b**.

As Jill's accountant, analyze and record the transactions in T account form. Set up the T accounts on the basis of the chart of accounts on page 75. Enter each transaction in the appropriate T account and label it with the letter of the transaction.

Chart of Accounts

Assets
Cash 111
Office Equipment 121

Liabilities
Accounts Payable 211

Owner's Equity
Jill Jay, Capital 311
Jill Jay, Withdrawals 312

Revenue
Consulting Fees Earned 411

Expenses
Advertising Expense 511
Rent Expense 512

Preparing a trial balance from the T accounts

2A-3. From the following T accounts of Mike's Window Washing Service of Yarmouth, (a) record and foot the balances on the appropriate pages in the *Study Guide with Working Papers*, and (b) prepare a trial balance in proper form for May 31, 2010.

	Cash 111		
(A)	5,000	100	(D)
(G)	3,500	200	(E)
		400	(F)
		200	(H)
		900	(I)

	Accounts Payable 211		
(D)	100	1,300	(C)

Fees Earned 411		
	6,500	(B)

Check Figure

Trial Balance Total $12,700

	Accounts Receivable 112		
(B)	6,500	3,500	(G)

Mike Frank, Capital 311		
	5,000	(A)

	Rent Expense 511	
(F)	400	

	Office Equipment 121	
(C)	1,300	
(H)	200	

	Mike Frank, Withdrawals 312	
(I)	900	

	Utilities Expense 512	
(E)	200	

Preparing financial reports from the trial balance

2A-4. From the trial balance of Grace Lantz, Barrister and Solicitor, of Winnipeg, prepare (a) an income statement for the month of May, (b) a statement of owner's equity for the month ended May 31, and (c) a balance sheet as of May 31, 2011.

Check Figure

Total Assets $6,400

GRACE LANTZ, Barrister and Solicitor
TRIAL BALANCE
MAY 31, 2011

	Dr.	Cr.
Cash	5 0 0 0 00	
Accounts Receivable	6 5 0 00	
Office Equipment	7 5 0 00	
Accounts Payable		4 3 0 0 00
Salaries Payable		6 7 5 00
G. Lantz, Capital		1 2 7 5 00
G. Lantz, Withdrawals	3 0 0 00	
Revenue from Legal Fees		2 3 5 0 00
Utilities Expense	3 0 0 00	
Rent Expense	4 5 0 00	
Salaries Expense	1 1 5 0 00	
Totals	8 6 0 0 00	8 6 0 0 00

Comprehensive problem

2A-5. The chart of accounts for Angel's Delivery Service of Flin Flon is as follows:

Chart of Accounts

Assets
Cash 111
Accounts Receivable 112
Office Equipment 121
Delivery Trucks 122

Liabilities
Accounts Payable 211

Owner's Equity
Alice Angel, Capital 311
Alice Angel, Withdrawals 312

Revenue
Delivery Fees Earned 411

Expenses
Advertising Expense 511
Gas Expense 512
Salaries Expense 513
Telephone Expense 514

Check Figure

Trial Balance Total $38,100

Angel's Delivery Service completed the following transactions during the month of March 2010:

Transaction A: Alice Angel invested $16,000 in the delivery service from her personal savings account.

Transaction B: Bought delivery trucks on account, $18,000.

Transaction C: Bought office equipment for cash, $600.

Transaction D: Paid advertising expense, $250.

Transaction E: Collected cash for delivery services rendered, $2,600.

Transaction F: Paid drivers' salaries, $900.

Transaction G: Paid gas expense for trucks, $1,200.

Transaction H: Performed delivery services for a customer on account, $800.

Transaction I: Telephone expense was due but not yet paid, $700.

Transaction J: Received $300 as partial payment of transaction H.

Transaction K: Alice Angel withdrew cash for personal use, $300.

As Alice's newly employed accountant, you must:

1. Set up T accounts in a ledger.
2. Record transactions in the T accounts. (Place the letter of the transaction next to the entry.)
3. Foot the T accounts where appropriate.
4. Prepare a trial balance at the end of March 2010.
5. Prepare from the trial balance, in proper form, (a) an income statement for the month of March, (b) a statement of owner's equity for the month of March, and (c) a balance sheet as of March 31, 2010.

Group B Problems

(The forms you need are on pages 2-11 to 2-16 of the *Study Guide with Working Papers*.)

Using a transaction analysis chart

2B-1. MayBell Lee decided to open a shuttle service in Charlottetown. Record the following transactions in the transaction analysis charts:

Transaction A: MayBell invested $2,500 in the shuttle service from her personal savings account.

What did the bookkeeper tell Cookie? Which accounts were overstated and which were understated? Which were correct? Explain in writing how mistakes can be avoided in the future.

CONTINUING PROBLEM

The Precision Computer Centre created its chart of accounts as follows:

Chart of Accounts
as of July 1, 2010

Assets
1000   Cash
1020   Accounts Receivable
1025   Prepaid Rent
1030   Supplies
1080   Computer Shop Equipment
1090   Office Equipment

Liabilities
2000   Accounts Payable

Owner's Equity
3000   T. Freedman, Capital
3010   T. Freedman, Withdrawals

Revenue
4000   Service Revenue

Expenses
5010   Advertising Expense
5020   Rent Expense
5030   Utilities Expense
5040   Phone Expense
5050   Supplies Expense
5060   Insurance Expense
5070   Postage Expense

You will use this chart of accounts to complete the Continuing Problem.

The following problem continues from Chapter 1. The balances as of July 31 have been brought forward in your *Study Guide with Working Papers* on pages 2-24 to 2-25. Additional transactions in August were:

(k) Received the phone bill for the month of July, $155
(l) Paid $150 (cheque No. 205) for insurance for the month
(m) Paid $200 (cheque No. 206) of the amount due from transaction (d) in Chapter 1
(n) Paid advertising expense for the month, $1,400 (cheque No. 207)
(o) Billed a client (Jeannine Sparks) for services rendered, $850
(p) Collected $900 for services rendered
(q) Paid the electric bill in full for the month of July (cheque No. 208—transaction (h), Chapter 1)
(r) Paid cash (cheque No. 209) for $50 in stamps
(s) Purchased $200 worth of supplies from Computer Connection on account

Assignment

1. Set up T accounts in a ledger.
2. Record the transactions (k) through (s) in the appropriate T accounts.
3. Foot the T accounts where appropriate.
4. Prepare a trial balance at the end of August 2010
5. From the trial balance, prepare an income statement, a statement of owner's equity, and a balance sheet for the two months ending August 31, 2010.

3 Beginning the Accounting Cycle

Journalizing, Posting, and the Trial Balance

THE BIG PICTURE

When you take your next vacation, will you buy your airline ticket online or visit a travel agency? Chances are good that even if you don't book online, you'll compare prices or check out hotels on your computer.

Travel companies know that an Internet presence is increasingly important to customers. In a tough Canadian market, smart companies are doing everything they can to maintain and grow their customer base.

For a generation of students who have grown up with online shopping, it may come as a surprise to know that just ten years ago, ticket sales on WestJet's website accounted for only 1% of bookings. Nowadays, the majority of tickets are purchased this way, and passengers can even use the site to check in for their flight 24 hours beforehand.

But WestJet understands that while having a strong Web presence is essential, nothing beats old-fashioned customer service. The airline revolutionized the way Canadians fly, staffing its flights with casually dressed flight attendants who tell jokes and sing songs to passengers in addition to running through the safety features of the aircraft.

WestJet keeps its maintenance and training costs low by using only one type of aircraft—the 737—and maximizes the use of its fleet, flying to 38 destinations with only 65 aircraft. All these efficiencies result in lower costs for the company, which translates into lower fares.

Whatever the future holds for the Canadian airline industry, companies will continue to look at ways to combine high-tech services with a personal touch. In this, they are like savvy accountants who hope to thrive in the new economy. Most likely, you will accomplish all the activities in the *accounting cycle* on the computer. Yet, in order to help your client or company—let's say it's a local travel company—you'll need to be familiar with every step so you can explain results and correct any errors.

In this chapter, you'll learn how to perform the first activities in the accounting cycle: keeping a *journal* of business transactions, transferring journal information to a *general ledger*, and preparing a *trial balance*. Whether you do it manually or on a computer, the first step of the accounting cycle is the same: business transactions occur and generate source documents. At WestJet, customers pay online with credit cards or in person with credit cards, cash, or debit cards. Source documents for such purchases will run the gamut from credit card receipts to cash register receipts and deposit slips. All must be recorded accurately as business transactions either in a computerized journal or with ink in a traditional journal. Accuracy is extremely important, because errors will throw off the rest of the accounting cycle.

Sources: Based on Paul Knowles, "The Little Airline That Could," *Tourist*, September 2001; information from Industry Canada, "Success Stories: WestJet Airlines," Electronic Commerce in Canada Website, www.e-com.ic.gc.ca; WestJet Airlines website, www.westjet.com.

◆ **Journalizing—analyzing and recording business transactions into a journal (p. 84)**
◆ **Posting—transferring information from a journal to a ledger (p. 92)**
◆ **Preparing a trial balance (p. 99)**

The normal accounting procedures that are performed over a period of time are called the **accounting cycle**. The accounting cycle takes place in a period of time called an **accounting period**. An accounting period is the period of time covered by the income statement. Although it can be any time period up to one year (e.g., one month or three months), most businesses use a one-year accounting period. The year can be either a **calendar year** (January 1 through December 31) or a fiscal year.

A **fiscal year** is an accounting period that runs for any 12 consecutive months, so it can be the same as a calendar year. A business can choose any fiscal year that is convenient. For example, some retailers may decide to end their fiscal year when inventories and business activity are at a low point, such as after the Christmas season. This is called a **natural business year.** Using a natural business year allows the business to count its year-end inventory when it is easiest to do so.

Businesses would not be able to operate successfully if they prepared financial statements only at the end of their calendar or fiscal year. That is why most businesses prepare **interim reports** on a monthly, quarterly, or semiannual basis.

In this chapter, as well as in Chapters 4 and 5, we will follow Brenda Clark's new business, Clark's Desktop Publishing Services. We will follow the normal accounting procedures that the business performs over a period of time. Clark has chosen to use a fiscal period of January 1 to December 31.

> This chapter covers steps 1 to 4 of the accounting cycle.

Learning Unit 3-1

Analyzing and Recording Business Transactions in a Journal: Steps 1 and 2 of the Accounting Cycle

THE GENERAL JOURNAL

> A business uses a journal to record transactions in chronological order. A ledger accumulates information from a journal. The journal and the ledger are in two different books.

> Journal—book of original entry
> Ledger—book of final entry

> Journal—from the French word *jour: day* (chronological)

Chapter 2 taught us how to analyze and record business transactions in T accounts, or ledger accounts. However, recording a debit in an account on one page of the ledger and recording the corresponding credit on a different page of the ledger can make it difficult to find errors. It would be much easier if all of the business's transactions were located in the same place. That is the function of the **journal** or **general journal**. Transactions are entered in the journal in chronological order (January 1, 8, 15, etc.) and then this recorded information is used to update the ledger accounts. In computerized accounting, a journal may be recorded on disk.

We will use a general journal, the simplest form of a journal, to record the transactions of Clark's Desktop Publishing Services. A transaction (debit[s] + credit[s]) that has been analyzed and recorded in a journal is called a **journal entry**. The process of recording the journal entry in the journal is called **journalizing.**

The journal is called the **book of original entry** since it contains the first formal information about the business transactions. The ledger is known as the **book of final entry** because the information it contains has been transferred from the journal. Like the ledger, the journal may be a bound or loose-leaf book. Each of the journal pages looks like the one in Figure 3-1. The pages of the journal are

Figure 3-1
The General Journal

CLARK'S DESKTOP PUBLISHING SERVICES
GENERAL JOURNAL

Page 1

Date	Account Titles and Description	PR	Dr.	Cr.

numbered consecutively from page 1. Keep in mind that the journal and the ledger are separate books. Also note that both journals and ledgers exist in computerized accounting although they may look different from the manual formats.

Relationship Between the Journal and the Chart of Accounts

The accountant must refer to the business's chart of accounts for the account name that is to be used in the journal. Every company has its own "unique" chart of accounts.

The chart of accounts for Clark's Desktop Publishing Services appears below. By the end of Chapter 5, we will have discussed each of these accounts.

Note that we will continue to use transaction analysis charts as a teaching aid in the journalizing process.

Journalizing the Transactions of Clark's Desktop Publishing Services

Certain formalities must be followed in making journal entries: The debit portion of the transaction is always recorded first. The credit portion of a transaction is indented about 1 centimetre and placed below the debit portion. The explanation of the journal entry follows immediately after the credit and about 2 centimetres

---

Clark's Desktop Publishing Services
Chart of Accounts

Assets (100–199)
111 Cash
112 Accounts Receivable
114 Office Supplies
115 Prepaid Rent
121 Desktop Publishing Equipment
122 Accumulated Amortization,
      Desktop Publishing Equipment

Liabilities (200–299)
211 Accounts Payable
212 Salaries Payable

Owner's Equity (300–399)
311 Brenda Clark, Capital
312 Brenda Clark, Withdrawals
313 Income Summary

Revenue (400–499)
411 Desktop Publishing Fees

Expenses (500–599)
511 Office Salaries Expense
512 Advertising Expense
513 Telephone Expense
514 Office Supplies Expense
515 Rent Expense
516 Amortization Expense,
      Desktop Publishing Equipment

from the date column. A one-line space follows each transaction and explanation. This makes the journal easier to read, and there is less chance of mixing transactions. Finally, as always, the total amount of debits must equal the total amount of credits. The same format is used for each of the entries in the journal.

May 1, 2010: Brenda Clark began the business by investing $10,000 in cash.

1 Accounts Affected	2 Category	3 ↑ ↓	4 Rules of Dr. and Cr.
Cash	Asset	↑	Dr.
Brenda Clark, Capital	Owner's Equity	↑	Cr.

CLARK'S DESKTOP PUBLISHING SERVICES
GENERAL JOURNAL

Page 1

For now the PR (posting reference) column is blank; we will discuss it later.

Date			Account Titles and Description	PR	Dr.	Cr.
2010 May	1		Cash		10000 00	
			Brenda Clark, Capital			10000 00
			Initial investment of cash by owner			

Let's now look at the structure of this journal entry. The entry contains the following information:

1. Year of the journal entry   2010
2. Month of the journal entry   May
3. Day of the journal entry   1
4. Name(s) of account(s) debited   Cash
5. Name(s) of account(s) credited   Brenda Clark, Capital
6. Explanation of transaction   Investment of cash
7. Amount of debit(s) $10,000
8. Amount of credit(s) $10,000

May 1: Purchased desktop publishing equipment from Ben Co. for $6,000, paying $1,000 and promising to pay the balance within 30 days.

1 Accounts Affected	2 Category	3 ↑ ↓	4 Rules of Dr. and Cr.
Desktop Publishing Equipment	Asset	↑	Dr.
Cash	Asset	↓	Cr.
Accounts Payable	Liability	↑	Cr.

Note that in this compound entry we have one debit and two credits—but the total amount of debits equals the total amount of credits.

This transaction affects three accounts. When a journal entry has more than two accounts, it is called a **compound journal entry.**

	1	Desktop Publishing Equipment		6 0 0 0 00			
		Cash				1 0 0 0 00	
		Accounts Payable				5 0 0 0 00	
		Purchase of equipment from Ben Co.					

In this entry, only the day is entered in the date column. That is because the year and month were entered at the top of the page from the first transaction. There is no need to repeat this information until a new page is needed or a change of month occurs.

May 1: Rented office space, paying $1,200 in advance for the first three months.

1 Accounts Affected	2 Category	3 ↑ ↓	4 Rules of Dr. and Cr.
Prepaid Rent	**Asset**	↑	**Dr.**
Cash	**Asset**	↓	**Cr.**

In this transaction, Clark gains an asset called prepaid rent and gives up an asset, cash. The prepaid rent does not become an expense until it expires.

	1	Prepaid Rent		1 2 0 0 00			
		Cash				1 2 0 0 00	
		Rent paid in advance (3 months)					

May 3: Purchased office supplies from Norris Co. on account, $600.

1 Accounts Affected	2 Category	3 ↑ ↓	4 Rules of Dr. and Cr.
Office Supplies	**Asset**	↑	**Dr.**
Accounts Payable	**Liability**	↑	**Cr.**

Remember, supplies are an asset when they are purchased. Once they are used up or consumed in the operation of business, they become an expense.

	3	Office Supplies		6 0 0 00			
		Accounts Payable				6 0 0 00	
		Purchase of supplies on account					
		from Norris Co.					

May 7: Completed sales promotion pieces for a client and immediately collected $3,000.

1 Accounts Affected	2 Category	3 ↑ ↓	4 Rules of Dr. and Cr.
Cash	Asset	↑	Dr.
Desktop Publishing Fees	Revenue	↑	Cr.

		7	Cash		3 0 0 0 00		
			Desktop Publishing Fees			3 0 0 0 00	
			Cash received for services rendered				

May 11: Paid office salaries, $650.

1 Accounts Affected	2 Category	3 ↑ ↓	4 Rules of Dr. and Cr.
Office Salaries Expense	Expense	↑	Dr.
Cash	Asset	↓	Cr.

		11	Office Salaries Expense		6 5 0 00		
			Cash			6 5 0 00	
			Payment of office salaries				

> Remember, expenses are recorded when they are incurred, no matter when they are paid.

May 18: Bill from Al's News Co. comes in but not paid.

1 Accounts Affected	2 Category	3 ↑ ↓	4 Rules of Dr. and Cr.
Advertising Expense	Expense	↑	Dr.
Accounts Payable	Liability	↑	Cr.

		18	Advertising Expense		2 5 0 00		
			Accounts Payable			2 5 0 00	
			Bill in but not paid from Al's News Co.				

Keep in mind that as withdrawals *increase*, owner's equity *decreases*.

May 20: Brenda Clark wrote a cheque on the bank account of the business to pay her home mortgage payment of $625.

1 Accounts Affected	2 Category	3 ↑ ↓	4 Rules of Dr. and Cr.
Brenda Clark, Withdrawals	Owner's Equity (Withdrawals)	↑	Dr.
Cash	Asset	↓	Cr.

		20	Brenda Clark, Withdrawals		625 00	
			Cash			625 00
			Personal withdrawal of cash			

Reminder: Revenue is recorded when it is earned, no matter when the cash is actually received.

May 22: Billed Morris Company for a sophisticated desktop publishing job, $5,000.

1 Accounts Affected	2 Category	3 ↑ ↓	4 Rules of Dr. and Cr.
Accounts Receivable	Asset	↑	Dr.
Desktop Publishing Fees	Revenue	↑	Cr.

		22	Accounts Receivable		5000 00	
			Desktop Publishing Fees			5000 00
			Billed Morris Co. for fees earned			

May 25: Paid office salaries, $650.

1 Accounts Affected	2 Category	3 ↑ ↓	4 Rules of Dr. and Cr.
Office Salaries Expense	Expense	↑	Dr.
Cash	Asset	↓	Cr.

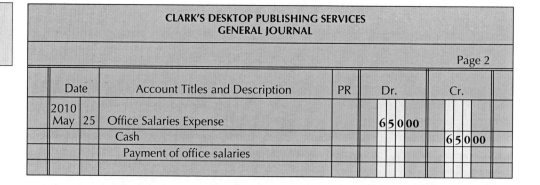

CLARK'S DESKTOP PUBLISHING SERVICES
GENERAL JOURNAL

Page 2

Date		Account Titles and Description	PR	Dr.	Cr.
2010 May	25	Office Salaries Expense		6 5 0 00	
		Cash			6 5 0 00
		Payment of office salaries			

May 28: Paid half the amount owed for desktop publishing equipment purchased May 1 from Ben Co., $2,500.

1 Accounts Affected	2 Category	3 ↑ ↓	4 Rules of Dr. and Cr.
Accounts Payable	Liability	↓	Dr.
Cash	Asset	↓	Cr.

	28	Accounts Payable		2 5 0 0 00	
		Cash			2 5 0 0 00
		Paid half the amount owed Ben Co.			

May 29: Received and paid telephone bill, $220.

1 Accounts Affected	2 Category	3 ↑ ↓	4 Rules of Dr. and Cr.
Telephone Expense	Expense	↑	Dr.
Cash	Asset	↓	Cr.

	29	Telephone Expense		2 2 0 00	
		Cash			2 2 0 00
		Paid telephone bill			

This concludes the journal transactions of Clark's Desktop Publishing Services. (See pages 95 and 96 for a summary of all the transactions.)

LEARNING UNIT 3-1 REVIEW

AT THIS POINT you should be able to:

- Explain the purpose of the accounting cycle. (p. 84)
- Define and explain the relationship of the accounting period to the income statement. (p. 84)
- Compare and contrast a calendar year and a fiscal year. (p. 84)
- Explain the term "natural business year." (p. 84)
- Explain the function of interim reports. (p. 84)
- Define and state the purpose of a journal. (p. 84)
- Compare and contrast a book of original entry and a book of final entry. (p. 84)
- Differentiate between a chart of accounts and a journal. (p. 85)
- Explain a compound entry. (p. 87)
- Journalize business transactions. (p. 86)

Self-Review Quiz 3-1

(The blank forms you need are on pages 3-1 and 3-2 of the *Study Guide with Working Papers*.)

The following are the transactions of Lowe's Repair Service. Journalize the transactions in proper form. The chart of accounts includes Cash; Accounts Receivable; Prepaid Rent; Repair Supplies; Repair Equipment; Accounts Payable; A. Lowe, Capital; A. Lowe, Withdrawals; Repair Fees Earned; Salaries Expense; Advertising Expense; and Supplies Expense.

2009
June 1 A. Lowe invested $7,000 cash and $5,000 worth of repair equipment in the business.
1 Paid two months' rent in advance, $1,200.
4 Bought repair supplies from Melvin Co. on account, $600. (These supplies have not yet been consumed or used up.)
15 Performed repair work, received $600 in cash, and had to bill Doe Co. for remaining balance of $300.
18 A. Lowe paid his home telephone bill, $50, using a company cheque.
22 Advertising bill for $400 from Jones Co. was received, but payment was not due yet. (Advertising has already appeared in the newspaper.)
24 Paid salaries, $1,400.

Solution to Self-Review Quiz 3-1

Quiz Tip

All titles for the debits and credits come from the chart of accounts. Debits are against the date column and credits are indented. The description is indented further. The PR column is left blank in the journalizing process.

LOWE'S REPAIR SERVICE
GENERAL JOURNAL

Page 1

Date			Account Titles and Description	PR*	Dr.	Cr.
2009 June	1		Cash		7 0 0 0 00	
			Repair Equipment		5 0 0 0 00	
			A. Lowe, Capital			1 2 0 0 0 00
			Owner investment			
	1		Prepaid Rent		1 2 0 0 00	
			Cash			1 2 0 0 00
			Rent paid in advance (2 months)			
	4		Repair Supplies		6 0 0 00	
			Accounts Payable			6 0 0 00
			Purchase of supplies on account			
	15		Cash		6 0 0 00	
			Accounts Receivable		3 0 0 00	
			Repair Fees Earned			9 0 0 00
			Performed repairs			
	18		A. Lowe, Withdrawals		5 0 00	
			Cash			5 0 00
			Personal withdrawal			
	22		Advertising Expense		4 0 0 00	
			Accounts Payable			4 0 0 00
			Advertising bill			
	24		Salaries Expense		1 4 0 0 00	
			Cash			1 4 0 0 00
			Paid salaries			

*Note that the PR column is left blank in the journalizing process.

Learning Unit 3-2

Posting to the Ledger: Step 3 of the Accounting Cycle

The **general journal** serves a particular purpose: it puts every transaction that the business makes in one place. There are things it cannot do, however. For example, if you were asked to find the balance of the Cash account from the general journal, you would have to go through the entire journal and look for only the cash entries. Then you would have to add up the debits and the credits for the Cash account (separately) and determine the difference between the two totals.

What we really need to do to find balances of accounts is transfer the information from the journal to the **general ledger**. This is called **posting**. In the general ledger, we will accumulate an ending balance for each account so that we can prepare financial statements.

POSTING

Footings are not needed in three-column accounts.

In Chapter 2, we used the T account form to make our ledger entries. T accounts are very simple, but they are not used in the real business world. They are used only for demonstration purposes. In practice, accountants often use a **three-column account** form that includes a column for each account's running balance. Figure 3-2 shows a standard three-column account (all the details are made up). We will use that format in the text from now on to illustrate general ledger accounts.

Now let's look at how to post the transactions of Clark's Desktop Publishing Services from its journal. The diagram in Figure 3-3 shows how to post the cash line from the journal to the ledger. The steps in the posting process are numbered and illustrated in the figure.

Step 1: In the Cash account in the ledger, record the date (May 1, 2010) and the amount of the entry ($10,000).

Step 2: Record the page number of the journal "GJ1" in the posting reference (PR) column of the Cash account.

Step 3: Calculate the new balance of the account. You keep a running balance in each account as you would in your chequebook. To do this, you take the present balance in the account on the previous line and add or subtract the transaction as necessary to arrive at your new balance.

Step 4: Record the account number of Cash (111) in the posting reference (PR) column of the journal. This is called **cross-referencing**.

The same sequence of steps occurs for each line in the journal. In a manual system like Clark's, the debits and credits in the journal may be posted in the order in which they were recorded, or all the debits may be posted first and then all the credits. If Clark used a computer system, the program would post at the press of a menu button.

Using Posting References

The posting references are very helpful. In the journal, the PR column tells us which transactions have or have not been posted and also to which accounts they have been posted. In the ledger, the posting reference leads us back to the original transaction in its entirety so that we can see why the debit or credit was recorded and what other accounts were affected. (It leads us back to the original transaction by identifying the journal and the page in the journal from which the information came.)

Figure 3-2
Three-Column Account

GENERAL LEDGER						
Accounts Payable						Account No. 211
Date 2010	Explanation	Post. Ref.	Debit	Credit	DR or CR	Balance
May 1		GJ1		5 0 0 00	CR	5 0 0 00
3		GJ1		6 0 00	CR	5 6 0 00
18		GJ1		2 5 00	CR	5 8 5 00
28		GJ2	2 5 0 00		CR	3 3 5 00

Figure 3-3
How to Post from
Journal to Ledger

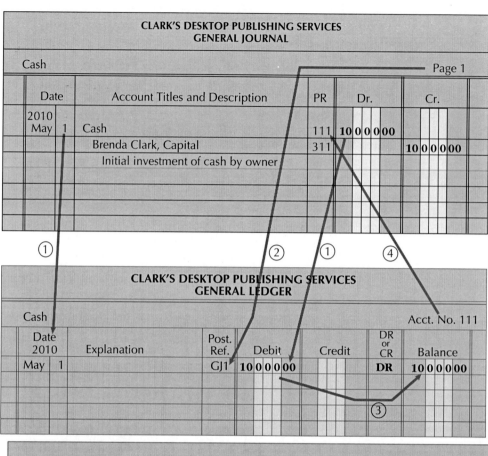

Figure 3-3 — How to Post from Journal to Ledger

LEARNING UNIT 3-2 REVIEW

AT THIS POINT you should be able to:

◆ State the purpose of posting. (p. 92)

◆ Discuss the advantages of the three-column account. (p. 93)

◆ Identify the elements to be posted. (p. 93)

◆ From journalized transactions, post to the general ledger. (p. 93)

Self-Review Quiz 3-2

(The forms you need are on pages 3-3 to 3-6 of the *Study Guide with Working Papers.*)

The following are the journalized transactions of Clark's Desktop Publishing Services. Your task is to post information to the ledger. The ledger in your workbook has all the account titles and numbers that were used from the chart of accounts.

Date		Account Titles and Description	PR	Dr.	Cr.
2010 May	1	Cash		10 000 00	
		Brenda Clark, Capital			10 000 00
		Initial investment of cash by owner			
	1	Desktop Publishing Equipment		6 000 00	
		Cash			1 000 00
		Accounts Payable			5 000 00
		Purchase of equipment from Ben Co.			
	1	Prepaid Rent		1 200 00	
		Cash			1 200 00
		Rent paid in advance (3 months)			
	3	Office Supplies		6 00 00	
		Accounts Payable			6 00 00
		Purchase of supplies on account from			
		Norris Co.			
	7	Cash		3 000 00	
		Desktop Publishing Fees			3 000 00
		Cash received for services rendered			
	11	Office Salaries Expense		6 50 00	
		Cash			6 50 00
		Payment of office salaries			
	18	Advertising Expense		2 50 00	
		Accounts Payable			2 50 00
		Bill received but not paid from			
		Al's News Co.			
	20	Brenda Clark, Withdrawals		6 25 00	
		Cash			6 25 00
		Personal withdrawal of cash			
	22	Accounts Receivable		5 000 00	
		Desktop Publishing Fees			5 000 00
		Billed Morris Co. for fees earned			

CLARK'S DESKTOP PUBLISHING SERVICES
GENERAL JOURNAL

Page 2

Date		Account Titles and Description	PR	Dr.	Cr.
2010 May	25	Office Salaries Expense		6 5 0 00	
		Cash			6 5 0 00
		Payment of office salaries			
	28	Accounts Payable		2 5 0 0 00	
		Cash			2 5 0 0 00
		Paid half the amount owed Ben Co.			
	29	Telephone Expense		2 2 0 00	
		Cash			2 2 0 00
		Paid telephone bill			

Solution to Self-Review Quiz 3-2

Posting references

Remember: The PR column remains empty until the entries have been posted.

CLARK'S DESKTOP PUBLISHING SERVICES
GENERAL JOURNAL

Page 1

Date		Account Titles and Description	PR	Dr.	Cr.
2010 May	1	Cash	111	10 0 0 0 00	
		Brenda Clark, Capital	311		10 0 0 0 00
		Initial investment of cash by owner			
	1	Desktop Publishing Equipment	121	6 0 0 0 00	
		Cash	111		1 0 0 0 00
		Accounts Payable	211		5 0 0 0 00
		Purchase of equipment from Ben Co.			
	1	Prepaid Rent	115	1 2 0 0 00	
		Cash	111		1 2 0 0 00
		Rent paid in advance (3 months)			
	3	Office Supplies	114	6 0 0 00	
		Accounts Payable	211		6 0 0 00
		Purchase of supplies on account from Norris Co.			
	7	Cash	111	3 0 0 0 00	
		Desktop Publishing Fees	411		3 0 0 0 00
		Cash received for services rendered			
	11	Office Salaries Expense	511	6 5 0 00	
		Cash	111		6 5 0 00
		Payment of office salaries			

	18	Advertising Expense	512	2 5 0 00	
		Accounts Payable	211		2 5 0 00
		Bill received but not paid from			
		Al's News Co.			
	20	Brenda Clark, Withdrawals	312	6 2 5 00	
		Cash	111		6 2 5 00
		Personal withdrawal of cash			
	22	Accounts Receivable	112	5 0 0 0 00	
		Desktop Publishing Fees	411		5 0 0 0 00
		Billed Morris Co. for fees earned			

CLARK'S DESKTOP PUBLISHING SERVICES
GENERAL JOURNAL

Page 2

Date		Account Titles and Description	PR	Dr.	Cr.
2010 May	25	Office Salaries Expense	511	6 5 0 00	
		Cash	111		6 5 0 00
		Payment of office salaries			
	28	Accounts Payable	211	2 5 0 0 00	
		Cash	111		2 5 0 0 00
		Paid half the amount owed Ben Co.			
	29	Telephone Expense	513	2 2 0 00	
		Cash	111		2 2 0 00
		Paid telephone bill			

Posting to ledger accounts

CLARK'S DESKTOP PUBLISHING SERVICES
PARTIAL GENERAL LEDGER

Cash

Acct. No. 111

Date 2010		Explanation	Post. Ref.	Debit	Credit	DR or CR	Balance
May	1		GJ1	10 0 0 0 00		DR	10 0 0 0 00
	1		GJ1		1 0 0 0 00	DR	9 0 0 0 00
	1		GJ1		1 2 0 0 00	DR	7 8 0 0 00
	7		GJ1	3 0 0 0 00		DR	10 8 0 0 00
	11		GJ1		6 5 0 00	DR	10 1 5 0 00
	20		GJ1		6 2 5 00	DR	9 5 2 5 00
	25		GJ2		6 5 0 00	DR	8 8 7 5 00
	28		GJ2		2 5 0 0 00	DR	6 3 7 5 00
	29		GJ2		2 2 0 00	DR	6 1 5 5 00

Accounts Receivable   Acct. No. 112

Date 2010		Explanation	Post. Ref.	Debit	Credit	DR or CR	Balance
May	22		GJ1	5 0 0 0 00		DR	5 0 0 0 00

Office Supplies   Acct. No. 114

Date 2010		Explanation	Post. Ref.	Debit	Credit	DR or CR	Balance
May	3		GJ1	6 0 0 00		DR	6 0 0 00

Prepaid Rent   Acct. No. 115

Date 2010		Explanation	Post. Ref.	Debit	Credit	DR or CR	Balance
May	1		GJ1	1 2 0 0 00		DR	1 2 0 0 00

Desktop Publishing Equipment   Acct. No. 121

Date 2010		Explanation	Post. Ref.	Debit	Credit	DR or CR	Balance
May	1		GJ1	6 0 0 0 00		DR	6 0 0 0 00

Accounts Payable   Acct. No. 211

Date 2010		Explanation	Post. Ref.	Debit	Credit	DR or CR	Balance
May	1		GJ1		5 0 0 0 00	CR	5 0 0 0 00
	3		GJ1		6 0 0 00	CR	5 6 0 0 00
	18		GJ1		2 5 0 00	CR	5 8 5 0 00
	28		GJ2	2 5 0 0 00		CR	3 3 5 0 00

Brenda Clark, Capital   Acct. No. 311

Date 2010		Explanation	Post. Ref.	Debit	Credit	DR or CR	Balance
May	1		GJ1		1 0 0 0 0 00	CR	1 0 0 0 0 00

Brenda Clark, Withdrawals   Acct. No. 312

Date 2010	Explanation	Post. Ref.	Debit	Credit	DR or CR	Balance
May 20		GJ1	625 00		DR	625 00

Desktop Publishing Fees   Acct. No. 411

Date 2010	Explanation	Post. Ref.	Debit	Credit	DR or CR	Balance
May 7		GJ1		3000 00	CR	3000 00
22		GJ1		5000 00	CR	8000 00

Office Salaries Expense   Acct. No. 511

Date 2010	Explanation	Post. Ref.	Debit	Credit	DR or CR	Balance
May 11		GJ1	650 00		DR	650 00
25		GJ2	650 00		DR	1300 00

Advertising Expense   Acct. No. 512

Date 2010	Explanation	Post. Ref.	Debit	Credit	DR or CR	Balance
May 18		GJ1	250 00		DR	250 00

Telephone Expense   Acct. No. 513

Date 2010	Explanation	Post. Ref.	Debit	Credit	DR or CR	Balance
May 29		GJ2	220 00		DR	220 00

Quiz Tip

The Post. Ref. column in the ledger tells from which part of the journal the information came. The PR column in the journal (the last to be filled in) tells to what account number in the ledger the information was posted.

Learning Unit 3-3

Preparing the Trial Balance: Step 4 of the Accounting Cycle

Did you notice in Self-Review Quiz 3-2 that each account had a running balance figure? Did you know the normal balance of each account in Clark's ledger? As we discussed in Chapter 2, the list of the individual accounts with their balances taken from the ledger is called a **trial balance.**

The trial balance shown in Figure 3-4 was developed from the ledger accounts of Clark's Desktop Publishing Services that were posted and balanced in Self-Review Quiz 3-2. If the information is journalized or posted incorrectly, the trial balance will not be correct.

There are some things the trial balance will not show:

The totals of a trial balance can balance and yet be incorrect.

◆ The capital figure on the trial balance may not be the beginning capital figure. For instance, if Brenda Clark had made additional investments during the period, the additional investment would have been journalized and posted to

CLARK'S DESKTOP PUBLISHING SERVICES TRIAL BALANCE MAY 31, 2010	Debit	Credit
Cash	6 1 5 5 00	
Accounts Receivable	5 0 0 0 00	
Office Supplies	6 0 0 00	
Prepaid Rent	1 2 0 0 00	
Desktop Publishing Equipment	6 0 0 0 00	
Accounts Payable		3 3 5 0 00
Brenda Clark, Capital		10 0 0 0 00
Brenda Clark, Withdrawals	6 2 5 00	
Desktop Publishing Fees		8 0 0 0 00
Office Salaries Expense	1 3 0 0 00	
Advertising Expense	2 5 0 00	
Telephone Expense	2 2 0 00	
Totals	21 3 5 0 00	21 3 5 0 00

The trial balance lists the accounts in the same order as in the ledger. The $6,155 figure for cash came from the ledger.

Figure 3-4 The Trial Balance

the capital account. The only way to tell if the capital balance on the trial balance is the original balance is to check the ledger capital account to see whether any additional investments were made. This will be important when we make financial reports.

◆ There is no guarantee that transactions have been properly recorded. For example, the following errors would remain undetected: (1) a transaction that may have been omitted in the journalizing process; (2) a transaction incorrectly analyzed and recorded in the journal; (3) a journal entry journalized or posted twice. (4) a journal entry posted to an incorrect account.

WHAT TO DO IF A TRIAL BALANCE DOESN'T BALANCE

The trial balance of Clark's Desktop Publishing Services shows that the total of debits is equal to the total of credits. However, what happens if the trial balance is in balance, but the correct amount is not recorded in each ledger account? Accuracy in the journalizing and posting process will help ensure that no errors are made.

Even if there is an error, the first rule is "Don't panic." Everyone makes mistakes and there are accepted ways of correcting them. Once an entry has been made in ink, correcting an error must always show that the entry has been changed and who changed it. Sometimes the change has to be explained.

SOME COMMON MISTAKES

Correcting the trial balance: what to do if your trial balance doesn't balance

If the trial balance does not balance, the cause could be something relatively simple. Here are some common errors and how they can be fixed:

◆ If the difference (the amount you are off) is 10, 100, 1,000, etc., there probably is a mathematical error.

Did you clear your adding machine?

◆ If the difference is equal to an individual account balance in the ledger, the amount could have been omitted. It is also possible that the figure was not posted from the general journal.

◆ Divide the difference by 2; then check to see if a debit should have been a credit and vice versa in the ledger or trial balance. *Example*: $150 difference ÷ 2 = $75. This means that you may have placed $75 as a debit to an account instead of a credit or vice versa.

- If the difference is evenly divisible by 9, a slide or a transposition may have occurred. A **slide** is an error resulting from adding or deleting zeros in writing numbers. For example, $4,175.00 may have been copied as $41.75. A **transposition** is the accidental rearrangement of the digits of a number. For example, $4,175 might have been accidentally written as $4,157.
- Compare the balances in the trial balance with the ledger accounts to check for copying errors.
- Recompute balances in each ledger account.
- Trace all postings from journal to ledger.

If you cannot find the error after you have done all of this, take a break. Then start all over again.

MAKING A CORRECTION BEFORE POSTING

Before posting, error correction is straightforward. Simply draw a line through the incorrect entry in the journal, write the correct information above the line, and write your initials near the change.

Correcting an Error in an Account Title   The following illustration shows an error and its correction in an account title:

		1	Desktop Publishing Equipment		6 0 0 0 00		
			Cash			1 0 0 0 00	
			~~Accounts Payable~~ amp ~~Accounts Receivable~~			5 0 0 0 00	
			Purchase of equipment from Ben Co.				

Correcting a Numerical Error   Numbers are handled the same way as account titles, as the next change, from 520 to 250, shows:

		18	Advertising Expense		2 5 0 00		
			Accounts Payable			amp 2 5 0 00 ~~5 2 0 00~~	
			Bill from Al's News				

Correcting an Entry Error   If a number has been entered in the wrong column, a straight line is drawn through it, and the number is then written in the correct column:

		1	Desktop Publishing Equipment		6 0 0 0 00		
			Cash			1 0 0 0 00	
			Accounts Payable	amp ~~5 0 0 0 00~~		5 0 0 0 00	
			Purchase of equipment from Ben Co.				

MAKING A CORRECTION AFTER POSTING

It is also possible to correct an amount that is correctly entered in the journal but posted incorrectly to the ledger of the proper account. The first step is to draw a line through the error and write the correct figure above it. The next step is to change the running balance to reflect the corrected posting. Here, too, a line is drawn through the balance and the corrected balance is written above it. Both changes must be initialled.

Desktop Publishing Fees						Acct. No. 411	
Date 2010		Explanation	Post. Ref.	Debit	Credit	DR or CR	Balance
May	7		GJ1		3 0 0 0 00	CR	3 0 0 0 00
	22		GJ1		~~5 0 0 00~~ ⟨5 0 0 0 00⟩	CR	~~8 0 0 0 00~~ ⟨3 5 0 0 0⟩

CORRECTING AN ENTRY POSTED TO THE WRONG ACCOUNT

Drawing a line through an error and writing the correction above it is possible when a mistake has occurred within the proper account, but when an error involves a posting to the wrong account, the journal must include a correction accompanied by an explanation. In addition, the correct information must be posted to the appropriate ledger accounts.

Suppose, for example, that as a result of tracing postings from journal entries to ledger accounts, you find that a $180 telephone bill was incorrectly debited as an advertising expense. The following illustration shows how this is done.

Step 1: The error is corrected by making a new entry in the journal, dated with the date when the correction is entered, and the correction is explained.

GENERAL JOURNAL						Page 3	
Date 2010		Account Titles and Description	PR	Dr.		Cr.	
May	29	Telephone Expense	513	1 8 0 00			
		Advertising Expense	512			1 8 0 00	
		To correct error in which					
		Advertising Expense was debited					
		for charges to Telephone Expense					

Step 2: The Advertising Expense ledger account is also corrected, by posting the new entry.

Advertising Expense							Acct. No. 512	
Date 2010		Explanation	Post. Ref.	Debit	Credit	DR or CR	Balance	
May	18			1 7 5 00		DR	1 7 5 00	
	23			1 8 0 00		DR	3 5 5 00	
	29	*Correcting entry*	GJ3		1 8 0 00	DR	1 7 5 00	

Step 3: The Telephone Expense ledger is corrected.

Telephone Expense							Acct. No. 513	
Date 2010		Explanation	Post. Ref.	Debit	Credit	DR or CR	Balance	
May	29		GJ3	1 8 0 00		DR	1 8 0 00	

LEARNING UNIT 3-3 REVIEW

AT THIS POINT you should be able to:

◆ Prepare a trial balance from a ledger, which uses three-column accounts. (p. 99)
◆ Analyze and correct a trial balance that doesn't balance. (p. 100)
◆ Correct journal and posting errors. (p. 101)

Self-Review Quiz 3-3

(The blank forms you need are on page 3-7 of the *Study Guide with Working Papers.*)

1.

Interoffice Memo

To: Al Vincent
From: Professor Jones
Re: Trial Balance

You have submitted to me an incorrect trial balance. Could you please rework and turn it in to me before next Friday?

Note: Individual amounts look okay.

A. RICE
TRIAL BALANCE
OCTOBER 31, 2011

	Dr.	Cr.
Cash		8 0 6 0 00
Operating Expenses		1 7 0 0 00
A. Rice, Withdrawals		4 0 0 00
Service Revenue		5 4 0 0 00
Equipment	5 0 0 0 00	
Accounts Receivable	3 5 4 0 00	
Accounts Payable	2 0 0 0 00	
Supplies	3 0 0 00	
A. Rice, Capital		1 1 6 0 0 00

2. An $8,000 debit to Office Equipment was mistakenly journalized and posted on June 9, 2011, to Office Supplies. Prepare the appropriate journal entry to correct this error.

Quiz Tip

Items in a trial balance are listed in the same order as in the ledger or the chart of accounts. Expect each account to have its normal balance (either debit or credit).

1.

A. RICE TRIAL BALANCE OCTOBER 31, 2011	Dr.	Cr.
Cash	8 0 6 0 00	
Accounts Receivable	3 5 4 0 00	
Supplies	3 0 0 00	
Equipment	5 0 0 0 00	
Accounts Payable		2 0 0 0 00
A. Rice, Capital		11 6 0 0 00
A. Rice, Withdrawals	4 0 0 00	
Service Revenue		5 4 0 0 00
Operating Expenses	1 7 0 0 00	
Totals	19 0 0 0 00	19 0 0 0 00

2.

	GENERAL JOURNAL				Page 4
Date	Account Titles and Description	PR	Dr.	Cr.	
2011 June 9	Office Equipment		8 0 0 0 0 0		
	Office Supplies			8 0 0 0 0 0	
	To correct error in which Office Supplies				
	was debited for purchase of				
	Office Equipment				

DEMONSTRATION PROBLEM: STEPS 1–4 OF THE ACCOUNTING CYCLE

(The blank forms you need are on pages 3-8 to 3-10 in the *Study Guide with Working Papers.*)

In March, Abby's Employment Agency had the following transactions:

2010

March	1	Abby Todd invested $5,000 in the new employment agency.
	4	Bought equipment for cash, $800.
	5	Earned employment fee commission, $200, but the payment from Blue Co. will not be received until June.
	8	Paid wages expense, $300.
	9	Abby Todd paid her home utility bill from the company bank account, $75.
	11	Placed Rick Wool at VCR Corporation, receiving $1,200 cash.
	15	Paid cash for supplies, $600.
	29	Telephone bill was received but not yet paid, $180.
	30	Advertising bill was received but not yet paid, $400.

The chart of accounts includes: Cash, 111; Accounts Receivable, 112; Supplies, 131; Equipment, 141; Accounts Payable, 211; A. Todd, Capital, 311; A. Todd, Withdrawals, 321; Employment Fees Earned, 411; Wages Expense, 511; Telephone Expense, 521; Advertising Expense, 531.

Assignment

a. Set up a ledger based on the chart of accounts.
b. Journalize (all page 1).
c. Post transactions to ledger.
d. Prepare a trial balance for March 31.

Solution to Demonstration Problem

a. See solution to **c.**, General Ledger, on page 107.
b. Journalizing
c. Posting

<table>
<tr><th colspan="7">ABBY'S EMPLOYMENT AGENCY
GENERAL JOURNAL</th></tr>
<tr><td colspan="7" align="right">Page 1</td></tr>
<tr><th colspan="2">Date</th><th>Account Titles and Description</th><th>PR</th><th>Dr.</th><th>Cr.</th></tr>
<tr><td>2010
Mar.</td><td>1</td><td>Cash</td><td>111</td><td>5 0 0 0 00</td><td></td></tr>
<tr><td></td><td></td><td>A. Todd, Capital</td><td>311</td><td></td><td>5 0 0 0 00</td></tr>
<tr><td></td><td></td><td>Owner investment</td><td></td><td></td><td></td></tr>
<tr><td></td><td></td><td></td><td></td><td></td><td></td></tr>
<tr><td></td><td>4</td><td>Equipment</td><td>141</td><td>8 0 0 00</td><td></td></tr>
<tr><td></td><td></td><td>Cash</td><td>111</td><td></td><td>8 0 0 00</td></tr>
<tr><td></td><td></td><td>Bought equipment for cash</td><td></td><td></td><td></td></tr>
<tr><td></td><td></td><td></td><td></td><td></td><td></td></tr>
<tr><td></td><td>5</td><td>Accounts Receivable</td><td>112</td><td>2 0 0 00</td><td></td></tr>
<tr><td></td><td></td><td>Employment Fees Earned</td><td>411</td><td></td><td>2 0 0 00</td></tr>
<tr><td></td><td></td><td>Fees on account from Blue Co.</td><td></td><td></td><td></td></tr>
<tr><td></td><td></td><td></td><td></td><td></td><td></td></tr>
<tr><td></td><td>8</td><td>Wages Expense</td><td>511</td><td>3 0 0 00</td><td></td></tr>
<tr><td></td><td></td><td>Cash</td><td>111</td><td></td><td>3 0 0 00</td></tr>
<tr><td></td><td></td><td>Paid wages</td><td></td><td></td><td></td></tr>
<tr><td></td><td></td><td></td><td></td><td></td><td></td></tr>
<tr><td></td><td>9</td><td>A. Todd, Withdrawals</td><td>321</td><td>7 5 00</td><td></td></tr>
<tr><td></td><td></td><td>Cash</td><td>111</td><td></td><td>7 5 00</td></tr>
<tr><td></td><td></td><td>Personal withdrawals</td><td></td><td></td><td></td></tr>
<tr><td></td><td></td><td></td><td></td><td></td><td></td></tr>
<tr><td></td><td>11</td><td>Cash</td><td>111</td><td>1 2 0 0 00</td><td></td></tr>
<tr><td></td><td></td><td>Employment Fees Earned</td><td>411</td><td></td><td>1 2 0 0 00</td></tr>
<tr><td></td><td></td><td>Cash fees</td><td></td><td></td><td></td></tr>
<tr><td></td><td></td><td></td><td></td><td></td><td></td></tr>
<tr><td></td><td>15</td><td>Supplies</td><td>131</td><td>6 0 0 00</td><td></td></tr>
<tr><td></td><td></td><td>Cash</td><td>111</td><td></td><td>6 0 0 00</td></tr>
<tr><td></td><td></td><td>Bought supplies for cash</td><td></td><td></td><td></td></tr>
<tr><td></td><td></td><td></td><td></td><td></td><td></td></tr>
<tr><td></td><td>29</td><td>Telephone Expense</td><td>521</td><td>1 8 0 00</td><td></td></tr>
<tr><td></td><td></td><td>Accounts Payable</td><td>211</td><td></td><td>1 8 0 00</td></tr>
<tr><td></td><td></td><td>Telephone bill owed</td><td></td><td></td><td></td></tr>
<tr><td></td><td></td><td></td><td></td><td></td><td></td></tr>
<tr><td></td><td>30</td><td>Advertising Expense</td><td>531</td><td>4 0 0 00</td><td></td></tr>
<tr><td></td><td></td><td>Accounts Payable</td><td>211</td><td></td><td>4 0 0 00</td></tr>
<tr><td></td><td></td><td>Advertising bill received</td><td></td><td></td><td></td></tr>
</table>

Cash — Acct. No. 111

Date 2010	Explanation	Post. Ref.	Debit	Credit	DR or CR	Balance
Mar. 1		GJ1	5000 00		DR.	5000 00
4		GJ1		800 00	DR.	4200 00
8		GJ1		300 00	DR.	3900 00
9		GJ1		75 00	DR.	3825 00
11		GJ1	1200 00		DR.	5025 00
15		GJ1		600 00	DR.	4425 00

A. Todd, Capital — Acct. No. 311

Date 2010	Explanation	Post. Ref.	Debit	Credit	DR or CR	Balance
Mar. 1		GJ1		5000 00	CR.	5000 00

A. Todd, Withdrawals — Acct. No. 321

Date 2010	Explanation	Post. Ref.	Debit	Credit	DR or CR	Balance
Mar. 9		GJ1	75 00		DR.	75 00

Accounts Receivable — Acct. No. 112

Date 2010	Explanation	Post. Ref.	Debit	Credit	DR or CR	Balance
Mar. 5		GJ1	200 00		DR.	200 00

Employment Fees Earned — Acct. No. 411

Date 2010	Explanation	Post. Ref.	Debit	Credit	DR or CR	Balance
Mar. 5		GJ1		200 00	CR.	200 00
11		GJ1		1200 00	CR.	1400 00

Supplies — Acct. No. 131

Date 2010	Explanation	Post. Ref.	Debit	Credit	DR or CR	Balance
Mar. 15		GJ1	600 00		DR.	600 00

Wages Expense — Acct. No. 511

Date 2010	Explanation	Post. Ref.	Debit	Credit	DR or CR	Balance
Mar. 8		GJ1	300 00		DR.	300 00

Equipment — Acct. No. 141

Date 2010	Explanation	Post. Ref.	Debit	Credit	DR or CR	Balance
Mar. 4		GJ1	800 00		DR.	800 00

Telephone Expense — Acct. No. 521

Date 2010	Explanation	Post. Ref.	Debit	Credit	DR or CR	Balance
Mar. 29		GJ1	180 00		DR.	180 00

Accounts Payable — Acct. No. 211

Date 2010	Explanation	Post. Ref.	Debit	Credit	DR or CR	Balance
Mar. 29		GJ1		180 00	CR.	180 00
30		GJ1		400 00	CR.	580 00

Advertising Expense — Acct. No. 531

Date 2010	Explanation	Post. Ref.	Debit	Credit	DR or CR	Balance
Mar. 30		GJ1	400 00		DR.	400 00

Solution Tips to Journalizing

1. When journalizing, the PR column is not filled in.
2. Write the name of the debit against the date column. Indent credits and list them below debits. Be sure total debits for each transaction equal total credits.
3. Skip a line after each transaction.

| March 1 | Cash | A | ↑ | Dr. | $5,000 |
| | A. Todd, Capital | O.E. | ↑ | Cr. | $5,000 |

| 4 | Equipment | A | ↑ | Dr. | $ 800 |
| | Cash | A | ↓ | Cr. | $ 800 |

| 5 | Accts. Receivable | A | ↑ | Dr. | $ 200 |
| | Empl. Fees Earned | Rev. | ↑ | Cr. | $ 200 |

| 8 | Wages Expense | Exp. | ↑ | Dr. | $ 300 |
| | Cash | A | ↓ | Cr. | $ 300 |

| 9 | A. Todd, Withdrawals | O.E. (Withdrawals) | ↑ | Dr. | $ 75 |
| | Cash | A | ↓ | Cr. | $ 75 |

| 11 | Cash | A | ↑ | Dr. | $1,200 |
| | Empl. Fees Earned | Rev. | ↑ | Cr. | $1,200 |

| 15 | Supplies | A | ↑ | Dr. | $ 600 |
| | Cash | A | ↓ | Cr. | $ 600 |

| 29 | Telephone Expense | Exp. | ↑ | Dr. | $ 180 |
| | Accounts Payable | L | ↑ | Cr. | $ 180 |

| 30 | Advertising Expense | Exp. | ↑ | Dr. | $ 400 |
| | Accounts Payable | L | ↑ | Cr. | $ 400 |

Solution Tips to Posting

The Post. Ref. column in the ledger cash account tells you from which page in the general journal the information came (page 1). After the ledger cash account is posted, account number "111" is put in the PR column of the journal. (This is called *cross-referencing*.)

Note that we keep a running balance in the cash account. A $5,000 Dr. balance and an $800 credit entry result in a new debit balance of $4,200.

d. Trial balance

Abby's Employment Agency
Trial Balance
March 31, 2010

	Dr.	Cr.
Cash	4,425	
Accounts Receivable	200	
Supplies	600	
Equipment	800	
Accounts Payable		580
A. Todd, Capital		5,000
A. Todd, Withdrawals	75	
Employment Fees Earned		1,400
Wages Expense	300	
Telephone Expense	180	
Advertising Expense	400	
Totals	**6,980**	**6,980**

Solution Tip to Trial Balance

The trial balance lists the ending balance of each account, with the accounts in the order in which they appear in the ledger. The total of $6,980 on the left equals $6,980 on the right.

SUMMARY OF KEY POINTS

Learning Unit 3-1

1. The accounting cycle is a sequence of accounting procedures that are usually performed during an accounting period.
2. An accounting period is the time period for which the income statement is prepared. The time period can be any period up to one year.
3. A calendar year is from January 1 to December 31. The fiscal year is any 12-month period. A fiscal year could be a calendar year but does not have to be.
4. Interim reports are statements that are usually prepared for a portion of the business's calendar or fiscal year (e.g., a month or a quarter).
5. A general journal is a book that records transactions in chronological order. Here debits and credits are shown together on one page. It is the book of original entry.
6. The ledger is a collection of accounts where information is accumulated from the postings of the journal. The ledger is the book of final entry.
7. Journalizing is the process of recording journal entries.
8. The chart of accounts provides the specific titles of accounts to be entered in the journal.
9. When journalizing, the posting reference (PR) column is left blank.
10. A compound journal entry occurs when more than two accounts are affected in the journalizing process of a business transaction.

Learning Unit 3-2

1. Posting is the process of transferring information from the journal to the ledger.

2. The journal and ledger contain the same information but in a different form.

3. The three-column ledger account keeps a running balance of an account.

4. The normal balance of an account will be located on the side that increases according to the rules of debits and credits. For example, the normal balances of liabilities occur on the credit side.

5. The mechanical process of posting requires care in accurately transferring dates, posting references, titles, and amounts.

Learning Unit 3-3

1. A trial balance can balance but be incorrect. For example, an entire journal entry may not have been posted.

2. If a trial balance doesn't balance, check for errors in addition, omission of postings, slides, transpositions, copying errors, and so on.

3. Specific procedures should be followed in making corrections in journals and ledgers.

KEY TERMS

Accounting cycle   For each accounting period, the process that begins with the recording of business transactions or procedures into a journal and ends with the completion of a post-closing trial balance (p. 84)

Accounting period   The period of time for which an income statement is prepared (p. 84)

Book of final entry   A ledger that receives information about business transactions from a book of original entry (a journal) (p. 84)

Book of original entry   Book that records the first formal information about business transactions—a journal (p. 84)

Calendar year   January 1 to December 31 (p. 84)

Compound journal entry   A journal entry that affects more than two accounts (p. 87)

Cross-referencing   Adding the account number of the ledger account that was updated to the PR column of the journal, and inserting the journal page on the ledger account (p. 93)

Fiscal year   The 12-month period a business chooses for its accounting year (p. 84)

General journal   The simplest form of a journal, which records information from transactions in chronological order as they occur. This journal links the debit and credit parts of transactions. (p. 84, 92)

General ledger   A collection of accounts that includes all those needed to contain the individual balances that show up on any of the financial statements (asset accounts, liability and equity accounts, revenue accounts, and expense accounts) (p. 92)

Interim reports   Financial reports that are prepared for a month, quarter, or some other portion of the fiscal year (p. 84)

Journal   A listing of business transactions in chronological order. The journal links the debit and credit parts of transactions on one page. (p. 84)

Journal entry   The transaction (debits and credits) that is recorded in a journal once it is analyzed (p. 84)

Journalizing   The process of recording a transaction entry in the journal (p. 84)

Natural business year A business's fiscal year that ends at the same time as a slow seasonal period begins (p. 84)

Posting The transferring, copying, or recording of information from a journal to a ledger (p. 92)

Slide The error of adding or deleting zeros when a number is written; for example, 79,200 & 7,920 (p. 101)

Three-column account A running balance account that records debits and credits, has a column for an ending balance (debit or credit), and replaces the standard two-column account we used earlier (p. 93)

Transposition The accidental rearrangement of the digits of a number; for example, 152 for 125 (p. 101)

Trial balance An informal listing of the ledger accounts and their balances that aids in proving the equality of debits and credits (p. 99)

BLUEPRINT OF FIRST FOUR STEPS OF THE ACCOUNTING CYCLE

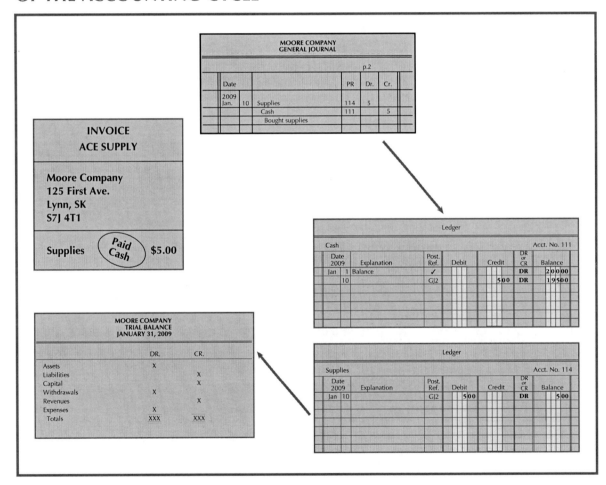

QUESTIONS, CLASSROOM DEMONSTRATION EXERCISES, EXERCISES, AND PROBLEMS

Discussion Questions and Critical Thinking/Ethical Case

1. Explain the concept of the accounting cycle.
2. An accounting period is based on the balance sheet. Agree or disagree.
3. Compare and contrast a calendar year versus a fiscal year.
4. What are interim reports?
5. Why is the ledger called the book of final entry?
6. How do transactions get "linked" in a general journal?
7. What is the relationship of the chart of accounts to the general journal?
8. What is a compound journal entry?
9. Posting means updating the journal. Agree or disagree. Please comment.
10. The side that decreases an account is the normal balance. True or false?
11. The PR column of a general journal is the last item to be filled in during the posting process. Agree or disagree.
12. Discuss the concept of cross-referencing.
13. What is the difference between a transposition and a slide?
14. Jay Simons, the accountant of See Co., wanted to buy a new computer software package for his general ledger. He couldn't do it because all funds were frozen for the rest of the fiscal period. Jay called his friend at Joor Industries and asked whether he could copy their software. Why should or shouldn't Jay do that?

Classroom Demonstration Exercises

(The blank forms you need are on page 3-11 of the *Study Guide with Working Papers*.)

Set A

General Journal

1. Complete the following from the general journal of Lang Company.

									LANG COMPANY GENERAL JOURNAL												Page 1	

Date			Account Titles and Descriptions	PR	Dr.	Cr.
2009 Nov.	18	Cash			7 0 0 0 00	
		Equipment			6 0 0 0 00	
		J. Lang, Capital				13 0 0 0 00
		Initial investment by owner				

    a. Year of journal entry
    b. Month of journal entry
    c. Day of journal entry
    d. Name(s) of account(s) debited
    e. Name(s) of account(s) credited
    f. Explanation of transaction

g. Amount of debit(s)

h. Amount of credit(s)

i. Page of journal

General Journal

2. Provide the explanation for each of these general journal entries.

		GENERAL JOURNAL					Page 4
Date		Account Titles and Descriptions	PR	Debit		Credit	
2009 June	10	Cash		17 00 0 00			
		Office Equipment		26 00 0 00			
		B. Blue, Capital				43 00 0 00	
		(A)					
	16	Cash		4 0 00			
		Accounts Receivable		7 0 00			
		Legal Fees Earned				11 0 00	
		(B)					
	22	Salary Expense		4 0 00			
		Cash				4 0 00	
		(C)					

Posting and Balancing

3. Balance this three-column account. What function does the Post. Ref. column serve? When will Account 111 be used in the journalizing and posting process?

Name: Cash								Account No. 111	
Date 2009		Explanation	Post. Ref.	Debit		Credit	DR or CR	Balance	
May	1		GJ1	19 00					
	4		GJ1	9 00					
	11		GJ2			6 00			
	12		GJ3	2 00					

The Trial Balance

4. The following trial balance was prepared *incorrectly.*

Lee Company
Trial Balance
October 31, 2011

	Dr.	Cr.
D. Lee, Capital	30	
Equipment	112	
Rent Expense		17
Advertising Expense		3
Accounts Payable		108
Taxi Fare Income	16	
Cash	17	
D. Lee, Withdrawals		5
Totals	**175**	**133**

a. Rearrange the accounts in proper order.

b. Calculate the total of the trial balance. (Small numbers are used intentionally so that you can do the calculations in your head.) Assume that each account has a normal balance.

Correcting Entry

5. On June 1, 2011, a telephone expense for $210 was debited to Repair Expense. On July 12, 2011, this error was found. Prepare the correcting journal entry. When would a correcting entry *not* be needed?

Set B

General Journal

1. Complete the following from the general journal of Swan Company.

SWAN COMPANY GENERAL JOURNAL						Page 1
Date	Account Titles and Descriptions	PR	Dr.		Cr.	
2009 Aug. 18	Cash		6 0 0 0 00			
	Equipment		4 0 0 00			
	L. Swan, Capital				6 4 0 0 00	
	Initial investment by owner					

a. Year of journal entry

b. Month of journal entry

c. Day of journal entry

d. Name(s) of account(s) debited

e. Name(s) of account(s) credited

f. Explanation of transaction

g. Amount of debit(s)

h. Amount of credit(s)

i. Page of journal

General Journal

2. Provide the explanation for each of these general journal entries.

GENERAL JOURNAL					Page 4	
Date	Account Titles and Descriptions	PR	Debit		Credit	
2009 July 10	Cash		8 0 0 0 00			
	Office Equipment		5 0 0 0 00			
	J. Walsh, Capital				1 3 0 0 0 00	
	(A)					
15	Cash		3 0 00			
	Accounts Receivable		6 0 00			
	Hair Fees Earned				9 0 00	
	(B)					
20	Advertising Expense		4 0 00			
	Accounts Payable				4 0 00	
	(C)					

Posting and Balancing

3. Balance this three-column account. What function does the Post. Ref. column serve? When will Account 111 be used in the journalizing and posting process?

Name: Cash			Account No. 111			
Date 2009	Explanation	Post. Ref.	Debit	Credit	DR or CR	Balance
June 2		GJ1	15 00			
5		GJ1	6 00			
9		GJ2		4 00		
10		GJ3	1 00			

The Trial Balance

4. The following trial balance was prepared *incorrectly.*

   a. Rearrange the accounts in proper order.

   b. Calculate the total of the trial balance. (Small numbers are used intentionally so that you can do the calculations in your head.) Assume that each account has a normal balance.

Lee Company
Trial Balance
October 31, 2011

	Dr.	Cr.
D. Lee, Capital	17	
Equipment	12	
Rent Expense		4
Advertising Expense		3
Accounts Payable		8
Taxi Fare Income	16	
Cash	17	
D. Lee, Withdrawals		5
Totals	**62**	**20**

Correcting Entry

5. On May 2, 2011, a telephone expense for $180 was debited to Repair Expense. On June 13, 2011, this error was found. Prepare the correcting journal entry. When would a correcting entry *not* be needed?

Exercises

(The forms you need are on pages 3-12 to 3-16 of the *Study Guide with Working Papers.*)

Preparing journal entries

3-1. Prepare journal entries for the following transactions that occurred during October:

2011
Oct.   3   Grace Stafford invested $60,000 cash and $4,000 worth of equipment in her new business.
      6   Purchased building for $60,000 on account.
    13   Purchased a truck from Lange Co. for $18,000 cash.
    17   Bought supplies from Green Co. on account, $700.

3-2. Record the following in the general journal of Reggie's Auto Repair Shop.

2010

Jan. 4 Reggie Long invested $16,000 cash in the auto repair shop.
      5 Paid $7,000 for auto repair equipment.
      8 Bought auto repair equipment for $6,000 on account from Lowell Co.
      15 Received $900 for repair fees earned.
      18 Billed Sullivan Co. $900 for services rendered.
      22 Reggie withdrew $300 for personal use.

3-3. Post the following transactions to the ledger of King Company. The partial ledger of King Company includes Cash, 111; Equipment, 121; Accounts Payable, 211; and A. King, Capital, 311. Please use three-column accounts in the posting process.

Date 2009			PR	Dr.	Cr.
April	6	Cash		15 000 00	
		A. King, Capital			15 000 00
		Cash investment			
	14	Equipment		9 000 00	
		Cash			4 000 00
		Accounts Payable			5 000 00
		Purchase of equipment			

Page 4

3-4. From the following transactions for Lowe Company for the month of July, (a) prepare journal entries (assume that it is page 1 of the journal), (b) post to the ledger (use three-column account style), and (c) prepare a trial balance.

2011

July 4 Joan Lowe invested $6,000 in the business.
      6 Bought equipment on account, $800 from Lax Co.
      15 Billed Friend Co. for services rendered, $4,000.
      18 Received $5,000 cash for services rendered.
      25 Paid salaries expense, $1,800.
      28 Joan withdrew $400 for personal use.

A partial chart of accounts includes: Cash, 111; Accounts Receivable, 112; Equipment, 121; Accounts Payable, 211; J. Lowe, Capital, 311; J. Lowe, Withdrawals, 312; Fees Earned, 411; Salaries Expense, 511.

3-5. You have been hired to correct the following trial balance that has been recorded improperly from the ledger to the trial balance.

SUN CO.
TRIAL BALANCE
MARCH 31, 2009

	Dr.	Cr.
Accounts Payable	2 0 0 0 00	
A. Sun, Capital		6 5 0 0 00
A. Sun, Withdrawals		3 0 0 00
Services Earned		4 7 0 0 00
Concessions Earned	2 5 0 0 00	
Rent Expense	4 0 0 00	
Salaries Expense	2 5 0 0 00	
Miscellaneous Expense		1 3 0 0 00
Cash	10 0 0 0 00	
Accounts Receivable		1 2 0 0 00
Totals	17 4 0 0 00	14 0 0 0 00

3-6. On February 5, 2010, Mike Sullivan made the following journal entry to record the purchase of office equipment priced at $1,400 on account. This transaction had not yet been posted when the error was discovered. Make the appropriate correction.

GENERAL JOURNAL

Date		Account Titles and Description	PR	Dr.	Cr.
2010 Feb.	5	Office Equipment		9 0 0 00	
		Accounts Payable			9 0 0 00
		Purchase of office equipment on account			

Group A Problems

(The forms you need are on pages 3-17 to 3-26 of the *Study Guide with Working Papers*.)

3A-1. Pete Rey operates Pete's Fitness Centre in Victoria. As the bookkeeper, you have been requested to journalize the following transactions:

2010
Nov.　1　Paid rent for two months in advance, $7,000.
　　　3　Purchased exercise equipment on account from Leek's Supply House, $4,400.
　　　10　Purchased exercise room supplies from Angel's Wholesale for $500 cash.
　　　15　Received $1,700 cash from fitness fees earned.
　　　19　Pete withdrew $700 for his personal use.
　　　22　Advertising bill was received from *Daily Sun* but was still unpaid, $200.
　　　24　Paid cleaning expense, $110.
　　　26　Paid salaries expense, $600.
　　　29　Performed fitness work for $1,900; however, payment will not be received until January.

Nov.　30　Paid Leek's Supply House half the amount owed from November 3 transaction.

Your task is to journalize the above transactions. The chart of accounts for Pete's Fitness Centre is as follows:

Chart of Accounts

Assets	Owner's Equity
111　Cash	311　Pete Rey, Capital
112　Accounts Receivable	312　Pete Rey, Withdrawals
114　Prepaid Rent	
116　Exercise Room Supplies	
120　Office Equipment	**Revenue**
121　Exercise Equipment	411　Fitness Fees Earned
Liabilities	**Expenses**
211　Accounts Payable	511　Advertising Expense
	512　Salaries Expense
	514　Cleaning Expense

Comprehensive problem: journalizing, posting, and preparing a trial balance

3A-2. On June 1, 2011, Betty Rice opened Betty's Art Studio in Toronto. The following transactions occurred in June:

2011
June　1　Betty Rice invested $12,000 in the art studio.
　　　2　Paid three months' rent in advance, $1,200.
　　　3　Purchased $600 worth of equipment from Astor Co. on account.
　　　6　Received $900 cash for art training workshop for teachers.
　　　9　Purchased $400 worth of art supplies for cash.
　　　10　Billed Lester Co. $2,100 for group art lessons for its employees.
　　　10　Paid salaries of assistants, $600.
　　　16　Betty withdrew $200 from the business for her personal use.
　　　27　Paid electrical expense, $140.
　　　30　Paid telephone bill for June, $210.

Required

a. Set up the ledger based on the chart of accounts below.
b. Journalize (using journal page 1) and post the June transactions.
c. Prepare a trial balance as of June 30, 2011.

Check Figure

Trial Balance Total $15,600

The chart of accounts for Betty's Art Studio is as follows:

Chart of Accounts

Assets	Owner's Equity
111　Cash	311　Betty Rice, Capital
112　Accounts Receivable	312　Betty Rice, Withdrawals
114　Prepaid Rent	
121　Art Supplies	**Revenue**
131　Equipment	411　Art Fees Earned
Liabilities	**Expenses**
211　Accounts Payable	511　Electrical Expense
	521　Salaries Expense
	531　Telephone Expense

3A-3. The following transactions occurred in June 2009 for A. French Placement Agency of Fredericton:

2009

June	1	A. French invested $9,000 cash in the placement agency.
	1	Bought equipment on account from Hook Co., $2,000.
	2	Earned placement fees of $1,600, but payment will not be received until July.
	5	A. French withdrew $100 for his personal use.
	8	Paid wages expense, $300.
	9	Placed a client on a local TV show, receiving $600 cash.
	15	Bought supplies on account from Lyon Co., $500.
	29	Paid telephone bill for June, $160.
	30	Advertising bill from Shale Co. was received but not yet paid, $900.

The chart of accounts for A. French Placement Agency is as follows:

Chart of Accounts

Assets
111 Cash
112 Accounts Receivable
131 Supplies on Hand
141 Equipment

Liabilities
211 Accounts Payable

Owner's Equity
311 A. French, Capital
321 A. French, Withdrawals

Revenue
411 Placement Fees Earned

Expenses
511 Wages Expense
521 Telephone Expense
531 Advertising Expense

Required

a. Set up the ledger based on the chart of accounts.

b. Journalize (page 1) and post the June transactions.

c. Prepare a trial balance as of June 30, 2009.

d. PREPARE I/S, O/E AND BALANCE

Group B Problems

(The forms you need are on pages 3-17 to 3-26 of the *Study Guide with Working Papers*.)

3B-1. In April 2010, Pete Rey opened a new fitness centre in Victoria. Please assist him by journalizing the following business transactions:

2010

April	1	Pete Rey invested $6,000 worth of exercise equipment as well as $3,000 cash in the new business.
	2	Purchased exercise room supplies on account from Rex Co., $500.
	9	Purchased office equipment on account from Ross Stationery, $400.
	12	Pete paid his home telephone bill from the company bank account, $60.
	20	Received $600 cash for fitness services performed.
	22	Advertising bill was received but not yet paid, $75.
	23	Cleaning bill was received but not yet paid, $90.

CONTINUING PROBLEM

Tony's computer centre is picking up in business, so he has decided to expand his bookkeeping system to a general journal/ledger system. The balances from August have been forwarded to the ledger accounts.

The forms are in the *Study Guide with Working Papers*, pages 3-39 to 3-44.

Assignment

1. Use the chart of accounts provided in Chapter 2 (page 82) to record the transactions illustrated by the following documents.

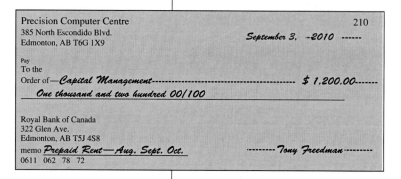

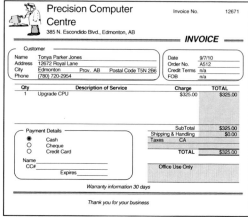

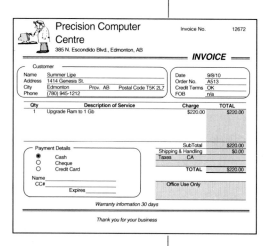

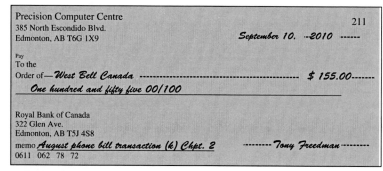

Refer back to Chapter 2, transaction (k).

Refer back to Chapter 2, transaction (o).

Refer back to Chapter 2, transaction (s).

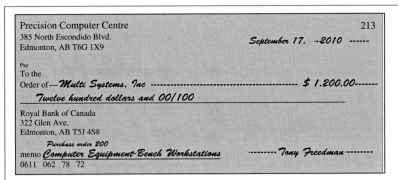

Precision Computer Centre
385 North Escondido Blvd.
Edmonton, AB T6G 1X9

213

September 17, 2010

Pay
To the
Order of — *Multi Systems, Inc* -- $ *1,200.00*------

Twelve hundred dollars and 00/100

Royal Bank of Canada
322 Glen Ave.
Edmonton, AB T5J 4S8

Purchase order 200
memo *Computer Equipment-Bench Workstations*   --------- *Tony Freedman* ---------
0611 062 78 72

Purchased computer shop equipment.

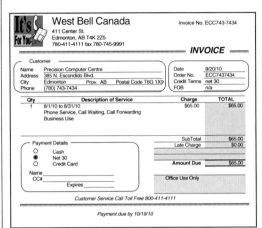

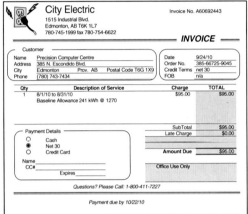

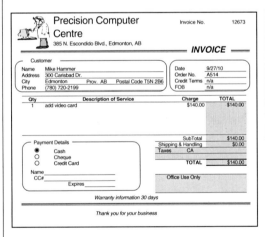

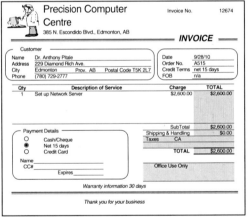

2. Post all transactions to the general ledger accounts (the Prepaid Rent account No. 1025 has been added to the chart of accounts).

3. Prepare a trial balance for September 30, 2010.

4. Prepare the financial statements for the three months ended September 30, 2010.

4 The Accounting Cycle Continued

Preparing Worksheets and Financial Statements

THE BIG PICTURE

What is the largest reporting entity in Canada? Put another way, where would you look if you wanted to see the country's largest dollar figures on a set of financial statements?

For an answer, check out www.fin.gc.ca. As you may have guessed, the Government of Canada easily qualifies as the largest Canadian fiscal entity. It is not a business, of course, so it does not have sales revenue, but it does take in nearly $200 billion every year.

All accounting students in Canada should visit this site and review Canada's financial position. Lots of people may have the impression that the federal government's financial statements are too complex to bother with. Well, it is true that the numbers are really large, and 2002 introduced some important changes in the way the government reports its financial affairs, but the statements are surprisingly understandable to most Canadians.

Up until 2001, the government used the cash basis of accounting (modified somewhat) for preparing its financial statements. This means that no accruals were used in calculating the numbers shown in the financial statements—tax revenue, for example, was simply the amount of tax received by the government in its fiscal year, not the amount of tax the various taxpayers in Canada owed in that year. One other really important aspect of this cash-based approach is that the majority of funds expended on assets were simply written off. If the federal government spent a few million on an upgrade to an airport, for instance, that just showed up as an expense in the year it happened.

Starting in 2002, the federal government based its financial statements on the accrual basis of accounting—much as it asks all businesses in Canada to do. This meant a substantial increase in the number of adjustments the government departments made in their financial records.

This chapter introduces you to the process of adjustments. You will discover that, rather than recording only the cash in and out, really useful accounting reports are prepared only after a number of adjustments are calculated and recorded in the entity's accounting records. Now, Canada's largest government does the same—and the results dramatically change the details of what our federal government reports to Canadians.

Keep watching Canada's largest fiscal entity. You will learn a lot about accounting, and be a much better informed voter besides!

◆ **Making adjustments for prepaid rent, office supplies, amortization on equipment, and accrued salaries (p. 129)**
◆ **Preparing an adjusted trial balance on the worksheet (p. 135)**
◆ **Completing the income statement and balance sheet sections of the worksheet (p. 138)**
◆ **Preparing financial statements from the worksheet (p. 141)**

In the accompanying diagram, steps 1–4 show the steps of the accounting cycle that were completed for Clark's Desktop Publishing Services in the last chapter. This chapter continues the cycle with steps 5 and 6, the preparation of a worksheet and the three financial statements.

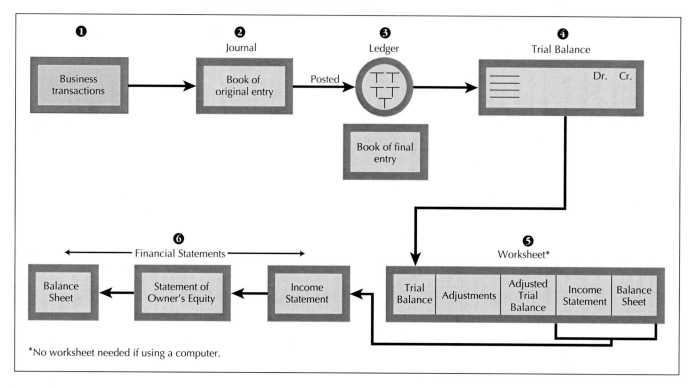

*No worksheet needed if using a computer.

> The worksheet is not a formal report, so no dollar signs appear on it. Because it is a ruled form, there are no commas either.

An accountant uses a **worksheet** to organize and check data before preparing the financial reports necessary to complete the accounting cycle. The most important function of the worksheet is to allow the accountant to find and correct errors before financial statements are prepared. In a way, a worksheet acts as the accountant's scratch pad. No one sees the worksheet once the formal reports are prepared. The beginning of a sample worksheet is shown in Figure 4-1.

Learning Unit 4-1

Step 5 of the Accounting Cycle: Preparing a Worksheet

The accounts listed on the far left of the worksheet are taken from the ledger. The rest of the worksheet has five sections: trial balance, adjustments, adjusted trial balance, income statement, and balance sheet. Each of these sections is divided into debit and credit columns. Refer often to the special overlays in Figure 4-5 (see page 138b) as you

Account Titles	Trial Balance		Adjustments		Adjusted Trial Balance		Income Statement	
	Dr.	Cr.	Dr.	Cr.	Dr.	Cr.	Dr.	Cr.
Cash	6 1 5 5 00							
Accounts Receivable	5 0 0 0 00							
Office Supplies	6 0 0 00							
Prepaid Rent	1 2 0 0 00							
Desktop Publishing Equipment	6 0 0 0 00							
Accounts Payable		3 3 5 0 00						
Brenda Clark, Capital		10 0 0 0 00						
Brenda Clark, Withdrawals	6 2 5 00							
Desktop Publishing Fees		8 0 0 0 00						
Office Salaries Expense	1 3 0 0 00							
Advertising Expense	2 5 0 00							
Telephone Expense	2 2 0 00							
	21 3 5 0 00	21 3 5 0 00						

Figure 4-1 Sample Worksheet—Started, with Trial Balance

> As is true for all accounting statements, the heading includes the name of the company, the name of the report, the date, and the accounting period covered.

> Worksheets can be completed using spreadsheet software like Excel. If your worksheets are carefully designed, several types of errors can be prevented.

study this learning unit. The transparencies illustrating the completion of a worksheet can be very useful to your understanding of the process.

THE TRIAL BALANCE SECTION

We discussed how to prepare a trial balance in Chapter 3. Some companies prepare a separate trial balance; others, such as Clark's Desktop Publishing Services, prepare the trial balance directly on the worksheet. Every account in the ledger that has a balance is entered in the trial balance. Additional titles from the ledger are added as they are needed. (We will show this later.)

THE ADJUSTMENTS SECTION

Chapters 1 to 3 discussed transactions that occurred with outside suppliers and companies. In a real business, inside transactions also occur during the accounting cycle. These transactions must be recorded too. At the end of the worksheet process, the accountant will have all of the business's accounts up to date and ready to be used to prepare the formal financial statements. By analyzing each of Clark's accounts on the worksheet, the accountant will be able to identify specific accounts that must be **adjusted** to bring them up to date. The accountant for Clark's Desktop Publishing Services needs to adjust the following accounts:

A. Office Supplies
B. Prepaid Rent
C. Desktop Publishing Equipment
D. Office Salaries Expense

Let's look at how to analyze and adjust each of these accounts.

A. Adjusting the Office Supplies Account

On May 31, the accountant found out that the company had only $100 worth of office supplies on hand. When the company originally purchased the $600 worth of office supplies, they were considered an asset. However, as the supplies were used up, they became an expense.

The adjustment for supplies deals with the amount of supplies used up.

◆ Office supplies available, $600
◆ Office supplies left or on hand as of May 31, $100
◆ Office supplies used up in the operation of the business for the month of May, $500

As a result, the asset Office Supplies on the trial balance is too high (it should be $100, not $600). At the same time, if we don't show the additional expense of supplies used, the company's *net income* will be too high.

Adjustments affect both the income statement and the balance sheet.

Office Supplies Expense 514

| 500 | |

This is supplies used up.

Office Supplies 114

| 600 | 500 |

100 ↗

This is supplies on hand.

If Clark's accountant does not adjust the trial balance to reflect the change, the company's net income would be too high on the income statement and both sides (assets and owner's equity) of the balance sheet also would be too high.

Now let's look at the adjustment for office supplies in terms of the transaction analysis chart.

Will go on income statement.

Accounts Affected	Category	↑ ↓	Rules
Office Supplies Expense	Expense	↑	Dr.
Office Supplies	Asset	↓	Cr.

Will go on balance sheet.

For our discussion, the letter A is used to code the Office Supplies adjustment because it is the first adjustment.

The Office Supplies Expense account comes from the Chart of Accounts on page 85. Since it is not listed in the trial balance account titles, it must be listed below the trial balance. Let's see how we enter this adjustment on the worksheet.

Note: All accounts listed below the trial balance will be *increasing*.

Place $500 in the debit column of the adjustments section on the same line as Office Supplies Expense. Place $500 in the credit column of the adjustments section on the same line as Office Supplies. The numbers in the adjustment column show what is used, *not* what is on hand.

CLARK'S DESKTOP PUBLISHING SERVICES
WORKSHEET
FOR MONTH ENDED MAY 31, 2010

Account Titles	Trial Balance Dr.	Trial Balance Cr.	Adjustments Dr.	Adjustments Cr.
Cash	6 1 5 5 00			
Accounts Receivable	5 0 0 0 00			
Office Supplies	6 0 0 00			(A) 5 0 0 00
Prepaid Rent	1 2 0 0 00			
Desktop Publishing Equipment	6 0 0 0 00			
Accounts Payable		3 3 5 0 00		
Brenda Clark, Capital		1 0 0 0 0 00		
Brenda Clark, Withdrawals	6 2 5 00			
Desktop Publishing Fees		8 0 0 0 00		
Office Salaries Expense	1 3 0 0 00			
Advertising Expense	2 5 0 00			
Telephone Expense	2 2 0 00			
	21 3 5 0 00	21 3 5 0 00		
Office Supplies Expense			(A) 5 0 0 00	

A decrease in Office Supplies, $500

An increase in Office Supplies Expense, $500

The Office Supplies Expense account (on page 130) indicates the amount of supplies used up. It is listed below other trial balance accounts since it was not on the original trial balance.

A debit will increase the account Office Supplies Expense; a credit will reduce the asset account Office Supplies.

Adjusting Prepaid Rent: On page 87 the trial balance showed a figure for Prepaid Rent of $1,200. The amount of rent *expired* is the adjustment figure used to update Prepaid Rent and Rent Expense.

Rent Expense 515

| 400 | |

Prepaid Rent 115

| 1,200 | 400 |
| 800 | |

Take this one slowly.

Original cost of $6,000 for desktop publishing equipment remains *unchanged* after adjustments.

B. Adjusting the Prepaid Rent Account

Back on May 1, Clark's Desktop Publishing Services paid three months' rent in advance. The accountant realized that the rent expense would be $400 per month ($1,200 ÷ 3 months = $400).

Remember, when rent expense is paid in advance, it is considered an asset called *prepaid rent.* When the asset, prepaid rent, begins to expire or be used up it becomes an expense. Now it is May 31, and one month's prepaid rent has become an expense.

How is this handled? Should the account be $1,200, or is there really only $800 of prepaid rent left as of May 31? What do we need to do to bring prepaid rent to the "true" balance? The answer is that we must increase Rent Expense by $400 and decrease Prepaid Rent by $400.

Without this adjustment, the expenses for Clark's Desktop Publishing Services for May will be too low, and the asset Prepaid Rent will be too high. If unadjusted amounts were used in the formal reports, the net income shown on the income statement would be too high, and both sides (assets and owner's equity) would be too high on the balance sheet.

In terms of our transaction analysis chart, the adjustment would look like this:

Will go on income statement.

Accounts Affected	Category	↑ ↓	Rules
Rent Expense	Expense	↑	Dr.
Prepaid Rent	Asset	↓	Cr.

Will go on balance sheet.

Like the Office Supplies Expense account, the Rent Expense account comes from the chart of accounts on page 85.

The worksheet on page 132 shows how to enter an adjustment to Prepaid Rent.

C. Adjusting the Desktop Publishing Equipment Account for Amortization

The life of the asset affects how it is adjusted. The two accounts we discussed above, Office Supplies and Prepaid Rent, involved things that are used up relatively quickly. Equipment—like desktop publishing equipment—is expected to last much longer. Also, it is expected to help produce revenue over a longer period. That is why accountants treat it differently. The balance sheet reports the **historical cost**, or original cost, of the equipment. The original cost also is reflected in the ledger. The adjustment shows how the cost of the equipment is allocated (spread) over its expected useful life. This spreading is called **amortization**. To amortize the equipment, we have to figure out how much its value goes down each month. Then we have to keep a running total of how that amortization mounts up over time. Canada Revenue Agency has a specific set of rules (called **Capital Cost Allowance** rules), which tell how businesses in Canada may amortize their assets for tax purposes. For accounting reports, however, different methods can be used to calculate amortization. We will use the simplest method—straight-line amortization—to calculate the amortization of Clark's Desktop Publishing Services' equipment. Under the straight-line method, equal amounts are taken over successive periods of time. Chapter 15 includes many detailed examples and illustrations of amortization, but for now, only a very simple example is being used.

CLARK'S DESKTOP PUBLISHING SERVICES
WORKSHEET
FOR MONTH ENDED MAY 31, 2010

Account Titles	Trial Balance Dr.	Trial Balance Cr.	Adjustments Dr.	Adjustments Cr.
Cash	6 1 5 5 00			
Accounts Receivable	5 0 0 0 00			
Office Supplies	6 0 0 00			(A) 5 0 0 00
Prepaid Rent	1 2 0 0 00			(B) 4 0 0 00
Desktop Publishing Equipment	6 0 0 0 00			
Accounts Payable		3 3 5 0 00		
Brenda Clark, Capital		10 0 0 0 00		
Brenda Clark, Withdrawals	6 2 5 00			
Desktop Publishing Fees		8 0 0 0 00		
Office Salaries Expense	1 3 0 0 00			
Advertising Expense	2 5 0 00			
Telephone Expense	2 2 0 00			
	21 3 5 0 00	21 3 5 0 00		
Office Supplies Expense			(A) 5 0 0 00	
Rent Expense			(B) 4 0 0 00	

A decrease in Prepaid Rent, $400

An increase in Rent Expense, $400

The calculation of amortization for the year for Clark's Desktop Publishing Services is as follows:

$$\frac{\text{Cost of Equipment} - \text{Residual Value}}{\text{Estimated Years of Usefulness}}$$

Desktop Publishing equipment has an expected life of approximately five years. At the end of that time, the property's value is called its "residual value." Think of **residual value** as the estimated value of the equipment at the end of the fifth year. For Clark, the equipment has an estimated residual value of $1,200.

$$\frac{\$6,000 - \$1,200}{5 \text{ Years}} = \frac{\$4,800}{5} = \$960 \text{ amortization per year}$$

Our trial balance is for one month, so we must determine the adjustment for that month:

$$\frac{\$960}{12 \text{ Months}} = \$80 \text{ amortization per month}$$

This $80 is known as *Amortization Expense* and will be shown on the income statement.

Next, we have to create a new account that can keep a running total of the amortization amount apart from the original cost of the equipment. That account is called **Accumulated Amortization.**

The Accumulated Amortization account shows the amount of amortization that has been taken or accumulated over a period of time. This is a **contra-asset account**; it has a normal balance opposite that of an asset such as equipment. Accumulated Amortization will summarize, accumulate, or build up the amount of amortization that is taken on the desktop publishing equipment over its estimated useful life.

This is how it would look on a partial balance sheet of Clark's Desktop Publishing Services.

❶ Historical cost of $6,000 for equipment is not changed.

❷ Amount of accumulated amortization is $80.

❸ This shows the remaining portion of the historical cost of the equipment that may be amortized in future periods of time. This figure, the cost of the asset less its accumulated amortization, is often termed **book value** or carrying value.

CLARK'S DESKTOP PUBLISHING SERVICES
BALANCE SHEET
MAY 31, 2010

Assets

			XXXX
Desktop Publishing Equipment	$6,000		
Less: Accumulated Amortization		80	5,920

Let's summarize the key points before going on to enter the adjustment on the worksheet:

1. Amortization Expense goes on the income statement, which results in:
   a. An increase in total expenses
   b. A decrease in net income

2. Accumulated amortization is a contra-asset account found on the balance sheet next to its related equipment account.
3. The original cost of equipment is not reduced; it stays the same until the equipment is sold or removed.
4. Each month, the amount in the Accumulated Amortization account grows larger, while the cost of the equipment remains the same.
5. Businesses may reduce their income tax expense by deducting Capital Cost Allowance (CCA). This CCA is similar to amortization, and some smaller businesses may use CCA values for their amortization expense. Chapter 15 has further details.

Now, let's analyze the adjustment on the transaction analysis chart.

Will go on income statement.

Accounts Affected	Category	↑ ↓	Rules
Amortization Expense, Desktop Publishing Equipment	**Expense**	↑	**Dr.**
Accumulated Amortization, Desktop Publishing Equipment	**Asset (Contra)**	↑	**Cr.**

Will go on balance sheet.

Remember, the original cost of the equipment never changes: the equipment account is not included among the affected accounts because the original cost of equipment remains the same. When the Accumulated Amortization increases (as a credit), the equipment's **book value** decreases.

The worksheet on page 134 shows how we enter the adjustment for amortization of desktop publishing equipment.

CLARK'S DESKTOP PUBLISHING SERVICES
WORKSHEET
FOR MONTH ENDED MAY 31, 2010

Account Titles	Trial Balance Dr.	Trial Balance Cr.	Adjustments Dr.	Adjustments Cr.
Cash	6 1 5 5 00			
Accounts Receivable	5 0 0 0 00			
Office Supplies	6 0 0 00			(A) 5 0 0 00
Prepaid Rent	1 2 0 0 00			(B) 4 0 0 00
Desktop Publishing Equipment	6 0 0 0 00			
Accounts Payable		3 3 5 0 00		
Brenda Clark, Capital		10 0 0 0 00		
Brenda Clark, Withdrawals	6 2 5 00			
Desktop Publishing Fees		8 0 0 0 00		
Office Salaries Expense	1 3 0 0 00			
Advertising Expense	2 5 0 00			
Telephone Expense	2 2 0 00			
	21 3 5 0 00	21 3 5 0 00		
Office Supplies Expense			(A) 5 0 0 00	
Rent Expense			(B) 4 0 0 00	
Amortization Exp., DTP Equip.			(C) 8 0 00	
Acc. Amortization, DTP Equip.				(C) 8 0 00

An increase in Amortization Expense, Desktop Publishing Equipment

An increase in Accumulated Amortization, Desktop Publishing Equipment

The third account to be adjusted is assigned the letter C.

Because this is a new business, neither account had a previous balance. Therefore, neither is listed in the account titles of the trial balance. We need to list both accounts below Rent Expense in the account titles section. On the worksheet, put $80 in the debit column of the adjustments section on the same line as Amortization Expense, DTP Equipment, and put $80 in the credit column of the adjustments section on the same line as Accumulated Amortization, DTP Equipment.

Next month (June in our example), accumulated amortization will appear listed in the original trial balance.

Next month, on June 30, a further $80 would be entered under Amortization Expense, and Accumulated Amortization would show a balance of $160. Remember, Clark's was a new company in May, so no previous amortization was taken.

Now let's look at the last adjustment for Clark's Desktop Publishing Services.

Accumulated Amortization

Dr.	Cr.
	History of amount of amortization taken to date

Adjusting salaries

D. Adjusting the Salaries Payable Account

Clark's Desktop Publishing Services paid $1,300 in Office Salaries Expense (see the trial balance of any previous worksheet in this chapter). The last salary cheques for the month were paid on May 25. How can we update this account to show the salary expense as of May 31?

John Murray worked for Clark's on May 28, 29, 30, and 31, but his next paycheque is not due until June 8. John earned $350 for these four days. Is the $350 an expense to Clark's in May, when it was earned, or in June when it is due and is paid?

Month shown is for illustration only. It may not agree with any particular year.

May						
S	M	T	W	T	F	S
			1	2	3	4	5
6	7	8	9	10	11	12
13	14	15	16	17	18	19
20	21	22	23	24	25	26
27	28	29	30	31		

Think back to Chapter 1 when we first discussed revenue and expenses. We noted then that revenue is recorded when it is earned, not when the payment is received, and expenses are recorded when they are incurred, not when they are actually paid. This principle will be discussed further in a later chapter; for now, it is enough to remember that we record revenue and expenses when they occur because we want to match earned revenue with the expenses that resulted in earning those revenues. In this case, by working those four days, John Murray created some revenue for Clark's in May. Therefore, the office salaries expense must be shown in May—the month in which the revenue was earned.

The results are:

◆ Office Salaries Expense is increased by $350. This unpaid and unrecorded expense for salaries for which payment is not yet due is called **accrued salaries.** In effect, we now show the true expense for salaries ($1,650 instead of $1,300):

Office Salaries Expense

| 1,300 | |
| 350 | |

◆ The second result is that salaries payable is increased by $350. Clark's has created a liability called Salaries Payable, meaning that the firm owes money for salaries. When the firm pays John Murray, it will reduce its liability, Salaries Payable, as well as decrease its cash.

In terms of the transaction analysis chart, the following would be done:

Accounts Affected	Category	↑ ↓	Rules
Office Salaries Expense	Expense	↑	Dr.
Salaries Payable	Liability	↑	Cr.

How the adjustment for accrued salaries is entered on the worksheet is shown at the top of page 136.

The account Office Salaries Expense is already listed in the account titles, so $350 is placed in the debit column of the adjustments section on the same line as Office Salaries Expense. However, because the Salaries Payable is not listed in the account titles, the account title Salaries Payable is added below the trial balance, below Accumulated Amortization, DTP Equipment. Also, $350 is placed in the credit column of the adjustments section on the same line as Salaries Payable.

Now that we have finished all the adjustments that we intended to make, we total the adjustments section, as shown in Figure 4-2.

THE ADJUSTED TRIAL BALANCE SECTION

The adjusted trial balance is the next section on the worksheet. To fill it out, we must summarize the information in the trial balance and adjustments sections, as shown in Figure 4-3.

Note that when the numbers are brought across from the trial balance to the adjusted trial balance, two debits will be added together and two credits will be added together. If the numbers include a debit and a credit, take the difference between the two and place it on the side that has the larger figure.

Now that we have completed the adjustments and adjusted trial balance sections of the worksheet, it is time to move on to the income statement and the balance sheet sections. Before we do that, however, look at the chart shown in Table 4-1 on page 138. This table should be used as a reference to help you fill out the next two sections of the worksheet.

The Salaries Payable account is coded D because it is the fourth account to be adjusted.

Remember, all accounts added below the trial balance are increasing.

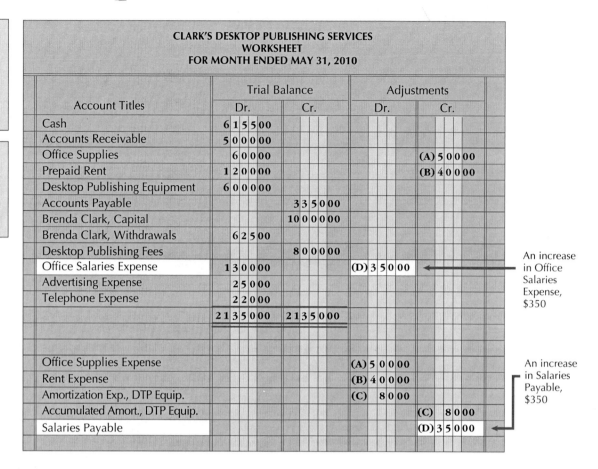

CLARK'S DESKTOP PUBLISHING SERVICES
WORKSHEET
FOR MONTH ENDED MAY 31, 2010

Account Titles	Trial Balance Dr.	Trial Balance Cr.	Adjustments Dr.	Adjustments Cr.
Cash	6 1 5 5 00			
Accounts Receivable	5 0 0 0 00			
Office Supplies	6 0 0 00			(A) 5 0 0 00
Prepaid Rent	1 2 0 0 00			(B) 4 0 0 00
Desktop Publishing Equipment	6 0 0 0 00			
Accounts Payable		3 3 5 0 00		
Brenda Clark, Capital		1 0 0 0 0 00		
Brenda Clark, Withdrawals	6 2 5 00			
Desktop Publishing Fees		8 0 0 0 00		
Office Salaries Expense	1 3 0 0 00		(D) 3 5 0 00	
Advertising Expense	2 5 0 00			
Telephone Expense	2 2 0 00			
	2 1 3 5 0 00	2 1 3 5 0 00		
Office Supplies Expense			(A) 5 0 0 00	
Rent Expense			(B) 4 0 0 00	
Amortization Exp., DTP Equip.			(C) 8 0 00	
Accumulated Amort., DTP Equip.				(C) 8 0 00
Salaries Payable				(D) 3 5 0 00

An increase in Office Salaries Expense, $350

An increase in Salaries Payable, $350

Figure 4-2
The Adjustments Section of the Worksheet

CLARK'S DESKTOP PUBLISHING SERVICES
WORKSHEET
FOR MONTH ENDED MAY 31, 2010

Account Titles	Trial Balance Dr.	Trial Balance Cr.	Adjustments Dr.	Adjustments Cr.
Cash	6 1 5 5 00			
Accounts Receivable	5 0 0 0 00			
Office Supplies	6 0 0 00			(A) 5 0 0 00
Prepaid Rent	1 2 0 0 00			(B) 4 0 0 00
Desktop Publishing Equipment	6 0 0 0 00			
Accounts Payable		3 3 5 0 00		
Brenda Clark, Capital		1 0 0 0 0 00		
Brenda Clark, Withdrawals	6 2 5 00			
Desktop Publishing Fees		8 0 0 0 00		
Office Salaries Expense	1 3 0 0 00		(D) 3 5 0 00	
Advertising Expense	2 5 0 00			
Telephone Expense	2 2 0 00			
	2 1 3 5 0 00	2 1 3 5 0 00		
Office Supplies Expense			(A) 5 0 0 00	
Rent Expense			(B) 4 0 0 00	
Amortization Expense, DTP Equip.			(C) 8 0 00	
Accum. Amort., DTP Equip.				(C) 8 0 00
Salaries Payable				(D) 3 5 0 00
			1 3 3 0 00	1 3 3 0 00

CLARK'S DESKTOP PUBLISHING SERVICES
WORKSHEET
FOR MONTH ENDED MAY 31, 2010

Account Titles	Trial Balance Dr.	Trial Balance Cr.	Adjustments Dr.	Adjustments Cr.	Adjusted Trial Balance Dr.	Adjusted Trial Balance Cr.
Cash	6155 00				6155 00	
Accounts Receivable	5000 00				5000 00	
Office Supplies	600 00			(A) 500 00	100 00	
Prepaid Rent	1200 00			(B) 400 00	800 00	
Desktop Publishing Equipment	6000 00				6000 00	
Accounts Payable		3350 00				3350 00
Brenda Clark, Capital		10000 00				10000 00
Brenda Clark, Withdrawals	625 00				625 00	
Desktop Publishing Fees		8000 00				8000 00
Office Salaries Expense	1300 00		(D) 350 00		1650 00	
Advertising Expense	250 00				250 00	
Telephone Expense	220 00				220 00	
	21350 00	21350 00				
Office Supplies Expense			(A) 500 00		500 00	
Rent Expense			(B) 400 00		400 00	
Amortization Exp., DTP Equip.			(C) 80 00		80 00	
Accum. Amort., DTP Equip.				(C) 80 00		80 00
Salaries Payable				(D) 350 00		350 00
			1330 00	1330 00	21780 00	21780 00

Annotations:

If no adjustment is made, just carry over amount from trial balance on same side.

Supplies were $600, but we used up $500, leaving us with a $100 balance in supplies. *Note:* If there is a debit and a credit, take the *difference* between the two and place it on the side that has the larger figure.

Note: Equipment is *not* adjusted here.

Two debits are added together. If two credits, they also would have been added together and shown in the credit column.

Carry these amounts over to adjusted trial balance in the same positions.

Note: The total of the left (debit) must equal the total of the right (credit) ($21,780).

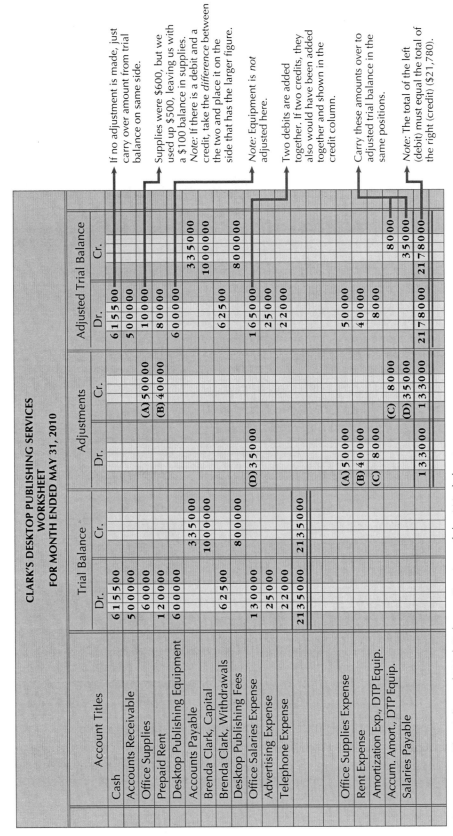

Figure 4-3 The Adjusted Trial Balance Section of the Worksheet

TABLE 4-1 Normal Balances and Account Categories

Account Title	Category	Normal Balance on Adjusted Trial Balance	Income Statement Dr.	Income Statement Cr.	Balance Sheet Dr.	Balance Sheet Cr.
Cash	Asset	Dr.			X	
Accounts Receivable	Asset	Dr.			X	
Office Supplies	Asset	Dr.			X	
Prepaid Rent	Asset	Dr.			X	
Desktop Publishing Equipment	Asset	Dr.			X	
Accounts Payable	Liability	Cr.				X
Brenda Clark, Capital	Owner's Equity	Cr.				X
Brenda Clark, Withdrawals	Owner's Equity	Dr.			X	
Desktop Publishing Fees	Revenue	Cr.		X		
Office Salaries Expense	Expense	Dr.	X			
Advertising Expense	Expense	Dr.	X			
Telephone Expense	Expense	Dr.	X			
Office Supplies Expense	Expense	Dr.	X			
Rent Expense	Expense	Dr.	X			
Amortization Expense, DTP Equipment	Expense	Dr.	X			
Accumulated Amortization, DTP Equipment	Asset (Contra)	Cr.				X
Salaries Payable	Liability	Cr.				X

Keep in mind that the numbers from the adjusted trial balance are carried over to one of the last four columns of the worksheet before the net income or net loss can be calculated.

THE INCOME STATEMENT SECTION

As shown in Figure 4-4, the income statement section lists only revenue and expenses from the adjusted trial balance. Note that Accumulated Amortization and Salaries Payable do not go on the income statement. Accumulated Amortization is a contra-asset account found on the balance sheet. Salaries Payable is a liability account found on the balance sheet.

The revenue ($8,000) and all the individual expenses are listed in the income statement section. The revenue is placed in the credit column of the income statement section because it has a credit balance. The expenses have debit balances, so they are placed in the debit column of the income statement section. The following steps must be taken after the debits and credits are placed in the correct columns:

> In the worksheet, net income is placed in the debit column of the income statement. Net loss goes in the credit column.

Step 1: Total the debits and the credits.

Step 2: Calculate the difference between the totals of the debit and credit columns and place this difference on the side with the smaller total.

Step 3: Total the two columns again.

The worksheet in Figure 4-4 shows that the label "Net Income" is added in the account title column on the same line as $4,900. When there is a net income, it will be placed in the debit column of the income statement section of the worksheet. If there is a net loss, it is placed in the credit column. The $8,000 total indicates that the two columns are in balance.

> The difference between $3,100 Dr. and $8,000 Cr. indicates a net income of $4,900. Do not think of the Net Income as a Dr. or Cr. The $4,900 is placed in the debit column to balance the two columns at $8,000. Actually, the credit side is larger by $4,900.

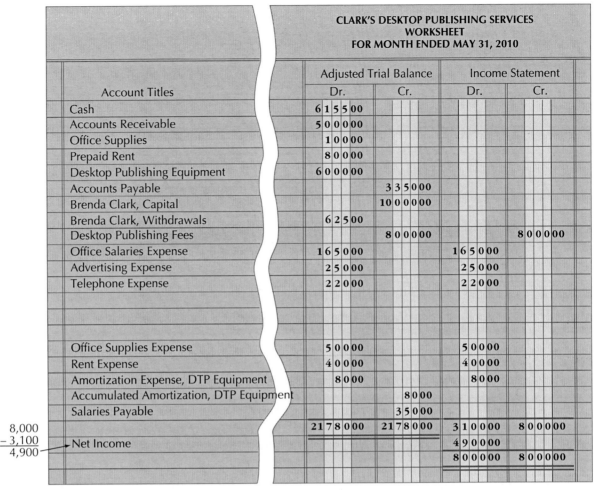

CLARK'S DESKTOP PUBLISHING SERVICES
WORKSHEET
FOR MONTH ENDED MAY 31, 2010

Account Titles	Adjusted Trial Balance Dr.	Adjusted Trial Balance Cr.	Income Statement Dr.	Income Statement Cr.
Cash	6 1 5 5 00			
Accounts Receivable	5 0 0 0 00			
Office Supplies	1 0 0 00			
Prepaid Rent	8 0 0 00			
Desktop Publishing Equipment	6 0 0 0 00			
Accounts Payable		3 3 5 0 00		
Brenda Clark, Capital		10 0 0 0 00		
Brenda Clark, Withdrawals	6 2 5 00			
Desktop Publishing Fees		8 0 0 0 00		8 0 0 0 00
Office Salaries Expense	1 6 5 0 00		1 6 5 0 00	
Advertising Expense	2 5 0 00		2 5 0 00	
Telephone Expense	2 2 0 00		2 2 0 00	
Office Supplies Expense	5 0 0 00		5 0 0 00	
Rent Expense	4 0 0 00		4 0 0 00	
Amortization Expense, DTP Equipment	8 0 00		8 0 00	
Accumulated Amortization, DTP Equipment		8 0 00		
Salaries Payable		3 5 0 00		
	21 7 8 0 00	21 7 8 0 00	3 1 0 0 00	8 0 0 0 00
Net Income			4 9 0 0 00	
			8 0 0 0 00	8 0 0 0 00

```
  8,000
– 3,100
  4,900
```
(Net Income)

Figure 4-4 The Income Statement Section of the Worksheet

THE BALANCE SHEET SECTION

To fill out the balance sheet section of the worksheet, the following are carried over from the adjusted trial balance section: assets, contra-assets, liabilities, capital, and withdrawals. The net income is brought over to the credit column of the balance sheet so the two columns balance. This net income will be added to the figure for capitalization on the statement of owner's equity.

Let's now look at the completed worksheet in Figure 4-5 to see how the balance sheet section is completed. The base worksheet here provides the trial balance. When Overlay No. 1 is placed over the base worksheet, we can see all the adjustments and the adjusted trial balance. Overlay No. 2 provides the income statement items and also the balance sheet items. Finally, Overlay No. 3 totals the income statement and balance sheet columns, determines the difference, enters the difference appropriately in each statement, and totals the columns again. Note how the net income of $4,900 is brought over to the credit column of the worksheet. The figure for capital is also in the credit column, while the figure for withdrawals is in the debit column. By placing the net income in the credit column, both sides total $18,680. If a net loss were to occur, it would be placed in the debit column of the balance sheet column.

Now that we have completed the worksheet, we can go on to the three financial statements. But let's summarize our progress first.

Remember: The ending figure for capital is *not* on the worksheet.

To see whether additional investments occurred for the period, you must check the capital account in the ledger.

The amounts come from the adjusted trial balance except the $4,900, which was carried over from the income statement section.

CLARK'S DESKTOP PUBLISHING SERVICES
WORKSHEET
FOR MONTH ENDED MAY 31, 2010

Account Titles	Trial Balance Dr.	Trial Balance Cr.	Adjustments Dr.	Adjustments Cr.	Adjusted Trial Balance Dr.	Adjusted Trial Balance Cr.	Income Statement Dr.	Income Statement Cr.	Balance Sheet Dr.	Balance Sheet Cr.
Cash	6 1 5 5 00									
Accounts Receivable	5 0 0 0 00									
Office Supplies	6 0 0 00									
Prepaid Rent	1 2 0 0 00									
Desktop Publishing Equipment	6 0 0 0 00									
Accounts Payable		3 3 5 0 00								
Brenda Clark, Capital		1 0 0 0 0 00								
Brenda Clark, Withdrawals	6 2 5 00									
Desktop Publishing Fees		8 0 0 0 00								
Office Salaries Expense	1 3 0 0 00									
Advertising Expense	2 5 0 00									
Telephone Expense	2 2 0 00									
	2 1 3 5 0 00	2 1 3 5 0 00								

Figure 4-5 Sample Worksheet

Flip to Overlay No. 1—Adjustments A, B, C, and D

LEARNING UNIT 4-1 REVIEW

AT THIS POINT you should be able to:

- Define and explain the purpose of a worksheet. (p. 128)
- Explain the need as well as the process for adjustments. (p. 129)
- Explain the concept of amortization. (p. 131)
- Explain the difference between amortization expense and accumulated amortization. (p. 132)
- Prepare a worksheet from a trial balance and adjustment data. (p. 135)

Self-Review Quiz 4-1

From the accompanying trial balance and adjustment data, complete a worksheet for P. Logan Company for the month ended December 31, 2009. (You can use a blank foldout worksheet located at the end of the *Study Guide with Working Papers.*)

Note: The numbers used in this quiz may seem impossibly small, but we have done that on purpose, so that at this point you don't have to worry about arithmetic, just about preparing the worksheet correctly.

P. LOGAN COMPANY
TRIAL BALANCE
DECEMBER 31, 2009

	Dr.	Cr.
Cash	15 00	
Accounts Receivable	3 00	
Prepaid Insurance	3 00	
Store Supplies	5 00	
Store Equipment	6 00	
Accumulated Amortization, Store Equipment		4 00
Accounts Payable		2 00
P. Logan, Capital		14 00
P. Logan, Withdrawals	3 00	
Revenue from Clients		25 00
Rent Expense	2 00	
Salaries Expense	8 00	
	45 00	45 00

Adjustment Data

a. Amortization Expense, Store Equipment, $1
b. Insurance expired, $2
c. Supplies on hand, $1
d. Salaries owed but not paid to employees, $3

Solution to Self-Review Quiz 4-1

Don't adjust this line! Store Equipment always contains the historical cost.

P. LOGAN COMPANY
WORKSHEET
FOR MONTH ENDED DECEMBER 31, 2009

Quiz Tip

The adjustment for supplies worth $4 represents the amount *used up*. The *on-hand* amount of $1 ends up on the adjusted trial balance.

Account Titles	Trial Balance Dr.	Trial Balance Cr.	Adjustments Dr.	Adjustments Cr.	Adjusted Trial Balance Dr.	Adjusted Trial Balance Cr.	Income Statement Dr.	Income Statement Cr.	Balance Sheet Dr.	Balance Sheet Cr.
Cash	1500				1500				1500	
Accounts Receivable	300				300				300	
Prepaid Insurance	300			(B) 200	100				100	
Store Supplies	500			(C) 400	100				100	
Store Equipment	600				600				600	
Accumulated Amortization, Store Equipment		400		(A) 100		500				500
Accounts Payable		200				200				200
P. Logan, Capital		1400				1400				1400
P. Logan, Withdrawals	300				300				300	
Revenue from Clients		2500				2500		2500		
Rent Expense	200				200		200			
Salaries Expense	800		(D) 300		1100		1100			
	4500	4500								
Amortization Expense, Store Equipment			(A) 100		100		100			
Insurance Expense			(B) 200		200		200			
Supplies Expense			(C) 400		400		400			
Salaries Payable				(D) 300		300				300
			1000	1000	4900	4900	2000	2500	2900	2400
Net Income							500			500
							2500	2500	2900	2900

Note that Accumulated Amortization is listed in the trial balance since this is not a new company. Store Equipment has already been amortized $4 from an earlier period.

Learning Unit 4-2

Step 6 of the Accounting Cycle: Preparing the Financial Statements from the Worksheet

The formal financial statements can be prepared from the worksheet completed in Learning Unit 4-1. Before beginning, we must check that the entries on the worksheet are correct and in balance. To do this, we have to be sure that (1) all entries are recorded in the appropriate columns, (2) the correct amounts are entered in the proper places, (3) the addition is correct across the columns (i.e., from the trial balance to the adjusted trial balance to the financial reports), and (4) the columns are added correctly.

PREPARING THE INCOME STATEMENT

The first statement to be prepared for Clark's Desktop Publishing Services is the income statement. When preparing the income statement, it is important to remember that:

1. Every figure on the formal report is on the worksheet. Figure 4-6 (page 142) shows where each of these figures goes on the income statement.
2. There are no debit or credit columns on the formal report.
3. The inside column on financial reports is used for subtotalling.
4. Withdrawals do not go on the income statement; they go on the statement of owner's equity.

   Take a moment to look at the income statement in Figure 4-6. Note which items go where from the income statement section of the worksheet onto the formal report.

PREPARING THE STATEMENT OF OWNER'S EQUITY

Figure 4-7 (page 142) is the statement of owner's equity for Clark's. The figure shows where on the worksheet the information comes from. It is important to remember that, if there were additional investments, the figure on the worksheet for capital would not be the beginning figure for capital. Checking the ledger account for capital will tell you whether the amount is correct. Note how net income and withdrawals aid in calculating the new figure for capital.

PREPARING THE BALANCE SHEET

In preparing the balance sheet (page 143), remember that the balance sheet section totals on the worksheet ($18,680) do *not* usually match the totals on the formal balance sheet ($17,975). This occurs because information is grouped differently on the formal report. First, in the formal report, Accumulated Amortization ($80) is subtracted from Desktop Publishing Equipment, reducing the balance. Second, Withdrawals ($625) are subtracted from Owner's Equity, reducing the balance further. These two reductions (–$80 + [–$625] = –$705) represent the difference between the worksheet and the formal version of the balance sheet ($17,975 – $18,680 = –$705). Figure 4-8 (page 143) shows how to prepare the balance sheet from the worksheet.

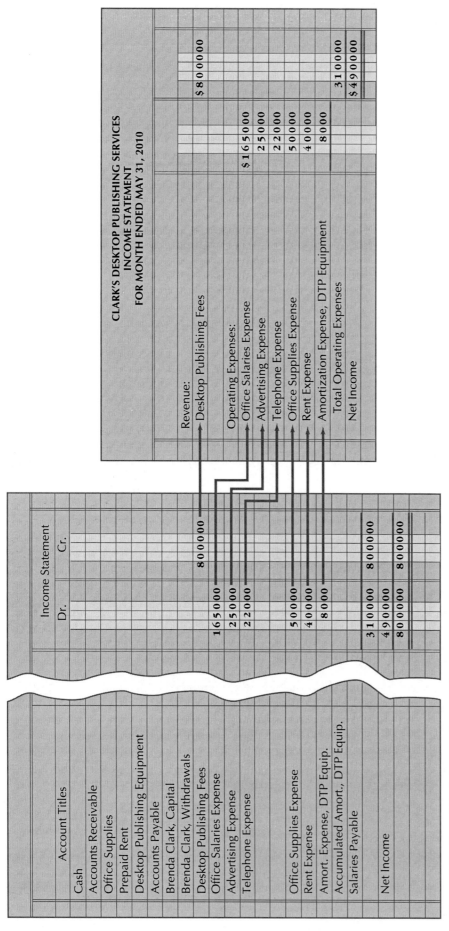

CLARK'S DESKTOP PUBLISHING SERVICES
INCOME STATEMENT
FOR MONTH ENDED MAY 31, 2010

Revenue:		
Desktop Publishing Fees		$8 000 00
Operating Expenses:		
Office Salaries Expense	$1 650 00	
Advertising Expense	2 500 0	
Telephone Expense	2 200 0	
Office Supplies Expense	5 000 0	
Rent Expense	4 000 0	
Amortization Expense, DTP Equipment	800 0	
Total Operating Expenses		3 100 00
Net Income		$4 900 00

Figure 4-6 From Worksheet to Income Statement

Account Titles	Income Statement	
	Dr.	Cr.
Cash		
Accounts Receivable		
Office Supplies		
Prepaid Rent		
Desktop Publishing Equipment		
Accounts Payable		
Brenda Clark, Capital		
Brenda Clark, Withdrawals		
Desktop Publishing Fees		8 000 00
Office Salaries Expense	1 650 00	
Advertising Expense	2 500 0	
Telephone Expense	2 200 0	
Office Supplies Expense	5 000 0	
Rent Expense	4 000 0	
Amort. Expense, DTP Equip.	800 0	
Accumulated Amort., DTP Equip.		
Salaries Payable		
	3 100 00	8 000 00
Net Income	4 900 00	
	8 000 00	8 000 00

CLARK'S DESKTOP PUBLISHING SERVICES
STATEMENT OF OWNER'S EQUITY
FOR MONTH ENDED MAY 31, 2010

Brenda Clark, Capital, May 1, 2010		$10 000 00
Net Income for May	$4 900 00	
Less: Withdrawals for May	625 00	
Increase in Capital		4 275 00
Brenda Clark, Capital, May 31, 2010		$14 275 00

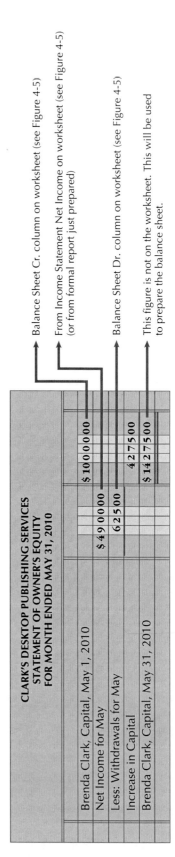

Balance Sheet Cr. column on worksheet (see Figure 4-5)

From Income Statement Net Income on worksheet (see Figure 4-5) (or from formal report just prepared)

Balance Sheet Dr. column on worksheet (see Figure 4-5)

This figure is not on the worksheet. This will be used to prepare the balance sheet.

Figure 4-7 Completing a Statement of Owner's Equity

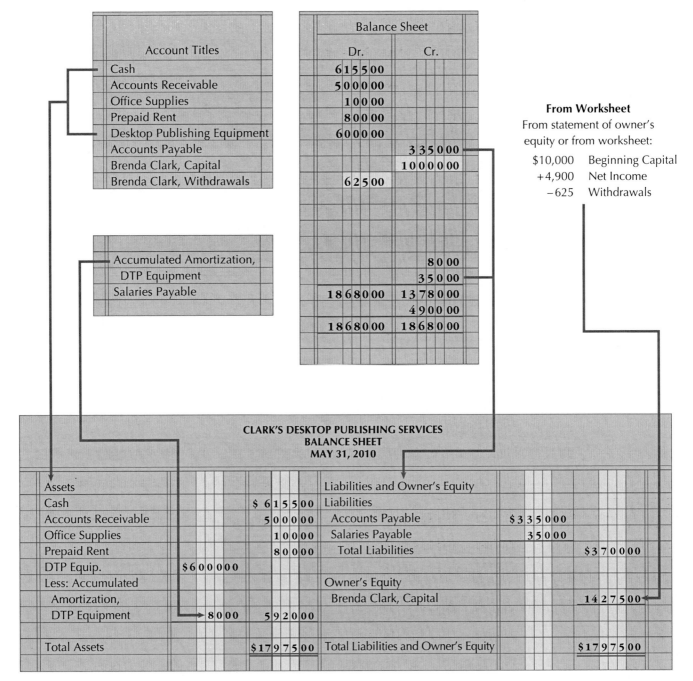

Figure 4-8 From Worksheet to Balance Sheet

LEARNING UNIT 4-2 REVIEW

AT THIS POINT you should be able to:

◆ Prepare the three financial statements from a worksheet. (p. 141)

◆ Explain why totals of the formal balance sheet don't match totals of balance sheet columns on the worksheet. (p. 141)

Self-Review Quiz 4-2

(The forms you need are located on pages 4-1 to 4-3 of the *Study Guide with Working Papers.*)

From the worksheet on page 140 for P. Logan, prepare (1) an income statement for December, (2) a statement of owner's equity, and (3) a balance sheet for December 31, 2009. No additional investments took place during the period.

Solution to Self-Review Quiz 4-2

P. LOGAN COMPANY
INCOME STATEMENT
FOR THE MONTH ENDED DECEMBER 31, 2009

Revenue:			
Revenue from Clients			$25 00
Operating Expenses:			
Rent Expense	$2 00		
Salaries Expense	11 00		
Amortization Expense, Store Equipment	1 00		
Insurance Expense	2 00		
Supplies Expense	4 00		
Total Operating Expenses		20 00	
Net Income		$5 00	

> **Quiz Tip**
>
> The income statement is made up of revenue and expenses. Use the inside column for subtotalling.

P. LOGAN COMPANY
STATEMENT OF OWNER'S EQUITY
FOR THE MONTH ENDED DECEMBER 31, 2009

P. Logan, Capital, December 1, 2009			$14 00
Net Income for December	$5 00		
Less: Withdrawals for December	3 00		
Increase in Capital		2 00	
P. Logan, Capital, December 31, 2009		$16 00	

> **Quiz Tip**
>
> The $5 on the income statement is used to update the statement of owner's equity.

> **Quiz Tip**
>
> The ending capital figure on the statement of owner's equity ($16) is used as the capital figure on the balance sheet.

P. LOGAN COMPANY
BALANCE SHEET
DECEMBER 31, 2009

Assets			Liabilities and Owner's Equity		
Cash		$15 00	Liabilities		
Accounts Receivable		3 00	Accounts Payable	$2 00	
Prepaid Insurance		1 00	Salaries Payable	3 00	
Store Supplies		1 00	Total Liabilities		$5 00
Store Equipment	$6 00		Owner's Equity		
Less Accumulated Amortization, Store Equipment	5 00	1 00	P. Logan, Capital		16 00
Total Assets		$21 00	Total Liabilities and Owner's Equity		$21 00

No matter how harried Stan Hernandez feels as the owner of his own Subway restaurant, the aroma of his fresh-baked gourmet breads always perks him up. However, the sales generated by Subway's line of gourmet seasoned breads perk Stan up even more. Subway restaurants introduced freshly baked bread in 1983, a practice that made it stand out from other fast-food chains and helped build its reputation for made-to-order freshness. Since then, Subway franchisees have introduced many types of gourmet seasoned breads—such as Hearty Italian or Monterey Cheddar—according to a schedule determined by headquarters.

SUBWAY
WHERE THE DOUGH GOES

Stan was one month into the "limited-time promotion" for the chain's new Roasted Garlic seasoned bread when his bake oven started faltering. "The temperature controls just don't seem quite right," said his employee and sandwich artist, Rashid. "It's taking incrementally longer to bake the bread."

"This couldn't happen at a worse time," moaned Stan. "We're baking enough Roasted Garlic bread to keep a whole town of vampires away, but if we don't get it out of the oven fast enough, we'll keep our customers away!"

That very day Stan called his field consultant, Mariah, to discuss what to do about his bake oven. Mariah reminded Stan that his oven trouble illustrated the flip side of buying an existing store from a retired franchisee—having to repair or replace worn or old equipment. After receiving a rather expensive repair estimate and considering the age of the oven, Stan ultimately decided it would make sense for him to purchase a new one. Mariah concurred, "At the rate your sales are going, Stan,

you're going to need that roomier new model."

"Wow, do you realize how much this new bake oven is going to cost me?—$3,000!" Stan exclaimed while meeting with his cousin-turned-Subway-accountant, Lila Hernandez. "Yes, it's a lot to lay out, Stan," said Lila, "but you'll be amortizing the cost over a period of 10 years, which will help you at tax time. Let's do the adjustment on your worksheet so that you can see it."

The two of them were sitting in Stan's small office, behind the Subway kitchen, and they pulled up this month's worksheet on Stan's QuickBooks® program. Lila laughed, "I'm sure glad you started entering your worksheets on QuickBooks again! The figures on those old ones were so doodled over and crossed out that I could barely decipher them! We may need your worksheets at tax time."

"Anything for you, mi prima," Stan said, "I may amortize my bake oven, but my gratitude for your accounting skills only appreciates with time!"

DISCUSSION QUESTIONS

1. If you are using a straight-line method of amortization and Stan's bake oven has a residual value of $1,000, how much amortization will he account for each year and what would be the adjustment for each month?

2. Where does Lila get the information on the useful life of Stan's bake oven and the estimate for its residual value? Why do you think she gets her information from this particular source?

3. Why is a clean worksheet helpful even after that month's statements have been prepared?

DEMONSTRATION PROBLEM: STEPS 5 AND 6 OF THE ACCOUNTING CYCLE

(The blank forms you need are on pages 4-4 and 4-5 of the *Study Guide with Working Papers*.)

From the following trial balance and additional data, (1) complete a worksheet and (2) prepare the three financial reports (the numbers are intentionally small so that you may concentrate on the theory).

Frost Company
Trial Balance
December 31, 2011

	Dr.	Cr.
Cash	14	
Accounts Receivable	4	
Prepaid Insurance	5	
Plumbing Supplies	3	
Plumbing Equipment	7	
Accumulated Amortization, Plumbing Equipment		5
Accounts Payable		1
J. Frost, Capital		12
J. Frost, Withdrawals	3	
Plumbing Fees		27
Rent Expense	4	
Salaries Expense	5	
Totals	45	45

Adjustment Data

a. Insurance expired, $3
b. Plumbing supplies on hand, $1
c. Amortization Expense, Plumbing Equipment, $1
d. Salaries owed but not paid to employees, $2

Solution Tips for Building a Worksheet

1. Adjustments

a.

Insurance Expense	Expense	↑	Dr.	$3
Prepaid Insurance	Asset	↓	Cr.	$3

Expired means used up.

b.

Plumbing Supplies Expense	Expense	↑	Dr.	$2
Plumbing Supplies	Asset	↓	Cr.	$2

$3 − $1 on hand = $2 *used up!*

c.

Amortization Expense, Plumbing Equipment	Expense	↑	Dr.	$1
Accumulated Amortization, Plumbing Equipment	Asset (Contra)	↑	Cr.	$1

The original cost of equipment of $7 is not "touched."

FROST COMPANY
WORKSHEET
FOR MONTH ENDED DECEMBER 31, 2011

Account Titles	Trial Balance Dr.	Trial Balance Cr.	Adjustments Dr.	Adjustments Cr.	Adjusted Trial Balance Dr.	Adjusted Trial Balance Cr.	Income Statement Dr.	Income Statement Cr.	Balance Sheet Dr.	Balance Sheet Cr.
Cash	1400				1400				1400	
Accounts Receivable	400				400				400	
Prepaid Insurance	500			(A) 300	200				200	
Plumbing Supplies	300			(B) 200	100				100	
Plumbing Equipment	700				700				700	
Accumulated Amortization, Plumbing Equipment		500		(C) 100		600				600
Accounts Payable		100				100				100
J. Frost, Capital		1200				1200				1200
J. Frost, Withdrawals	300				300				300	
Plumbing Fees		2700				2700		2700		
Rent Expense	400				400		400			
Salaries Expense	500		(D) 200		700		700			
	4500	4500								
Insurance Expense			(A) 300		300		300			
Plumbing Supplies Expense			(B) 200		200		200			
Amortization Expense, Plumbing Equipment			(C) 100		100		100			
Salaries Payable				(D) 200		200				200
			800	800	4800	4800	1700	2700	3100	2100
Net Income							1000			1000
							2700	2700	3100	3100

Original cost not adjusted

"used up"

"on hand"

d.

Salaries Expense	Expense	↑	Dr.	$2
Salaries Payable	Liability	↑	Cr.	$2

2. Last four columns of worksheet are prepared from adjusted trial balance.
3. Capital of $12 is the old figure. Net income of $10 (revenue − expenses) is brought over to same side as capital on the balance sheet Cr. column to balance columns.

Frost Company
Income Statement
for Month Ended December 31, 2011

Revenue:		
Plumbing Fees		$27
Operating Expenses:		
Rent Expense	$4	
Salaries Expense	7	
Insurance Expense	3	
Plumbing Supplies Expense	2	
Amortization Expense, Plumbing Equipment	1	
Total Operating Expenses		17
Net Income		$10

Frost Company
Statement of Owner's Equity
for Month Ended December 31, 2011

J. Frost, Capital, December 1, 2011		$12
Net Income for December	$10	
Less: Withdrawals for December	3	
Increase in Capital		7
J. Frost, Capital, December 31, 2011		$19

Frost Company
Balance Sheet
December 31, 2011

Assets			Liabilities and Owner's Equity		
Cash		$14	Liabilities:		
Accounts Receivable		4	Accounts Payable	$1	
Prepaid Insurance		2	Salaries Payable	2	
Plumbing Supplies		1	Total Liabilities		$3
Plumbing Equipment	$7				
Less: Accum. Amort.	6	1	Owner's Equity:		
			J. Frost, Capital		19
			Total Liabilities and		
Total Assets		$22	Owner's Equity		$22

Solution Tips for Preparing Financial Statements from a Worksheet

The inside columns of the three financial statements are used for subtotalling. There are no debits or credits on the formal statements.

Statement

Income statement From income statement columns of worksheet for revenue and expenses

Statement of owner's equity From balance sheet Cr. column for old figure for Capital; Net Income from income statement; from balance sheet Dr. column for Withdrawals figure

Balance sheet From balance sheet Dr. column for assets; from balance sheet Cr. column for liabilities and Accumulated Amortization; new figure for Capital from statement of owner's equity

Note how Plumbing Equipment, $7, and Accumulated Amortization, $6, are rearranged on the formal balance sheet. The total assets figure of $22 is not on the worksheet. Remember that there are no debits or credits on formal reports.

SUMMARY OF KEY POINTS

Learning Unit 4-1

1. The worksheet is not a formal statement.

2. Adjustments update certain accounts so that they will be up to their latest balance before financial reports are prepared. Adjustments are the result of internal transactions.

3. Adjustments will affect both the income statement and the balance sheet.

4. Accounts listed *below* the account titles on the trial balance of the worksheet are *increasing.*

5. The original cost of a piece of equipment is not adjusted; historical cost is not lost.

6. Amortization is the process of spreading the original cost of the asset over its expected useful life.

7. Accumulated amortization is a contra-asset on the balance sheet that summarizes, accumulates, or builds up the amount of amortization that an asset has accumulated.

8. Book value is the original cost less accumulated amortization.

9. Accrued salaries are unpaid and unrecorded expenses that are accumulating but for which payment is not yet due.

10. Revenue and expenses go on income statement sections of the worksheet. Assets, contra-assets, liabilities, capital, and withdrawals go on balance sheet sections of the worksheet.

Learning Unit 4-2

1. The formal statements prepared from a worksheet do not have debit or credit columns.

2. Revenue and expenses go on the income statement. Beginning capital plus net income less withdrawals (or beginning capital minus net loss, less withdrawals) goes on the statement of owner's equity. Be sure to check the capital account in the ledger to see if any additional investments took place. Assets, contra-assets, liabilities, and the new figure for capital go on the balance sheet.

KEY TERMS

Accrued salaries   Salaries that are earned by employees but unpaid and unrecorded during the period (and thus need to be recorded by an adjustment) and will not come due for payment until the next accounting period (p. 135)

Accumulated Amortization   A contra-asset account that summarizes or accumulates the amount of amortization that has been taken on an asset (p. 132)

Adjusting   The process of calculating the latest up-to-date balance of each account at the end of an accounting period (p. 129)

Amortization   The allocation (spreading) of the cost of an asset (such as an auto or equipment) over its expected useful life (p. 131)

Book value   Cost of equipment less accumulated amortization (p. 133)

Capital Cost Allowance   Another term for amortization as defined in law by the *Income Tax Act* and administered by the Canada Revenue Agency (p. 131)

Contra-asset account   An account that causes another, related account to be restated or revalued. Its normal balance is a credit, which reduces the net asset value (p. 132)

Historical cost   The actual cost of an asset at time of purchase (p. 131)

Residual value   Book value of an asset after all the allowable amortization has been deducted. Also, an estimate of disposal value at the end of an asset's useful life (p. 132)

Worksheet   A columnar device used by accountants to aid them in completing the accounting cycle. It is not a formal statement (p. 128)

BLUEPRINT OF STEPS 5 AND 6 OF THE ACCOUNTING CYCLE

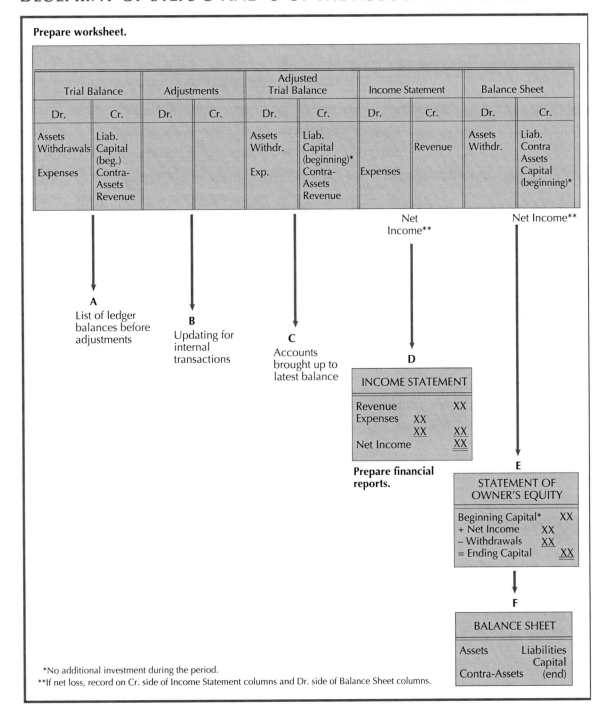

Prepare worksheet.

	Trial Balance		Adjustments		Adjusted Trial Balance		Income Statement		Balance Sheet	
	Dr.	Cr.	Dr.	Cr.	Dr.	Cr.	Dr.	Cr.	Dr.	Cr.
	Assets Withdrawals Expenses	Liab. Capital (beg.) Contra-Assets Revenue			Assets Withdr. Exp.	Liab. Capital (beginning)* Contra-Assets Revenue	Expenses	Revenue	Assets Withdr.	Liab. Contra Assets Capital (beginning)*

A List of ledger balances before adjustments

B Updating for internal transactions

C Accounts brought up to latest balance

Net Income**

Net Income**

D

INCOME STATEMENT

Revenue		XX
Expenses	XX	
	XX	XX
Net Income		XX

Prepare financial reports.

E

STATEMENT OF OWNER'S EQUITY

Beginning Capital*	XX
+ Net Income	XX
– Withdrawals	XX
= Ending Capital	XX

F

BALANCE SHEET

Assets	Liabilities
	Capital
Contra-Assets	(end)

*No additional investment during the period.
**If net loss, record on Cr. side of Income Statement columns and Dr. side of Balance Sheet columns.

QUESTIONS, CLASSROOM DEMONSTRATION EXERCISES, EXERCISES, AND PROBLEMS

Discussion Questions and Critical Thinking/Ethical Case

1. Worksheets are required in every company's accounting cycle. Please agree or disagree and explain why.

2. What is the purpose of adjusting accounts?

3. What is the relationship of internal transactions to the adjusting process?

4. Explain how an adjustment can affect both the income statement and balance sheet. Please give an example.

5. Why do we need the accumulated amortization account?

6. Amortization expense goes on the balance sheet. True or false? Why?

7. Each month the cost of accumulated amortization grows while the cost of equipment goes up. Agree or disagree. Defend your position.

8. Define accrued salaries.

9. Why don't the formal financial statements contain debit or credit columns?

10. Explain how the financial statements are prepared from the worksheet.

11. Janet Fox, President of Angel Co., went to a tax seminar. One of the speakers at the seminar advised the audience to put off showing expenses until next year because doing so would allow them to take advantage of a new tax law. When Janet returned to the office, she called in her accountant, Frieda O'Riley. She told Frieda to forget about making any adjustments for salaries in the old year so more expenses could be shown in the new year. Frieda told her that putting off these expenses would not follow generally accepted accounting principles. Janet said she should do it anyway. You make the call. Write your specific recommendations to Frieda.

Classroom Demonstration Exercises

(The blank forms you need are on pages 4-6 and 4-7 of the *Study Guide with Working Papers*.)

Set A

Adjustment for Supplies

1. Before adjustment:

Computer Supplies   900

Computer Supplies Expense

Given

At year-end, an inventory of supplies shows $200.

Required

a. How much is the adjustment for computer supplies?
b. Draw a transaction analysis box for this adjustment.
c. What will the balance of computer supplies be on the adjusted trial balance?

Adjustment for Prepaid Rent

2. Before adjustment:

Prepaid Rent   1,200

Rent Expense

Given

At year-end, rent expired is $700.

Required

a. How much is the adjustment for Prepaid Rent?
b. Draw a transaction analysis box for this adjustment.
c. What will be the balance of Prepaid Rent on the adjusted trial balance?

Adjustment for Amortization

3. Before adjustment:

Equipment	Accumulated Amortization, Equipment	Amortization Expense, Equipment
9,000	2,000	

Given

For the current year, amortization on equipment is $2,000.

Required

a. Which of the three T accounts is not affected?
b. Which title is a contra-asset?
c. Draw a transaction analysis box for this adjustment.
d. What will be the balance of each of these three accounts on the adjusted trial balance?

Adjustment for Accrued Salaries

4. Before adjustment:

Salaries Expense	Salaries Payable
1,400	

Given

Accrued Salaries, $300

Required

a. Draw a transaction analysis box for this adjustment.
b. What will be the balances of these two accounts on the adjusted trial balance?

Worksheet

5. From the following adjusted trial balance (ATB) titles on a worksheet of a lawyer, identify in which column each account will be listed in the last four columns of the worksheet.
(ID) Income statement, Dr. column
(IC) Income statement, Cr. column
(BD) Balance sheet, Dr. column
(BC) Balance sheet, Cr. column

ATB	ID	IC	BD	BC
a. Legal Fees				
b. Accounts Payable				
c. Cash				
d. Prepaid Advertising				
e. Salaries Payable				
f. Amortization Expense				

ATB	ID	IC	BD	BC
g. V., Capital	___	___	___	___
h. V., Withdrawals	___	___	___	___
i. Computer Supplies	___	___	___	___
j. Rent Expense	___	___	___	___
k. Supplies Payable	___	___	___	___
l. Advertising Expense	___	___	___	___
m. Accumulated Amortization	___	___	___	___
n. Wages Payable	___	___	___	___

6. From the following balance sheet (which was made from the worksheet and other financial statements), explain why the lettered numbers were not found on the worksheet. *Hint:* There are no debits or credits on the formal financial statements.

Laze Co.
Balance Sheet
December 31, 2009

Assets			Liabilities and Owner's Equity		
Cash		$ 6	Liabilities		
Accounts Receivable		2	Accounts Payable	$2	
Supplies		2	Salaries Payable	1	
Equipment	$10		Total Liabilities		$ 3 (B)
Less: Accumulated			Owner's Equity		
Amortization	4	6 (A)	H. Wells, Capital		13
			Total Liabilities and		
Total Assets		$16	Owner's Equity		$16

Set B

Adjustment for Supplies

1. Before adjustment:

Supplies	Supplies Expense
600	

Given

At year-end, an inventory of supplies shows $100.

Required

a. How much is the adjustment for supplies?
b. Draw a transaction analysis box for this adjustment.
c. What will the balance of supplies be on the adjusted trial balance?

Adjustment for Prepaid Rent

2. Before adjustment:

Prepaid Rent	Rent Expense
700	

Given

At year-end, rent expired is $300.

Required

a. How much is the adjustment for Prepaid Rent?

> **b.** Draw a transaction analysis box for this adjustment.
>
> **c.** What will be the balance of Prepaid Rent on the adjusted trial balance?

Adjustment for Amortization

3. Before adjustment:

Equipment	Accumulated Amortization, Equipment	Amortization Expense, Equipment
6,000	1,000	

Given

For the current year, amortization on equipment is $800.

Required

a. Which of the three T accounts is not affected?

b. Which title is a contra-asset?

c. Draw a transaction analysis box for this adjustment.

d. What will be the balance of each of these three accounts on the adjusted trial balance?

Adjustment for Accrued Salaries

4. Before adjustment:

Salaries Expense	Salaries Payable
900	

Given

Accrued Salaries, $200

Required

a. Draw a transaction analysis box for this adjustment.

b. What will be the balances of these two accounts on the adjusted trial balance?

Worksheet

5. From the following adjusted trial balance (ATB) titles on a worksheet, identify in which column each account will be listed in the last four columns of the worksheet.

(ID) Income statement, Dr. column
(IC) Income statement, Cr. column
(BD) Balance sheet, Dr. column
(BC) Balance sheet, Cr. column

ATB		ID	IC	BD	BC
a.	Supplies	___	___	___	___
b.	Accounts Receivable	___	___	___	___
c.	Cash	___	___	___	___
d.	Prepaid Rent	___	___	___	___
e.	Equipment	___	___	___	___
f.	Accumulated Amortization	___	___	___	___
g.	B., Capital	___	___	___	___
h.	B., Withdrawals	___	___	___	___

ATB		ID	IC	BD	BC
i.	Taxi Fare Income	___	___	___	___
j.	Advertising Expense	___	___	___	___
k.	Office Supplies Expense	___	___	___	___
l.	Rent Expense	___	___	___	___
m.	Amortization Expense	___	___	___	___
n.	Salaries Payable	___	___	___	___

6. From the following balance sheet (which was made from the worksheet and other financial statements), explain why the lettered numbers were not found on the worksheet. *Hint:* There are no debits or credits on the formal financial statements.

H. Wells
Balance Sheet
December 31, 2009

Assets			Liabilities and Owner's Equity		
Cash		$ 6	Liabilities		
Accounts Receivable		2	Accounts Payable	$2	
Supplies		2	Salaries Payable	1	
Equipment	$10		Total Liabilities	$ 3	(B)
Less: Accumulated			Owner's Equity		
Amortization	4	6	H. Wells, Capital	13	(C)
			Total Liabilities and		
Total Assets		$16 (A)	Owner's Equity	$16	(D)

Exercises

(The blank forms you need are on pages 4-8 and 4-9 of the *Study Guide with Working Papers.*)

4-1. Complete the following table.

Account	Category	Normal Balance	Found on Which Financial Statement(s)
Supplies Expense			
Prepaid Rent			
Office Equipment			
Amortization Expense			
B. Reel, Capital			
B. Reel, Withdrawals			
Office Supplies			
Accumulated Amortization			

Categorizing accounts

4-2. Use transaction analysis charts to analyze the following adjustments:

Reviewing adjustments and the transaction analysis charts

  a. Amortization on equipment, $600
  b. Rent expired, $400

4-3. From the following adjustment data, calculate the adjustment amount and record appropriate debits or credits:

Recording adjusting entries

  a. Supplies purchased, $700; Supplies on hand, $200
  b. Store equipment, $12,000; Accumulated amortization before adjustment, $900; Amortization expense, $200

4-4. From the following trial balance and adjustment data, complete a worksheet for J. Trent as of December 31, 2011:

    a. Amortization expense, equipment, $2.00

    b. Insurance expired, $1.00

    c. Store supplies on hand, $4.00

    d. Wages owed but not paid, $5.00 (they are an expense in the old year)

J. TRENT
TRIAL BALANCE
DECEMBER 31, 2011

	Dr.	Cr.
Cash	9 00	
Accounts Receivable	2 00	
Prepaid Insurance	7 00	
Store Supplies	6 00	
Store Equipment	7 00	
Accumulated Amortization, Equipment		2 00
Accounts Payable		4 00
J. Trent, Capital		17 00
J. Trent, Withdrawals	6 00	
Revenue from Clients		24 00
Rent Expense	4 00	
Wage Expense	6 00	
	47 00	47 00

4-5. From the completed worksheet in Exercise 4-4, prepare:

    a. An income statement for December

    b. A statement of owner's equity for December

    c. A balance sheet as of December 31, 2011

Group A Problems

(The blank forms you need are on pages 4-10 and 4-11 of the *Study Guide with Working Papers*.)

4A-1. The following is the trial balance for Jan's Cleaning Service of Etobicoke for December 31, 2010.

JAN'S CLEANING SERVICE
TRIAL BALANCE
DECEMBER 31, 2010

	Debit	Credit
Cash in Bank	9 0 0 0 00	
Accounts Receivable	6 0 0 0 00	
Cleaning Supplies	5 4 0 0 00	
Cleaning Equipment	7 2 0 0 00	
Accumulated Amortization, Cleaning Equipment		6 0 0 0 00
J. Welsh, Capital		14 3 5 0 00
J. Welsh, Withdrawals	3 0 0 0 00	
Cleaning Fees		11 3 0 0 00
Rent Expense	9 0 0 00	
Advertising Expense	1 5 0 00	
	31 6 5 0 00	31 6 5 0 00

Given

The following adjustment data on December 31:

a. Cleaning supplies on hand, $900

b. Amortization taken on cleaning equipment, $600

Complete a partial worksheet up to the adjusted trial balance.

Completing a worksheet

4A-2. The trial balance below is for Ling's Landscaping Service of Merritt for December 31, 2009.

Check Figure

Net Income $654

LING'S LANDSCAPING SERVICE
TRIAL BALANCE
DECEMBER 31, 2009

	Dr.	Cr.
Cash in Bank	4 0 0 0 00	
Accounts Receivable	7 0 0 00	
Prepaid Rent	8 0 0 00	
Landscaping Supplies	7 4 2 00	
Landscaping Equipment	1 4 0 0 00	
Accumulated Amortization, Landscaping Equipment		1 0 6 0 00
Accounts Payable		8 3 6 00
A. Ling, Capital		3 2 5 0 00
Landscaping Revenue		4 3 5 6 00
Heat Expense	4 0 0 00	
Advertising Expense	2 0 0 00	
Wages Expense	1 2 6 0 00	
	9 5 0 2 00	9 5 0 2 00

Adjustment data to update the trial balance:

a. Rent expired, $600

b. Landscaping supplies on hand (remaining), $200

c. Amortization expense, landscaping equipment, $300

d. Wages earned by workers but not paid and not due until January, $400

Required

Prepare a worksheet for Ling's Landscaping Service for the month of December.

Comprehensive problem

4A-3. The following is the trial balance for Kevin's Moving Co. of Dartmouth.

KEVIN'S MOVING CO.
TRIAL BALANCE
OCTOBER 31, 2011

Check Figure

Net Income $2,140

	Dr.	Cr.
Cash	5 0 0 0 00	
Prepaid Insurance	2 5 0 0 00	
Moving Supplies	1 2 0 0 00	
Moving Truck	1 1 0 0 0 00	
Accumulated Amortization, Moving Truck		9 0 0 0 00
Accounts Payable		2 7 6 8 00
K. Hoff, Capital		5 4 4 2 00
K. Hoff, Withdrawals	1 4 0 0 00	
Revenue from Moving		9 0 0 0 00
Wages Expense	3 7 1 2 00	
Rent Expense	1 0 8 0 00	
Advertising Expense	3 1 8 00	
	2 6 2 1 0 00	2 6 2 1 0 00

Adjustment data to update trial balance:

a. Insurance expired, $700
b. Moving supplies on hand, $900
c. Amortization on moving truck, $500
d. Wages earned but unpaid, $250

Required

1. Complete a worksheet for Kevin's Moving Co. for the month of October.
2. Prepare an income statement for October, a statement of owner's equity for October, and a balance sheet as of October 31, 2011.

Comprehensive problem

4A-4. The following is a trial balance for Dick's Repair Service of Moose Jaw.

DICK'S REPAIR SERVICE TRIAL BALANCE NOVEMBER 30, 2010	Dr.	Cr.
Cash	3 2 0 0 00	
Prepaid Insurance	4 0 0 0 00	
Repair Supplies	4 6 0 0 00	
Repair Equipment	3 0 0 0 00	
Accumulated Amortization, Repair Equipment		7 0 0 00
Accounts Payable		5 5 7 0 00
D. Horn, Capital		3 8 0 0 00
Revenue from Repairs		7 0 0 0 00
Wages Expense	1 8 0 0 00	
Rent Expense	3 6 0 00	
Advertising Expense	1 1 0 00	
	17 0 7 0 00	17 0 7 0 00

Check Figure

Net Income $1,830

Adjustment data to update the trial balance:

a. Insurance expired, $700
b. Repair supplies on hand, $3,000
c. Amortization on repair equipment, $200
d. Wages earned but not yet paid, $400

Required

1. Complete a worksheet for Dick's Repair Service for the month of November.
2. Prepare an income statement for November, a statement of owner's equity for November, and a balance sheet as of November 30, 2010.

Group B Problems

(The blank forms you need are on pages 4-10 and 4-11 of the *Study Guide with Working Papers*.)

Completing a partial worksheet up to adjusted trial balance

4B-1. For Jan's Cleaning Service of Etobicoke, complete a partial worksheet up to the adjusted trial balance using the following adjustment data and trial balance:

a. Cleaning supplies on hand, $3,000
b. Amortization taken on cleaning equipment, $500

CONTINUING PROBLEM

At the end of September, Tony took a complete inventory of his supplies and found the following:

5 dozen ¼" screws at a cost of $8 a dozen

2 dozen ½" screws at a cost of $5 a dozen

2 cartons of computer inventory paper at a cost of $14 a carton

3 feet of coaxial cable at a cost of $4 per foot

After speaking to his accountant, he found that a reasonable amortization amount for each of his long-term assets is as follows:

Computer purchased July 5, 2010	Amortization $33 a month
Office equipment purchased July 16, 2010	Amortization $10 a month
Computer workstations purchased September 17, 2010	Amortization $20 a month

Tony uses the straight-line method of amortization and declares no salvage value for any of the assets. If any long-term asset is purchased in the first 15 days of the month, he will charge amortization for the full month. If an asset is purchased on the 16th of the month, or later, he will not charge amortization in the month it was purchased.

September's rent has now expired.

Assignment

Use your trial balance from the completed problem in Chapter 3 and the above adjusting information to complete the worksheet for the three months ended September 30, 2010. From the worksheets, prepare the financial statements. (See pages 4-16 to 4-19 in your *Study Guide with Working Papers*.)

5 The Accounting Cycle Completed

Adjusting, Closing, and Post-Closing Trial Balance

THE BIG PICTURE

Warren Beesley is probably not a name that many accounting students would recognize, but you may get to know more about him and his company in the future. Warren's company, Beesley Exhibitions Inc., is the brains behind Canada's Financial Technology Show, which is held in Toronto and Vancouver in alternating years.

Each of the shows brings together most of Canada's accounting software firms to demonstrate their products' capabilities to hundreds of professional accountants. It is a kind of one-stop event where accountants can go to discover solutions for accounting problems they, or, more usually, their companies face. The show's website (www.financial-technologyshow.com) states proudly that if you cannot find a solution for your accounting needs, a solution probably does not exist.

Big words, to be sure. Does the show actually deliver? Judging by the list of exhibitors, one would have to say a definite "Yes!" Included are a virtual who's who of accounting software providers. And if

that were not enough, the show's sponsors include *The Bottom Line*, Canada's accounting newspaper, which has been keeping the accounting profession informed and up to date for more than two decades. Many other top companies are also proud to be associated with the show as sponsors.

Warren Beesley once worked for *The Bottom Line*, and still contributes an article or two as time permits. But for the past eight years, he has been devoting his attention mainly to ensuring the success of his two shows. Is he having fun yet? There are anxious moments, of course, but he really would not want to be doing anything else. Being the go-to guy for Canada's top show in accounting technology has its own rewards, and the future seems very bright indeed.

If you ever need details on how you can complete the accounting cycle, and close your company's books, you could do worse than attend one of Warren's shows. But you will definitely want to complete this chapter first.

♦ **Journalizing and posting adjusting entries (p. 169)**
♦ **Journalizing and posting closing entries (p. 173)**
♦ **Preparing a post-closing trial balance (p. 183)**

Remember: For ease of presentation, we are using a month as the accounting cycle for Clark's. In the business world, the cycle can be any time period but is usually one year.

In Chapters 3 and 4, we completed these steps of the manual accounting cycle for Clark's Desktop Publishing Services:

Step 1: Business transactions occurred and generated source documents.

Step 2: Business transactions were analyzed and recorded in a journal.

Step 3: Information was posted or transferred from journal to ledger.

Step 4: A trial balance was prepared.

Step 5: A worksheet was completed.

Step 6: Financial statements were prepared.

This chapter covers the following steps, which will complete Clark's accounting cycle for the month of May:

Step 7: Journalizing and posting adjusting entries

Step 8: Journalizing and posting closing entries

Step 9: Preparing a post-closing trial balance

Learning Unit 5-1
Journalizing and Posting Adjusting Entries: Step 7 of the Accounting Cycle

RECORDING JOURNAL ENTRIES FROM THE WORKSHEET

Purpose of adjusting entries

At this point, many ledger accounts are *not up to date.*

The information in the worksheet is up to date. The financial statements prepared from that information can give the business's management and other interested parties a good idea of where the business stands as of a particular date. The problem is that the worksheet is an informal report. The information concerning the adjustments has not been placed in the journal or posted to the ledger accounts. This means that the books are not up to date and ready for the next accounting cycle to begin. For example, the ledger shows $1,200 of prepaid rent (page 98), but the balance sheet we prepared in Chapter 4 shows an $800 balance. Essentially, the worksheet is a tool for preparing financial statements. Now we must use the adjustment columns of the worksheet as a basis for bringing the ledger up to date. We do this by **adjusting journal entries** (see Figure 5-1). Again, the updating must be done before the next accounting period starts. For Clark's Desktop Publishing Services, the next period begins on June 1.

Figure 5-1 shows the adjusting journal entries for Clark's taken from the adjustments section of the worksheet (see Figure 5-2). Once the adjusting journal entries are posted to the ledger, the accounts making up the financial statements that were prepared from the worksheet will correspond with the updated ledger. (Keep in mind that this is the same journal we have been using.) Let's look at some simplified T accounts to show how Clark's ledger looked before and after the adjustments were posted (see adjustments A to D on page 171).

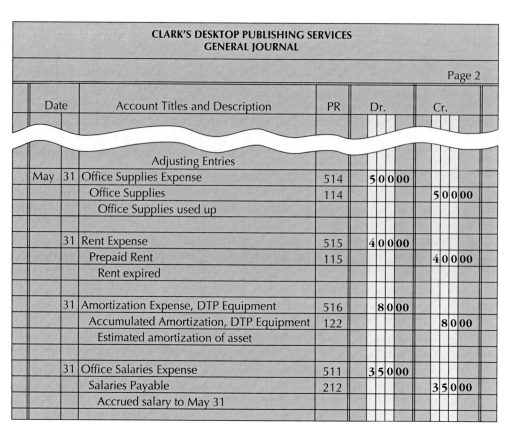

Figure 5-1
Adjusting Journal Entries

CLARK'S DESKTOP PUBLISHING SERVICES
GENERAL JOURNAL

Page 2

Date		Account Titles and Description	PR	Dr.	Cr.
		Adjusting Entries			
May	31	Office Supplies Expense	514	5 0 0 00	
		Office Supplies	114		5 0 0 00
		Office Supplies used up			
	31	Rent Expense	515	4 0 0 00	
		Prepaid Rent	115		4 0 0 00
		Rent expired			
	31	Amortization Expense, DTP Equipment	516	8 0 00	
		Accumulated Amortization, DTP Equipment	122		8 0 00
		Estimated amortization of asset			
	31	Office Salaries Expense	511	3 5 0 00	
		Salaries Payable	212		3 5 0 00
		Accrued salary to May 31			

Figure 5-2
Journalizing and Posting
Adjustments from the
Adjustments Section of the
Worksheet

Account Titles	Trial Balance		Adjustments	
	Dr.	Cr.	Dr.	Cr.
Cash	6 1 5 5 00			
Accounts Receivable	5 0 0 0 00			
Office Supplies	6 0 0 00			(A) 5 0 0 00
Prepaid Rent	1 2 0 0 00			(B) 4 0 0 00
Desktop Publishing Equipment	6 0 0 0 00			
Accounts Payable		3 3 5 0 00		
Brenda Clark, Capital		1 0 0 0 0 00		
Brenda Clark, Withdrawals	6 2 5 00			
Desktop Publishing Fees		8 0 0 0 00		
Office Salaries Expense	1 3 0 0 00		(D) 3 5 0 00	
Advertising Expense	2 5 0 00			
Telephone Expense	2 2 0 00			
	2 1 3 5 0 00	2 1 3 5 0 00		
Office Supplies Expense			(A) 5 0 0 00	
Rent Expense			(B) 4 0 0 00	
Amortization Expense, DTP Equipment			(C) 8 0 00	
Accumulated Amortization, DTP Equipment				(C) 8 0 00
Salaries Payable				(D) 3 5 0 00
			1 3 3 0 00	1 3 3 0 00

Adjustments A to D in the adjustments section of the worksheet must be recorded in the journal and posted to the ledger.

Adjustment A

Before posting:

Office Supplies 114	Office Supplies Expense 514
600	

After posting:

Office Supplies 114	Office Supplies Expense 514
600	500	500	

Adjustment B

Before posting:

Prepaid Rent 115	Rent Expense 515
1,200	

After posting:

Prepaid Rent 115	Rent Expense 515
1,200	400	400	

Adjustment C

Before posting:

Desktop Publishing Equipment 121	Amortization Expense, DTP Equipment 516	Accumulated Amortization, DTP Equipment 122
6,000		

After posting:

Desktop Publishing Equipment 121	Amortization Expense, DTP Equipment 516	Accumulated Amortization, DTP Equipment 122
6,000	80	80

This last adjustment shows the same balances for Amortization Expense and Accumulated Amortization. However, in subsequent adjustments, the Accumulated Amortization balance will keep getting larger, but the debit to Amortization Expense and the credit to Accumulated Amortization will be the same. We will see why in a moment.

Adjustment D

Before posting:

Office Salaries Expense 511	Salaries Payable 212
650	
650	

After posting:

Office Salaries Expense 511	Salaries Payable 212
650	350
650	
350	

LEARNING UNIT 5-1 REVIEW

AT THIS POINT you should be able to:

♦ Define and state the purpose of adjusting entries. (p. 169)

♦ Journalize adjusting entries from the worksheet. (p. 170)

♦ Post journalized adjusting entries to the ledger. (p. 170)

♦ Compare specific ledger accounts before and after posting of the journalized adjusting entries. (p. 171)

Self-Review Quiz 5-1

(The blank forms you need are on pages 5-1 and 5-2 of the *Study Guide with Working Papers*.)

Turn to the worksheet of P. Logan Company (p. 140) and (1) journalize and post the adjusting entries and (2) compare the adjusted ledger accounts before and after the adjustments are posted. T accounts with beginning balances are provided in your *Study Guide*.

Solution to Self-Review Quiz 5-1

Quiz Tip

These journal entries come from the adjustments column of the worksheet.

Page 2

Date		Account Titles and Description	PR	Dr.		Cr.	
		Adjusting Entries					
Dec.	31	Amortization Expense, Store Equipment	511	1	00		
		Accumulated Amortization, Store Equipment	122			1	00
		Estimated amortization of equipment					
	31	Insurance Expense	516	2	00		
		Prepaid Insurance	116			2	00
		Insurance expired					
	31	Supplies Expense	514	4	00		
		Store Supplies	114			4	00
		Store Supplies used					
	31	Salaries Expense	512	3	00		
		Salaries Payable	212			3	00
		Accrued salaries payable					

PARTIAL LEDGER

Before Posting		After Posting	

Before Posting

Amortization Expense, Store Equipment 511
```
        |
        |
```

Accumulated Amortization, Store Equipment 122
```
        | 4
        |
```

Prepaid Insurance 116
```
   3    |
```

Insurance Expense 516
```
        |
```

Store Supplies 114
```
   5    |
```

Supplies Expense 514
```
        |
```

Salaries Expense 512
```
   8    |
```

Salaries Payable 212
```
        |
```

After Posting

Amortization Expense, Store Equipment 511
```
   1    |
        |
```

Accumulated Amortization, Store Equipment 122
```
        | 4
        | 1
```

Prepaid Insurance 116
```
   3    | 2
```

Insurance Expense 516
```
   2    |
```

Store Supplies 114
```
   5    | 4
```

Supplies Expense 514
```
   4    |
```

Salaries Expense 512
```
   8    |
   3    |
```

Salaries Payable 212
```
        | 3
```

Learning Unit 5-2
Journalizing and Posting Closing Entries: Step 8 of the Accounting Cycle

To make recording of the next fiscal year's transactions easier, a mechanical step, called **closing**, is taken by the accountant at Clark's. Closing is used to end—or close off—the revenue, expense, and withdrawal accounts at the end of the fiscal year. The information needed to complete closing entries will be found in the income statement and balance sheet sections of the worksheet.

To make it easier to understand this process, we will first look at the difference between temporary (nominal) accounts and permanent (real) accounts.

Here is the expanded accounting equation that we used in an earlier chapter:

Assets = Liabilities + Capital – Withdrawals + Revenues – Expenses

> Permanent accounts are found on the balance sheet.

Three of the items in that equation—assets, liabilities, and capital—are known as **real** or **permanent accounts** because their balances are carried over from one fiscal year to another. The other three items—withdrawals, revenue, and expenses—are called **nominal** or **temporary accounts** because their balances are not carried over from one fiscal year to another. Instead, their balances are set to zero at the beginning of each fiscal year. This allows us to accumulate new data about revenue, expenses, and withdrawals in the new fiscal year. The process of closing summarizes the effects of the temporary accounts on capital for that period by using **closing journal entries** and by posting them to the ledger. When the closing process is complete, the accounting equation will be reduced to:

Assets = Liabilities + Ending Capital

> After all closing entries are journalized and posted to the ledger, all temporary accounts have a zero balance in the ledger. Closing is a step-by-step process.

If you look back at page 142 in Chapter 4, you will see that we have calculated the new capital on the balance sheet for Clark's Desktop Publishing Services to be $14,275. However, before the mechanical closing procedures are journalized and posted, the capital account of Brenda Clark in the ledger is only $10,000 (Chapter 3, page 98). Let's look now at how to journalize and post closing entries.

How to Journalize Closing Entries

There are four steps to be performed in journalizing closing entries:

Step 1: Clear the revenue balances and transfer them to Income Summary. **Income Summary** is a temporary account in the ledger needed for closing. At the end of the closing process, there will be no balance in Income Summary.

Revenue → Income Summary

Step 2: Clear the individual expense balances and transfer them to Income Summary.

Expenses → Income Summary

Step 3: Clear the balance in Income Summary and transfer it to Capital.

Income Summary → Capital

Step 4: Clear the balance in Withdrawals and transfer it to Capital.

Withdrawals → Capital

Figure 5-3 is a visual representation of these four steps. Keep in mind that this information must first be journalized and then posted to the appropriate ledger accounts. The worksheet presented in Figure 5-4 contains all the figures we will need for the closing process.

Step 1: Clear Revenue Balances and Transfer to Income Summary

Here is what is in the ledger before closing entries are journalized and posted:

Desktop Publishing Fees 411	Income Summary 313
| 8,000	|

The income statement section on the worksheet on page 175 shows that the Desktop Publishing Fees account has a credit balance of $8,000. To close or clear this to zero in the ledger, a debit of $8,000 is needed. However, if we add an amount to the debit side, we must also add a credit—so we add $8,000 on the credit side of the Income Summary account.

> An Income Summary is a temporary account located in the chart of accounts under Owner's Equity. It does not have a normal balance of a debit or a credit.

> Sometimes, closing the accounts is referred to as "clearing the accounts."

> *Don't forget two goals of closing:*
> 1. Clear all temporary accounts in the ledger.
> 2. Update Capital to a new balance that reflects a summary of all the temporary accounts.

> All numbers used in the closing process can be found on the worksheet in Figure 5-4. Note that the *account* Income Summary is *not* on the worksheet.

Figure 5-3
Four Steps in Journalizing Closing Entries

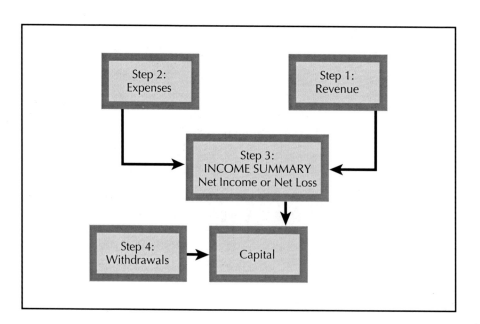

Figure 5-4
Closing Figures on the Worksheet

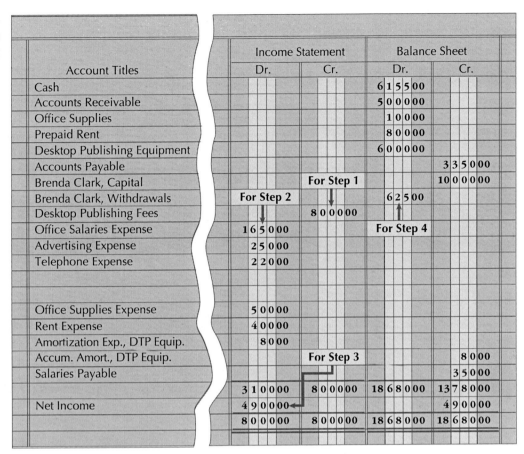

The following is the journalized closing entry for step 1:

			Desktop Publishing Fees	411	8 0 0 0 00				
May	31		Desktop Publishing Fees	411	8 0 0 0 00				
			Income Summary	313			8 0 0 0 00		
			To close income account						

This is what Desktop Publishing Fees and Income Summary should look like in the ledger after step 1 closing entries are journalized and posted:

Desktop Publishing Fees 411

8,000	8,000
	Closing

Income Summary 313

	8,000
	Revenue

Note that the revenue balance is cleared to zero and transferred to Income Summary, a temporary account also located in the ledger.

Step 2: Clear Individual Expense Balances and Transfer the Total to Income Summary

Here is what is in the ledger for each expense before step 2 closing entries are journalized and posted. Each expense is listed on the worksheet in the debit column of the income statement section as above.

Office Salaries Expense 511

650	
650	
350	

Advertising Expense 512

250	

Telephone Expense 513	Office Supplies Expense 514
220		500	

Rent Expense 515	Amortization Expense, DTP Equipment 516
400		80	

The income statement section of the worksheet lists all the expenses as debits. If we want to reduce each expense to zero, each one must be credited.

The following is the journalized closing entry for step 2:

	31	Income Summary	313	3 1 0 0|00		
		Office Salaries Expense	511		1 6 5 0	00
		Advertising Expense	512		2 5 0	00
		Telephone Expense	513		2 2 0	00
		Office Supplies Expense	514		5 0 0	00
		Rent Expense	515		4 0 0	00
		Amortization Expense, DTP Equipment	516		8 0	00
		To close expense accounts			

This is what individual expense accounts and the Income Summary should look like in the ledger after step 2 closing entries are journalized and posted:

Office Salaries Expense 511	Advertising Expense 512
650	Closing 1,650	250	Closing 250
650		
350		

Telephone Expense 513	Office Supplies Expense 514
220	Closing 220	500	Closing 500

Rent Expense 515	Amortization Expense 516
400	Closing 400	80	Closing 80

Income Summary 313

Expenses	Revenue
Step 2 3,100	8,000 Step 1

Step 3: Clear Balance in Income Summary (Net Income) and Transfer It to Capital

This is how the Income Summary and Brenda Clark, Capital, accounts look before step 3:

Income Summary 313	Brenda Clark, Capital 311
3,100	8,000		10,000
	4,900		

Note that the balance of Income Summary (Revenue minus Expenses, or $8,000 − $3,100) is $4,900. That is the amount we must clear from the Income Summary account and transfer to the Brenda Clark, Capital, account.

The opposite would take place if the business had a net loss.

In order to transfer the balance of $4,900 from Income Summary (check the bottom of the debit column of the income statement section on the worksheet; see Figure 5-4) to Capital, it will be necessary to debit Income Summary for $4,900 (the difference between the revenue and expenses) and credit or increase Capital of Brenda Clark with $4,900.

This is the journalized closing entry for step 3:

	31	Income Summary	313	4 9 0 0 00		
		Brenda Clark, Capital	311		4 9 0 0 00
		Transfer profit for period to Capital acct.			

At the end of these three steps, Income Summary has a zero balance. If we had a net loss, the end result would be to decrease capital. The entry would be to debit Capital and credit Income Summary for the loss.

This is what the Income Summary and Brenda Clark, Capital accounts will look like in the ledger after step 3 closing entries are journalized and posted:

Income Summary 313

Total of expenses → 3,100 | 8,000 ← Revenue

Debit to close account → 4,900 | 4,900 ← Net income

Brenda Clark, Capital 311

10,000

4,900 Net income

Step 4: Clear the Withdrawals Balance and Transfer It to Capital

Today's accounting software handles the closing process easily. However, accountants usually have to do step 4 separately.

Next, we must close the Withdrawals account. The Brenda Clark, Withdrawals, and Brenda Clark, Capital, accounts now look like this:

Brenda Clark, Withdrawals 312

625

Brenda Clark, Capital 311

10,000

4,900

To bring the Withdrawals account to a zero balance and summarize its effect on Capital, we must credit Withdrawals and debit Capital.

Note that the $10,000 is a beginning balance since no additional investments were made during the period.

Remember, withdrawals are a non-business expense and thus not transferred to Income Summary. The closing entry is journalized as follows:

	31	Brenda Clark, Capital	311	6 2 5 00	
		Brenda Clark, Withdrawals	312		6 2 5 00
		Transfer withdrawals to Capital account			

At this point, the Brenda Clark, Withdrawals, and Brenda Clark, Capital, accounts would look like this in the ledger:

Brenda Clark, Withdrawals 312

625 | Closing 625

Brenda Clark, Capital 311

→ 625 | 10,000 ↖

Withdrawals | **Beginning balance**

4,900 ↖

Net income

CLARK'S DESKTOP PUBLISHING SERVICES
GENERAL JOURNAL

Date 2010		Account Title and Description	Post. Ref.	Dr.	Cr.
May	31	Desktop Publishing Fees	411	8 0 0 0 00	
		Income Summary	313		8 0 0 0 00
		To close income account			
	31	Income Summary	313	3 1 0 0 00	
		Office Salaries Expense	511		1 6 5 0 00
		Advertising Expense	512		2 5 0 00
		Telephone Expense	513		2 2 0 00
		Office Supplies Expense	514		5 0 0 00
		Rent Expense	515		4 0 0 00
		Amortization Expense, DTP Equipment	516		8 0 00
		To close expense accounts			
	31	Income Summary	313	4 9 0 0 00	
		Brenda Clark, Capital	311		4 9 0 0 00
		Transfer profit to capital			
	31	Brenda Clark, Capital	311	6 2 5 00	
		Brenda Clark, Withdrawals	312		6 2 5 00
		Transfer withdrawals to capital			

Now let's look at a summary of the closing entries. The complete ledger for Clark's Desktop Publishing Services is shown in Figure 5-5 beginning on this page. Note that the word "adjusting" or "closing" is written in the explanation column of individual ledgers, as for example in the one for Office Supplies. If the goals of closing have been achieved, only permanent accounts will have balances carried to the next fiscal year. All temporary accounts should have zero balances.

Figure 5-5
Complete Ledger

CLARK'S DESKTOP PUBLISHING SERVICES
GENERAL LEDGER

Cash   Account No. 111

Date 2010		Explanation	Post. Ref.	Debit	Credit	DR or CR	Balance
May	1		GJ1	1 0 0 0 0 00		DR	1 0 0 0 0 00
	1		GJ1		1 0 0 0 00	DR	9 0 0 0 00
	1		GJ1		1 2 0 0 00	DR	7 8 0 0 00
	7		GJ1	3 0 0 0 00		DR	1 0 8 0 0 00
	11		GJ1		6 5 0 00	DR	1 0 1 5 0 00
	20		GJ1		6 2 5 00	DR	9 5 2 5 00
	25		GJ2		6 5 0 00	DR	8 8 7 5 00
	28		GJ2		2 5 0 0 00	DR	6 3 7 5 00
	29		GJ2		2 2 0 00	DR	6 1 5 5 00

Accounts Receivable
Acct. No. 112

Date 2010		Explanation	Post. Ref.	Debit	Credit	DR or CR	Balance
May	22		GJ1	5 0 0 0 00		DR	5 0 0 0 00

Office Supplies
Acct. No. 114

Date 2010		Explanation	Post. Ref.	Debit	Credit	DR or CR	Balance
May	3		GJ1	6 0 0 00		DR	6 0 0 00
	31	Adjusting	GJ2		5 0 0 00	DR	1 0 0 00

Prepaid Rent
Acct. No. 115

Date 2010		Explanation	Post. Ref.	Debit	Credit	DR or CR	Balance
May	1		GJ1	1 2 0 0 00		DR	1 2 0 0 00
	31	Adjusting	GJ2		4 0 0 00	DR	8 0 0 00

Desktop Publishing Equipment
Acct. No. 121

Date 2010		Explanation	Post. Ref.	Debit	Credit	DR or CR	Balance
May	1		GJ1	6 0 0 0 00		DR	6 0 0 0 00

Accumulated Amortization, Desktop Publishing Equipment
Acct. No. 122

Date 2010		Explanation	Post. Ref.	Debit	Credit	DR or CR	Balance
May	31	Adjusting	GJ2		80 00	CR	80 00

Accounts Payable
Acct. No. 211

Date 2010		Explanation	Post. Ref.	Debit	Credit	DR or CR	Balance
May	1		GJ1		5 0 0 0 00	CR	5 0 0 0 00
	3		GJ1		6 0 0 00	CR	5 6 0 0 00
	18		GJ1		2 5 0 00	CR	5 8 5 0 00
	28		GJ2	2 5 0 0 00		CR	3 3 5 0 00

Figure 5-5 (Continued)

Salaries Payable   Acct. No. 212

Date 2010		Explanation	Post. Ref.	Debit	Credit	DR or CR	Balance
May	31	Adjusting	GJ2		3 5 0 00	CR	3 5 0 00

Brenda Clark, Capital   Acct. No. 311

Date 2010		Explanation	Post. Ref.	Debit	Credit	DR or CR	Balance
May	1		GJ1		10 0 0 0 00	CR	10 0 0 0 00
	31	Closing (Net Income)	GJ2		4 9 0 0 00	CR	14 9 0 0 00
	31	Closing (Withdrawals)	GJ2	6 2 5 00		CR	14 2 7 5 00

Note that this is the same ending balance as on page 142.

Brenda Clark, Withdrawals   Acct. No. 312

Date 2010		Explanation	Post. Ref.	Debit	Credit	DR or CR	Balance
May	20		GJ1	6 2 5 00		DR	6 2 5 00
	31	Closing	GJ2		6 2 5 00		— 0 —

Income Summary   Acct. No. 313

Date 2010		Explanation	Post. Ref.	Debit	Credit	DR or CR	Balance
May	31	Closing (Revenue)	GJ2		8 0 0 0 00	CR	8 0 0 0 00
	31	Closing (Expense)	GJ2	3 1 0 0 00		CR	4 9 0 0 00
	31	Closing (Net Income)	GJ2	4 9 0 0 00			— 0 —

Desktop Publishing Fees   Acct. No. 411

Date 2010		Explanation	Post. Ref.	Debit	Credit	DR or CR	Balance
May	7		GJ1		3 0 0 0 00	CR	3 0 0 0 00
	22		GJ1		5 0 0 0 00	CR	8 0 0 0 00
	31	Closing	GJ2	8 0 0 0 00			— 0 —

Office Salaries Expense   Acct. No. 511

Date 2010		Explanation	Post. Ref.	Debit	Credit	DR or CR	Balance
May	11		GJ1	6 5 0 00		DR	6 5 0 00
	25		GJ2	6 5 0 00		DR	1 3 0 0 00
	31	Adjusting	GJ2	3 5 0 00		DR	1 6 5 0 00
	31	Closing	GJ2		1 6 5 0 00		— 0 —

Advertising Expense

Acct. No. 512

Date 2010		Explanation	Post. Ref.	Debit	Credit	DR or CR	Balance
May	18		GJ1	2 5 0 00		DR	2 5 0 00
	31	Closing	GJ2		2 5 0 00		—0—

Telephone Expense

Acct. No. 513

Date 2010		Explanation	Post. Ref.	Debit	Credit	DR or CR	Balance
May	29		GJ2	2 2 0 00		DR	2 2 0 00
	31	Closing	GJ2		2 2 0 00		—0—

Office Supplies Expense

Acct. No. 514

Date 2010		Explanation	Post. Ref.	Debit	Credit	DR or CR	Balance
May	31	Adjusting	GJ2	5 0 0 00		DR	5 0 0 00
	31	Closing	GJ2		5 0 0 00		—0—

Rent Expense

Acct. No. 515

Date 2010		Explanation	Post. Ref.	Debit	Credit	DR or CR	Balance
May	31	Adjusting	GJ2	4 0 0 00		DR	4 0 0 00
	31	Closing	GJ2		4 0 0 00		—0—

Amortization Expense, Desktop Publishing Equipment

Acct. No. 516

Date 2010		Explanation	Post. Ref.	Debit	Credit	DR or CR	Balance
May	31	Adjusting	GJ2	8 0 00		DR	8 0 00
	31	Closing	GJ2		8 0 00		—0—

LEARNING UNIT 5-2 REVIEW

AT THIS POINT you should be able to:

- ◆ Define closing. (p. 173)
- ◆ Differentiate between temporary (nominal) and permanent (real) accounts. (p. 173)
- ◆ List the four mechanical steps of closing. (p. 174)
- ◆ Explain the role of the Income Summary account. (p. 174)
- ◆ Explain the role of the worksheet in the closing process. (p. 174)

Self-Review Quiz 5-2

(The blank forms you need are on pages 5-2 and 5-3 of the *Study Guide with Working Papers*.)

Go to the worksheet for P. Logan on page 140. Then (1) journalize and post the closing entries and (2) calculate the new balance for P. Logan, Capital.

Solution to Self-Review Quiz 5-2

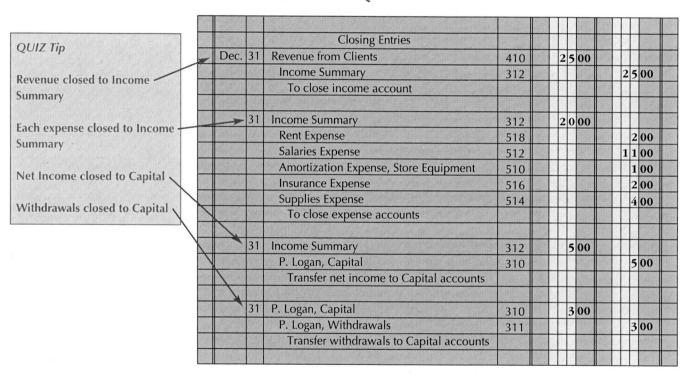

		Closing Entries			
Dec.	31	Revenue from Clients	410	25 00	
		Income Summary	312		25 00
		To close income account			
	31	Income Summary	312	20 00	
		Rent Expense	518		2 00
		Salaries Expense	512		11 00
		Amortization Expense, Store Equipment	510		1 00
		Insurance Expense	516		2 00
		Supplies Expense	514		4 00
		To close expense accounts			
	31	Income Summary	312	5 00	
		P. Logan, Capital	310		5 00
		Transfer net income to Capital accounts			
	31	P. Logan, Capital	310	3 00	
		P. Logan, Withdrawals	311		3 00
		Transfer withdrawals to Capital accounts			

QUIZ Tip

Revenue closed to Income Summary

Each expense closed to Income Summary

Net Income closed to Capital

Withdrawals closed to Capital

PARTIAL LEDGER

P. Logan, Capital 310		Revenue from Clients 410		Supplies Expense 514	
3	14	25	25	4	4
	5				
	16				

P. Logan, Withdrawals 311		Amortization Expense, Store Equipment 510		Insurance Expense 516	
3	3	1	1	2	2

Income Summary 312	Salaries Expense 512	Rent Expense 518
20 | 25	11 | 11	2 | 2
5 |		

P. Logan, Capital		$14
Net Income	$5	
Less: Withdrawals	3	
Increase in Capital		2
P. Logan, Capital (ending)		$16

Learning Unit 5-3

The Post-Closing Trial Balance: Step 9 of the Accounting Cycle and the Accounting Cycle Reviewed

PREPARING A POST-CLOSING TRIAL BALANCE

The post-closing trial balance helps prove the accuracy of the adjusting and closing process. It contains the true ending figure for capital.

The last step in the accounting cycle is the preparation of a **post-closing trial balance** (sometimes called an opening trial balance), which lists only permanent accounts in the ledger and their balances after adjusting and closing entries have been posted. This post-closing trial balance aids in checking whether the ledger is in balance. It is important to do this checking because so many new postings go to the ledger from the adjusting and closing process.

The procedure for taking a post-closing trial balance is the same as for a trial balance except that since closing entries have closed all temporary accounts, the post-closing trial balance will contain only permanent accounts (balance sheet). Keep in mind, however, that adjustments have occurred.

THE ACCOUNTING CYCLE REVIEWED

Table 5-1 lists the steps that we completed in the manual accounting cycle for Clark's Desktop Publishing Services for the month of May.

Insight: Most companies journalize and post adjusting and closing entries only at the end of their fiscal year. A company that prepares interim reports may complete only the first six steps of the cycle. Worksheets allow the preparation of interim reports without the formal adjusting and closing of the books.

Insight: To prepare a financial report for April, the data needed can be obtained by subtracting the worksheet accumulated totals for the end of March from the worksheet prepared at the end of April. In this chapter, we chose a month that would show the completion of an entire cycle for Clark's Desktop Publishing Services.

TABLE 5-1 Steps of the Manual Accounting Cycle

Step	Explanation
1. Business transactions occur and generate source documents.	Source documents are cash register tapes, sales tickets, bills, cheques, payroll cards, etc.
↓	↓
2. Analyze and record business transactions into a journal.	Called journalizing.
↓	↓
3. Post or transfer information from journal to ledger.	Copying the debits and credits of the journal entries into the ledger accounts.
↓	↓
4. Prepare a trial balance.	Summarizing each individual ledger account and listing these accounts and their balances to test for mathematical accuracy in recording transactions.
↓	↓
5. Prepare a worksheet.	A multicolumn form that summarizes accounting information to complete the accounting cycle.
↓	↓
6. Prepare financial statements.	Income statement, statement of owner's equity, and balance sheet.
↓	↓
7. Journalize and post adjusting entries.	Use figures in the adjustment columns of worksheet.
↓	↓
8. Journalize and post closing entries.	Use figures in the income statement and balance sheet sections of worksheet.
↓	↓
9. Prepare a post-closing trial balance.	Prove the mathematical accuracy of the adjusting and closing process of the accounting cycle.

LEARNING UNIT 5-3 REVIEW

AT THIS POINT you should be able to:

◆ Prepare a post-closing trial balance. (p. 183)
◆ Explain the relationship of interim reports to the accounting cycle. (p. 183)

Self-Review Quiz 5-3

(The blank forms you need are on page 5-3 of the *Study Guide with Working Papers.*)

From the ledger on pages 178–181, prepare a post-closing trial balance.

Solution to Self-Review Quiz 5-3

CLARK'S DESKTOP PUBLISHING SERVICES
POST-CLOSING TRIAL BALANCE
MAY 31, 2010

	Dr.	Cr.
Cash	6 1 5 5 00	
Accounts Receivable	5 0 0 0 00	
Office Supplies	1 0 0 00	
Prepaid Rent	8 0 0 00	
Desktop Publishing Equipment	6 0 0 0 00	
Accumulated Amortization, Desktop Publishing Equipment		8 0 00
Accounts Payable		3 3 5 0 00
Salaries Payable		3 5 0 00
Brenda Clark, Capital		14 2 7 5 00
Totals	18 0 5 5 00	18 0 5 5 00

"You wait and see," Stan told his new sandwich artist Wanda Kurtz, "Everything will fall into place soon." Wanda had a tough time serving customers quickly enough, and Stan was in the middle of giving her a pep talk when the phone rang.

"I'll let the machine pick up," Stan reassured Wanda, as he proceeded to train her in some crucial POS touch-screen manoeuvres.

"Stan!" an urgent voice came over the answering machine, "I think you've forgotten something!" Stan picked up the phone and said, "Lila, can I get back to you tomorrow? I'm in the middle of an important talk with Wanda." One of Stan's strong points as an employer was his ability to focus 100% on his employees' concerns. Yet, Lila simply would not wait.

"Stan," Lila said impatiently, "You absolutely must get me your worksheet by 12 noon tomorrow so that I can close your books," she insisted. "Tomorrow's the 31st of March and we close on the last day of the month!"

"*Ay caramba!*" Stan sighed, "Looks like I'm going to be up till the wee hours," he confided to Wanda when he put down the phone.

Although Subway company policy doesn't require a closing every month, closing the books is a key part of their accounting training for all new franchisees. By closing their books, business owners can clearly measure their net profit and loss for each period separate from all other periods. This makes activities like budgeting and comparing performance with similar businesses (or performance over time) possible.

At 9 a.m. the next morning, an exhausted Stan opened up the restaurant and emailed his worksheet to Lila. He was feeling quite pleased with himself—that is, until he heard Lila's urgent-sounding voice coming over the answering machine 10 minutes later.

"I've been over and over this," said Lila after Stan picked up, "And I can't get it to balance. I

CLOSING TIME

know it's hard for you to do this during working hours, but I need you to go back over the figures."

Stan opened up QuickBooks® and pored over his worksheets. Errors are hard to find when closing the books and, unfortunately, there is no set way to detect errors and even no set place to start. Stan chose payroll because it is one of the largest expenses and because of the new hire.

At 11:45 he called Lila, who sounded both exasperated and relieved to hear from him. "I think I've got it! It looks like I messed up on adjusting the Salaries Expense account. I looked at the Payroll Register and compared the total of the Salaries Payable account. It didn't match! When I hired Wanda Kurtz on the 26th, I should have increased both the Salaries Expense and the Salaries Payable lines because she has accrued wages."

"Yes," said Lila, "Salaries Expense is a debit and Salaries Payable is a credit and you skipped the payable. Great! With this adjusting entry in the general journal, the worksheet will balance."

Stan's sigh of relief turned into a big yawn and they both laughed. "I guess I just find it easier to hire people and train them than to account for them," said Stan.

DISCUSSION QUESTIONS

1. How would the adjustment be made if Wanda Kurtz received $7 per hour and worked 25 additional hours? Where do you place her accrued wages?

2. Stan bought three new Subway aprons and hats for Wanda Smith for $20 each but forgot to post it to the Uniforms account. How much will the closing balance be off? In what way will it be off?

3. Put yourself in Stan's shoes: What is the value of doing a monthly closing, no matter how much—or little—business you do?

DEMONSTRATION PROBLEM: REVIEWING THE ACCOUNTING CYCLE

(The blank forms you need are on pages 5-4 to 5-10 of the *Study Guide with Working Papers*.)

From the following transactions for Rolo Company, complete the entire accounting cycle. The chart of accounts includes:

Assets
111 Cash
112 Accounts Receivable
114 Prepaid Rent
115 Office Supplies
121 Office Equipment
122 Accumulated Amortization,
      Office Equipment

Liabilities
211 Accounts Payable
212 Salaries Payable

Owner's Equity
311 R. Kern, Capital
312 R. Kern, Withdrawals
313 Income Summary

Revenue
411 Fees Earned

Expenses
511 Salaries Expense
512 Advertising Expense
513 Rent Expense
514 Office Supplies Expense
515 Amortization Expense,
      Office Equipment

We will use unusually small numbers to simplify the calculations and to emphasize the theory.

2010
Jan.
  4 Rolo Kern invested $1,200 cash and $100 worth of office equipment to open Rolo Co.
  4 Paid rent for three months in advance, $300.
  5 Purchased office equipment on account, $50.
  6 Bought office supplies for cash, $40.
  8 Collected $400 for services rendered.
 12 Rolo paid his home electric bill from the company bank account, $20.
 14 Provided $100 worth of services to clients who will not pay until next month.
 15 Paid salaries, $60.
 18 Advertising bill for $70 was received but will not be paid until next month.

Adjustment Data on January 31

a. Supplies on Hand, $6
b. Rent Expired, $100
c. Amortization, Office Equipment, $20
d. Salaries Accrued, $50

Journalizing Transactions and Posting
to Ledger, Rolo Company

	Date		Account Titles and Description	PR	Dr.	Cr.
	2010 Jan.	4	Cash	111	1 2 0 0 00	
			Office Equipment	121	1 0 0 00	
			R. Kern, Capital	311		1 3 0 0 00
			Initial investment			
		4	Prepaid Rent	114	3 0 0 00	
			Cash	111		3 0 0 00
			Rent paid in advance—3 months			
		5	Office Equipment	121	5 0 00	
			Accounts Payable	211		5 0 00
			Purchased equipment on account			
		6	Office Supplies	115	4 0 00	
			Cash	111		4 0 00
			Supplies purchased for cash			
		8	Cash	111	4 0 0 00	
			Fees Earned	411		4 0 0 00
			Services rendered			
		12	R. Kern, Withdrawals	312	2 0 00	
			Cash	111		2 0 00
			Personal payment of a bill			
		14	Accounts Receivable	112	1 0 0 00	
			Fees Earned	411		1 0 0 00
			Services rendered on account			
		15	Salaries Expense	511	6 0 00	
			Cash	111		6 0 00
			Paid salaries			
		18	Advertising Expense	512	7 0 00	
			Accounts Payable	211		7 0 00
			Advertising bill, but not paid			

General Journal — Page 1

Solution Tips to Journalizing and Posting Transactions

Jan. 4	Cash	Asset	↑	Dr.	$1,200
	Office Equipment	Asset	↑	Dr.	$ 100
	R. Kern, Capital	Capital	↑	Cr.	$1,300

Jan. 4	Prepaid Rent	Asset	↑	Dr.	$ 300
	Cash	Asset	↓	Cr.	$ 300

| Jan. 5 | Office Equipment | Asset | ↑ | Dr. | $ 50 |
| | Accounts Payable | Liability | ↑ | Cr. | $ 50 |

| Jan. 6 | Office Supplies | Asset | ↑ | Dr. | $ 40 |
| | Cash | Asset | ↓ | Cr. | $ 40 |

| Jan. 8 | Cash | Asset | ↑ | Dr. | $ 400 |
| | Fees Earned | Revenue | ↑ | Cr. | $ 400 |

| Jan. 12 | R. Kern, Withdrawals | Owner's Equity (Withdr.) | ↑ | Dr. | $ 20 |
| | Cash | Asset | ↓ | Cr. | $ 20 |

| Jan. 14 | Accounts Receivable | Asset | ↑ | Dr. | $ 100 |
| | Fees Earned | Revenue | ↑ | Cr. | $ 100 |

| Jan.15 | Salaries Expense | Expense | ↑ | Dr. | $ 60 |
| | Cash | Asset | ↓ | Cr. | $ 60 |

| Jan. 18 | Advertising Expense | Expense | ↑ | Dr. | $ 70 |
| | Accounts Payable | Liability | ↑ | Cr. | $ 70 |

Note: All account titles come from the chart of accounts. When journalizing, the PR column of the general journal is blank. It is in the posting process that we update the ledger. The Post. Ref. columns in the ledger accounts tell us from which journal page the information came. After posting to the account in the ledger, we fill in the PR column of the journal, which tells us to what account number the information was transferred.

COMPLETING THE WORKSHEET

See the worksheet on page 190.

Solution Tips to the Trial Balance and Completion of the Worksheet

After the posting process from the journal to the ledger is complete, we take the ending balance in each account and prepare a trial balance on the worksheet. If an account title has no balance, it is not listed on the trial balance. New titles on the worksheet will be added below the trial balance as needed.

ROLO COMPANY
WORKSHEET
FOR MONTH ENDED JANUARY 31, 2010

Account Titles	Trial Balance Dr.	Trial Balance Cr.	Adjustments Dr.	Adjustments Cr.	Adjusted Trial Balance Dr.	Adjusted Trial Balance Cr.	Income Statement Dr.	Income Statement Cr.	Balance Sheet Dr.	Balance Sheet Cr.
Cash	118000				118000				118000	
Accounts Receivable	10000				10000				10000	
Prepaid Rent	30000			(B) 10000	20000				20000	
Office Supplies	4000			(A) 3400	600				600	
Office Equipment	15000				15000				15000	
Accounts Payable		12000				12000				12000
R. Kern, Capital		130000				130000				130000
R. Kern, Withdrawals	2000				2000				2000	
Fees Earned		50000				50000		50000		
Salaries Expense	6000		(D) 5000		11000		11000			
Advertising Expense	7000				7000		7000			
	192000	192000								
Office Supplies Expense			(A) 3400		3400		3400			
Rent Expense			(B) 10000		10000		10000			
Amort. Expense, Office Equip.			(C) 2000		2000		2000			
Accum. Amort., Office Equip.				(C) 2000		2000				2000
Salaries Payable				(D) 5000		5000				5000
			20400	20400	199000	199000	33400	50000	165600	149000
Net Income							16600			16600
							50000	50000	165600	165600

The amount of office supplies on hand ($6) is *not* the adjustment. The amount used up needs to be calculated.	**Office Supplies Expense** **Office Supplies**	Expense Asset	↑ ↓	Dr. Cr.	$ 34 $ 34	($40 − $6)

Expired	**Rent Expense** **Prepaid Rent**	Expense Asset	↑ ↓	Dr. Cr.	$100 $100	

Do not touch original cost of equipment.	**Amort. Exp., Office Equip.** **Accum. Amort., Office Equip.**	Expense Asset (Contra)	↑ ↓	Dr. Cr.	$ 20 $ 20	

Owed but not paid	**Salaries Expense** **Salaries Payable**	Expense Liability	↑ ↑	Dr. Cr.	$ 50 $ 50	

Note: This information is on the worksheet but has *not* been updated in the ledger. (This will happen when we journalize and post adjustments at the end of cycle.)

Note that the last four columns of the worksheet come from numbers on the adjusted trial balance.

We move Net Income of $166 to the balance sheet credit column since the capital figure is the old one on the worksheet.

PREPARING THE FORMAL FINANCIAL STATEMENTS

ROLO COMPANY INCOME STATEMENT FOR MONTH ENDED JANUARY 31, 2010		
Revenue:		
Fees Earned		$ 5 0 0 00
Operating Expenses:		
Salaries Expense	$ 1 1 0 00	
Advertising Expense	7 0 00	
Office Supplies Expense	3 4 00	
Rent Expense	1 0 0 00	
Amortization Expense, Office Equipment	2 0 00	
Total Operating Expenses		3 3 4 00
Net Income		$ 1 6 6 00

ROLO COMPANY STATEMENT OF OWNER'S EQUITY FOR MONTH ENDED JANUARY 31, 2010		
R. Kern, Capital, January 1, 2010		$ 1 3 0 0 00
Net Income for January	$ 1 6 6 00	
Less: Withdrawals for January	2 0 00	
Increase in Capital		1 4 6 00
R. Kern, Capital, January 31, 2010		$ 1 4 4 6 00

ROLO COMPANY
BALANCE SHEET
JANUARY 31, 2010

Assets			Liabilities and Owner's Equity		
Cash		$1 1 8 0 00	Liabilities:		
Accounts Receivable		1 0 0 00	Accounts Payable	$1 2 0 00	
Prepaid Rent		2 0 0 00	Salaries Payable	5 0 00	
Office Supplies		6 00	Total Liabilities		$ 1 7 0 00
Office Equipment	$1 5 0 00		Owner's Equity:		
Less: Acc. Amort.	2 0 00	1 3 0 00	R. Kern, Capital		1 4 4 6 00
			Total Liabilities and		
Total Assets		$1 6 1 6 00	Owner's Equity		$1 6 1 6 00

Solution Tips to Preparing the Financial Statements

The statements are prepared from the worksheet. (Many of the ledger accounts are not up to date.) The income statement lists revenue and expenses. The net income figure of $166 is used to update the statement of owner's equity. The statement of owner's equity calculates a new figure for Capital, $1,446 (Beginning Capital + Net Income – Withdrawals). This new figure is then listed on the balance sheet (Assets, Liabilities, and a new figure for Capital).

JOURNALIZING AND POSTING ADJUSTING AND CLOSING ENTRIES

See the journal at the top of page 193.

Solution Tips to Journalizing and Posting Adjusting and Closing Entries

ADJUSTMENTS

The adjustments from the worksheet are journalized (same journal) and posted to the ledger. Now ledger accounts will be brought up to date. Remember, we have already prepared the financial reports from the worksheet. Our goal now is to get the ledger up to date.

CLOSING

Note: Income Summary is a temporary account located in the ledger.

Goals

Where do I get my information for closing?

1. Adjust all temporary accounts in the ledger to zero balances.
2. Determine a new figure for capital in the ledger.

General Journal					Page 2	
Date		Account Titles and Description	PR	Dr.	Cr.	
		Adjusting Entries				
Jan.	31	Office Supplies Expense	514	3 4 00		
		Office Supplies	115		3 4 00	
		Supplies used				
	31	Rent Expense	513	1 0 0 00		
		Prepaid Rent	114		1 0 0 00	
		Rent expired				
	31	Amortization Expense, Office Equipment	515	2 0 00		
		Accumulated Amortization, Office Equip.	122		2 0 00	
		Estimated Amortization				
	31	Salaries Expense	511	5 0 00		
		Salaries Payable	212		5 0 00	
		Accrued salaries				
		Closing Entries				
Step 1 →	31	Fees Earned	411	5 0 0 00		
		Income Summary	313		5 0 0 00	
		To close income accounts				
Step 2 →	31	Income Summary	313	3 3 4 00		
		Salaries Expense	511		1 1 0 00	
		Advertising Expense	512		7 0 00	
		Office Supplies Expense	514		3 4 00	
		Rent Expense	513		1 0 0 00	
		Amortization Expense, Office Equipment	515		2 0 00	
		To close expense accounts				
Step 3 →	31	Income Summary	313	1 6 6 00		
		R. Kern, Capital	311		1 6 6 00	
		Transfer profit to Capital				
Step 4 →	31	R. Kern, Capital	311	2 0 00		
		R. Kern, Withdrawals	312		2 0 00	
		Transfer withdrawals to Capital				

(Closing brackets span Step 1 through Step 4, labeled **Closing**)

Steps in the Closing Process

Step 1: Close revenue to Income Summary.

Step 2: Close individual expenses to Income Summary.

Step 3: Close balance of Income Summary to Capital. (This really is the net income figure on the worksheet.)

Step 4: Close balance of Withdrawals to Capital.

All the journal closing entries are posted. (No new calculations are needed since all figures are on the worksheet.) The result in the ledger is that all temporary accounts have a zero balance.

Cash   Acct. No. 111

Date 2010		Explanation	Post. Ref.	Debit	Credit	DR or CR	Balance
Jan.	4		GJ1	1200 00		DR.	1200 00
	4		GJ1		300 00	DR.	900 00
	6		GJ1		40 00	DR.	860 00
	8		GJ1	400 00		DR.	1260 00
	12		GJ1		20 00	DR.	1240 00
	15		GJ1		60 00	DR.	1180 00

Accounts Receivable   Acct. No. 112

Date 2010		Explanation	Post. Ref.	Debit	Credit	DR or CR	Balance
Jan.	14		GJ1	100 00		DR.	100 00

Prepaid Rent   Acct. No. 114

Date 2010		Explanation	Post. Ref.	Debit	Credit	DR or CR	Balance
Jan.	4		GJ1	300 00		DR.	300 00
	31	Adjustment	GJ2		100 00	DR.	200 00

Office Supplies   Acct. No. 115

Date 2010		Explanation	Post. Ref.	Debit	Credit	DR or CR	Balance
Jan.	6		GJ1	40 00		DR.	40 00
	31	Adjustment	GJ2		34 00	DR.	6 00

Office Equipment   Acct. No. 121

Date 2010		Explanation	Post. Ref.	Debit	Credit	DR or CR	Balance
Jan.	4		GJ1	100 00		DR.	100 00
	5		GJ1	50 00		DR.	150 00

Accumulated Amortization, Office Equipment   Acct. No. 122

Date 2010		Explanation	Post. Ref.	Debit	Credit	DR or CR	Balance
Jan.	31	Adjustment	GJ2		20 00	CR.	20 00

Accounts Payable   Acct. No. 211

Date 2010		Explanation	Post. Ref.	Debit	Credit	DR or CR	Balance
Jan.	5		GJ1		50 00	CR.	50 00
	18		GJ1		70 00	CR.	120 00

Salaries Payable   Acct. No. 212

Date 2010		Explanation	Post. Ref.	Debit	Credit	DR or CR	Balance
Jan.	31	Adjustment	GJ2		50 00	CR.	50 00

R. Kern, Capital   Acct. No. 311

Date 2010		Explanation	Post. Ref.	Debit	Credit	DR or CR	Balance
Jan.	4		GJ1		1300 00	CR.	1300 00
	31	Closing	GJ2		166 00	CR.	1466 00
	31	Closing	GJ2	20 00		CR.	1446 00

R. Kern, Withdrawals   Acct. No. 312

Date 2010		Explanation	Post. Ref.	Debit	Credit	DR or CR	Balance
Jan.	12		GJ1	20 00		DR.	20 00
	31	Closing	GJ2		20 00		-0-

Income Summary   Acct. No. 313

Date 2010		Explanation	Post. Ref.	Debit	Credit	DR or CR	Balance
Jan.	31	Closing	GJ2		500 00	CR.	500 00
	31	Closing	GJ2	334 00		CR.	166 00
	31	Closing	GJ2	166 00			-0-

Fees Earned   Acct. No. 411

Date 2010		Explanation	Post. Ref.	Debit	Credit	DR. CR.	Balance
Jan.	8		GJ1		400 00	CR.	400 00
	14		GJ1		100 00	CR.	500 00
	31	Closing	GJ2	500 00			-0-

Salaries Expense   Acct. No. 511

Date 2010		Explanation	Post. Ref.	Debit	Credit	DR. CR.	Balance
Jan.	15		GJ1	60 00		DR.	60 00
	31	Adjusting	GJ2	50 00		DR.	110 00
	31	Closing	GJ2		110 00		-0-

Advertising Expense   Acct. No. 512

Date 2010		Explanation	Post. Ref.	Debit	Credit	DR. CR.	Balance
Jan.	18		GJ1	70 00		DR.	70 00
	31	Closing	GJ2		70 00		-0-

Rent Expense   Acct. No. 513

Date 2010		Explanation	Post. Ref.	Debit	Credit	DR. CR.	Balance
Jan.	31	Adjusting	GJ2	100 00		DR.	100 00
	31	Closing	GJ2		100 00		-0-

Office Supplies Expense   Acct. No. 514

Date 2010		Explanation	Post. Ref.	Debit	Credit	DR. CR.	Balance
Jan.	31	Adjusting	GJ2	34 00		DR.	34 00
	31	Closing	GJ2		34 00		-0-

Amortization Expense, Office Equipment   Acct. No. 515

Date 2010		Explanation	Post. Ref.	Debit	Credit	DR. CR.	Balance
Jan.	31	Adjusting	GJ2	20 00		DR.	20 00
	31	Closing	GJ2		20 00		-0-

ROLO CO. POST-CLOSING TRIAL BALANCE JANUARY 31, 2010	Dr.	Cr.
Cash	1 1 8 0 00	
Accounts Receivable	1 0 0 00	
Prepaid Rent	2 0 0 00	
Office Supplies	6 00	
Office Equipment	1 5 0 00	
Accumulated Amortization, Office Equipment		2 0 00
Accounts Payable		1 2 0 00
Salaries Payable		5 0 00
R. Kern, Capital		1 4 4 6 00
Total	1 6 3 6 00	1 6 3 6 00

Solution Tips for the Post-Closing Trial Balance

The post-closing trial balance is a list of the ledger balances *after* adjusting and closing entries have been completed. Note the figure for capital $1,446 is the new figure.

Beginning Capital	$1,300
+ Net Income	166
− Withdrawals	20
= Ending Capital	$1,446

Next accounting period, we will enter new amounts in the Revenues, Expenses, and Withdrawals accounts. For now, the post-closing trial balance is made up only of permanent accounts.

SUMMARY OF KEY POINTS

Learning Unit 5-1

1. After formal financial reports have been prepared, the ledger still has not been brought up to date.

2. Information for journalizing adjusting entries comes from the adjustments section of the worksheet.

Learning Unit 5-2

1. Closing is a mechanical process that is completed before the accountant can record transactions for the next fiscal year.

2. Assets, Liabilities, and Capital are permanent (real) accounts; their balances are carried over from one fiscal year to another. Withdrawals, Revenue, and Expenses are nominal (temporary) accounts; their balances are *not* carried over from one fiscal year to another.

3. Income Summary is a temporary account in the general ledger and does not have a normal balance. It will summarize revenue and expenses and transfer the balance to capital. Withdrawals do not go into Income Summary because they are *not* business expenses.

4. All information for closing can be obtained from the worksheet.

5. When closing is complete, all temporary accounts in the ledger will have a zero balance, and all this information will be updated in the Capital account.

6. Closing entries are usually done only at year-end. Interim reports can be prepared from worksheets that are prepared monthly, quarterly, et cetera.

Learning Unit 5-3

1. The post-closing trial balance is prepared from the ledger accounts after the adjusting and closing entries have been posted.

2. The accounts on the post-closing trial balance are all permanent accounts.

KEY TERMS

Adjusting journal entries Journal entries that are needed in order to update specific ledger accounts to reflect correct balances at the end of an accounting period (p. 169)

Closing The process of bringing the balances of all revenue, expense, and withdrawal accounts to zero, ready for a new fiscal year (p. 173)

Closing journal entries Journal entries that are prepared to (a) reduce or clear all temporary accounts to a zero balance and (b) update capital to a new closing balance (p. 173)

Income Summary A temporary account in the ledger that summarizes revenue and expenses and transfers its balance (net income or net loss) to capital. It does not have a normal balance. (p. 174)

Nominal accounts See Temporary accounts (p. 173)

Permanent accounts Balances of accounts that are carried over to the next fiscal year; examples: assets, liabilities, capital (p. 173)

Post-closing trial balance The final step in the accounting cycle that lists only permanent accounts in the ledger and their balances after adjusting and closing entries have been posted (p. 183)

Real accounts See Permanent accounts (p. 173)

Temporary accounts Balances of accounts at the end of a fiscal year that are not carried over to the next fiscal year. These accounts—Revenue, Expenses, Withdrawals—help to provide a new or ending figure for capital to begin the next fiscal year. Keep in mind that Income Summary is also a temporary account. (p. 173)

BLUEPRINT OF THE CLOSING PROCESS
FROM THE WORKSHEET

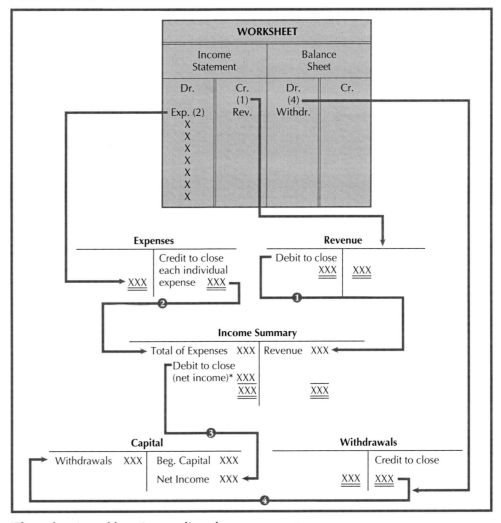

*If a net loss, it would require a credit to close.

The Closing Steps

1. Close revenue balances to Income Summary.
2. Close each *individual* expense and transfer the *total* of all expenses to Income Summary.
3. Transfer the balance in Income Summary (Net Income or Net Loss) to Capital.
4. Close Withdrawals to Capital.

QUESTIONS, CLASSROOM DEMONSTRATION EXERCISES, EXERCISES, AND PROBLEMS

Discussion Questions and Critical Thinking/Ethical Case

1. When a worksheet is completed, what balances are found in the general ledger?

2. Why must adjusting entries be journalized even though the formal reports have already been prepared?

3. "Closing slows down the recording of next year's transactions." Defend or reject this statement with supporting evidence.

4. What is the difference between temporary and permanent accounts?

5. What are the two major goals of the closing process?

6. List the four steps in closing.

7. What is the purpose of Income Summary and where is it located?

8. How can a worksheet aid the closing process?

9. What accounts are usually listed on a post-closing trial balance?

10. Closing entries are always prepared once a month. Agree or disagree. Why?

11. Todd Silver is the purchasing agent for Moore Company. One of his suppliers, Gem Company, offers Todd a free vacation to France if he buys at least 75 percent of Moore's supplies from Gem Company. Todd, who is angry because Moore Company has not given him a raise in over a year, is considering the offer. Write out your recommendation to Todd.

Classroom Demonstration Exercises

(The blank forms you need are on pages 5-11 and 5-12 of the *Study Guide with Working Papers.*)

Set A

Journalizing and Posting Adjusting Entries

1. Enter the beginning balances in the *Study Guide with Working Papers.* Post the following adjusting entries (be sure to cross-reference back to the journal) that came from the Adjustment columns of the worksheet.

General Journal						Page 3	
Date		Account Titles and Description	PR	Dr.		Cr.	
Dec.	31	Insurance Expense		6 00			
		Prepaid Insurance				6 00	
		Insurance expired					
	31	Supplies Expense		4 00			
		Store Supplies				4 00	
		Supplies used					
	31	Amortization Expense, Store Equipment		9 00			
		Accum. Amortization, Store Equipment				9 00	
		Estimated amortization					
	31	Salaries Expense		5 00			
		Salaries Payable				5 00	
		Accrued salaries					

LEDGER ACCOUNTS BEFORE ADJUSTING ENTRIES POSTED

Prepaid Insurance 115		Insurance Expense 510	
18			

Store Supplies 116		Amortization Expense, Store Equipment 512	
17			

Accumulated Amortization, Store Equipment 119		Supplies Expense 514	
	13		

Salaries Payable 210		Salaries Expense 516	
		9	

Closing Steps and Journalizing Closing Entries

2. Explain the four steps of the closing process given the following: Dec. 31 ending balances, before closing:

Fees Earned	$200
Rent Expense	100
Advertising Expense	60
J. Rice, Capital	3,000
J. Rice, Withdrawals	15

Journalizing Closing Entries

3. From the following accounts, journalize the closing entries (assume that December 31 is the closing date).

Mel Blanc, Capital 310		Gas Expense 510	
	40	8	

Mel Blanc, Withdrawals 312		Advertising Expense 512	
7		12	

Income Summary 314		Amortization Expense, Taxi 516	
		8	

Taxi Fare Income 410			
	39		

Posting to Income Summary

4. Draw a T account of Income Summary and post to it all entries from question 3 that affect it. Is Income Summary a temporary or permanent account?

Posting to Capital

5. Draw a T account for Mel Blanc, Capital, and post to it all entries from question 3 that affect it. What is the final balance of the capital account?

Set B

Journalizing and Posting Adjusting Entries

1. Enter the beginning balances in the *Study Guide with Working Papers*. Post the following adjusting entries (be sure to cross-reference back to the journal) that came from the Adjustment columns of the worksheet.

	Date		Account Titles and Description	PR	Dr.	Cr.
			General Journal			Page 3
	Dec.	31	Insurance Expense		4 00	
			Prepaid Insurance			4 00
			Insurance expired			
		31	Supplies Expense		3 00	
			Store Supplies			3 00
			Supplies used			
		31	Amortization Expense, Store Equipment		7 00	
			Accum. Amortization, Store Equipment			7 00
			Estimated amortization			
		31	Salaries Expense		4 00	
			Salaries Payable			4 00
			Accrued salaries			

LEDGER ACCOUNTS BEFORE ADJUSTING ENTRIES POSTED

Prepaid Insurance 115		Insurance Expense 510	
12			

Store Supplies 116		Amortization Expense, Store Equipment 512	
15			

Accumulated Amortization, Store Equipment 119		Supplies Expense 514	
	12		

Salaries Payable 210		Salaries Expense 516	
		7	

Closing Steps and Journalizing Closing Entries

2.

		Worksheet		
	IS		BS	
Dr. (2)	Cr. Revenue (1)	Dr. Withdrawals	Cr. (4)	
E X P E N S E S				
NI (3)				

Goals of Closing

1. Temporary accounts in the ledger should have a zero balance.
2. New figure for capital is determined in closing.

Note: All closing can be done from the worksheet. Income Summary is a temporary account in the ledger.

From the above worksheet, explain the four steps of closing. Keep in mind that each *individual* expense normally would be listed in the closing process.

Journalizing Closing Entries

3. From the following accounts, journalize the closing entries (assume that December 31 is the closing date).

Mel Blanc, Capital 310	Gas Expense 510
30	5

Mel Blanc, Withdrawals 312	Advertising Expense 512
6	4

Income Summary 314	Amortization Expense, Taxi 516
	6

Taxi Fare Income 410	
18	

Posting to Income Summary

4. Draw a T account of Income Summary and post to it all entries from question 3 that affect it. Is Income Summary a temporary or permanent account?

Posting to Capital

5. Draw a T account for Mel Blanc, Capital, and post to it all entries from question 3 that affect it. What is the final balance of the capital account?

(The blank forms you need are on pages 5-13 and 5-14 of the *Study Guide with Working Papers.*)

Journalizing adjusting entries

5-1. From the adjustments section of a worksheet presented here, prepare adjusting journal entries for the end of December.

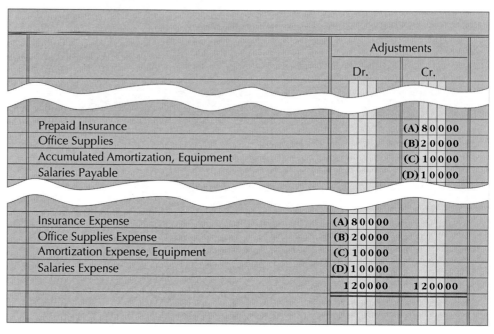

	Adjustments	
	Dr.	Cr.
Prepaid Insurance		(A) 8 0 0 00
Office Supplies		(B) 2 0 0 00
Accumulated Amortization, Equipment		(C) 1 0 0 00
Salaries Payable		(D) 1 0 0 00
Insurance Expense	(A) 8 0 0 00	
Office Supplies Expense	(B) 2 0 0 00	
Amortization Expense, Equipment	(C) 1 0 0 00	
Salaries Expense	(D) 1 0 0 00	
	1 2 0 0 00	1 2 0 0 00

Temporary versus permanent accounts

5-2. Complete this table by placing an X in the correct column for each item.

	Temporary	Permanent	Will Be Closed
Example: **Accounts Receivable**		X	
1. Income Summary			
2. Jen Rich, Capital			
3. Salary Expense			
4. Jen Rich, Withdrawals			
5. Fees Earned			
6. Accounts Payable			
7. Cash			

Closing entries

5-3. From the following T accounts, journalize the four closing entries on December 31, 2009.

J. King, Capital	
	14,000

Rent Expense	
5,000	

J. King, Withdrawals	
4,000	

Wages Expense	
7,000	

Income Summary	

Insurance Expense	
1,200	

Fees Earned	
	33,000

Amortization Expense, Office Equipment	
900	

5-4. From the following posted T accounts, reconstruct the closing journal entries for December 31, 2011.

M. Foster, Capital	
Withdrawals 100	2,000 (Dec. 1)
	Net Income 700

Insurance Expense	
50	Closing 50

M. Foster, Withdrawals	
100	Closing 100

Wages Expense	
100	Closing 100

Income Summary	
Expenses 600	Revenue 1,300
700	

Rent Expense	
200	Closing 200

Salon Fees	
Closing 1,300	1,300

Amortization Expense, Equipment	
250	Closing 250

5-5. From the following accounts (not in order), prepare a post-closing trial balance for Wey Co. on December 31, 2012. *Note:* These balances are *before* closing.

Accounts Receivable	18,875	P. Wey, Capital	63,450
Legal Library	14,250	P. Wey, Withdrawals	1,500
Office Equipment	59,700	Legal Fees Earned	12,000
Repair Expense	2,850	Accounts Payable	45,000
Salaries Expense	1,275	Cash	22,000

Group A Problems

(The blank forms you need are on pages 5-15 to 5-30 of the *Study Guide with Working Papers*.)

5A-1. The following data are given for Gerhard's Accounting Service of Vernon:

GERHARD'S ACCOUNTING SERVICE
TRIAL BALANCE
JUNE 30, 2011

	Dr.	Cr.
Cash	3 0 00 00	
Accounts Receivable	6 5 0 00	
Prepaid Insurance	4 0 0 00	
Supplies	1 5 0 00	
Equipment	3 0 0 00	
Accumulated Amortization, Equipment		1 9 0 0 00
Accounts Payable		1 1 0 0 00
Gerhard Franks, Capital		12 8 0 0 00
Gerhard Franks, Withdrawals	3 0 0 00	
Accounting Fees Earned		1 9 0 0 00
Salaries Expense	1 4 0 0 00	
Telephone Expense	1 0 0 0 00	
Advertising Expense	6 0 0 00	
	44 7 0 0 00	44 7 0 0 00

Adjustment Data

a. Insurance expired, $200

b. Supplies on hand, $600

c. Amortization on equipment, $200

d. Salaries earned by employees but not to be paid until July, $300

Required

1. Prepare a worksheet.
2. Journalize adjusting and closing entries.

5A-2. As the bookkeeper for Potter Cleaning Service, (1) from the trial balance columns of the worksheet on page 205, enter the beginning balance of each account in your working papers, (2) journalize and post adjusting entries, (3) journalize and post closing entries, and (4) from the ledger (after all posting is complete), prepare a post-closing trial balance at March 31, 2010.

5A-3. As the bookkeeper of Pete's Plowing of Fredericton, you have been asked to complete the entire accounting cycle for Pete from the following information:

2009

Jan.	2	Pete invested $7,000 cash and $6,000 worth of snow equipment in the plowing company.
	2	Paid rent in advance for garage space, $2,000.
	5	Purchased office equipment on account from Ling Corp., $7,200.
	6	Purchased snow supplies for $700 cash.
	9	Collected $15,000 from plowing local shopping centres.
	12	Pete Mack withdrew $1,000 from the business for personal use.
	20	Plowed North East Co. parking lots, payment not to be received until March, $5,000.
	26	Paid salaries to employees, $1,800.
	27	Paid Ling Corp. one-half amount owed for office equipment.
	29	Advertising bill was received from Bush Co. but will not be paid until March, $900.
	30	Paid telephone bill, $210.

Adjustment Data

a. Snow supplies on hand, $400

b. Rent expired, $600

c. Amortization on office equipment, $120
$$(\$7,200 \div 5 \text{ yr.} \rightarrow \frac{\$1,440}{12 \text{ mo.}} = \$120)$$

d. Amortization on snow equipment, $100 $(\$6,000 \div 5 \text{ yr.} \rightarrow \frac{\$1,200}{12 \text{ mo.}} = \$100)$

e. Accrued salaries, $190

Journalizing and posting adjusting and closing entries and preparing a post-closing trial balance

Check Figure (5A-2)

Post-Closing Trial Balance $3,504

Comprehensive review of the entire accounting cycle, Chapters 1–5

Check Figure

Net Income $15,780

POTTER CLEANING SERVICE
WORKSHEET
FOR MONTH ENDED MARCH 31, 2010

Account Titles	Trial Balance Dr.	Trial Balance Cr.	Adjustments Dr.	Adjustments Cr.	Adjusted Trial Balance Dr.	Adjusted Trial Balance Cr.	Income Statement Dr.	Income Statement Cr.	Balance Sheet Dr.	Balance Sheet Cr.
Cash	40000				40000				40000	
Prepaid Insurance	52000			(A) 18000	34000				34000	
Cleaning Supplies	14400			(B) 10000	4400				4400	
Auto	272000				272000				272000	
Accum. Amortization, Auto		86000		(C) 15000		101000				101000
Accounts Payable		22400				22400				22400
B. Potter, Capital		54000				54000				54000
B. Potter, Withdrawals	46000				46000				46000	
Cleaning Fees		468000				468000		468000		
Salaries Expense	144000		(D) 16000		160000		160000			
Telephone Expense	26400				26400		26400			
Advertising Expense	19600				19600		19600			
Gas Expense	16000				16000		16000			
	630400	630400								
Insurance Expense			(A) 18000		18000		18000			
Cleaning Supplies Expense			(B) 10000		10000		10000			
Amortization Expense, Auto			(C) 15000		15000		15000			
Salaries Payable				(D) 16000		16000				16000
			59000	59000	661400	661400	265000	468000	396400	193400
Net Income							203000			203000
							468000	468000	396400	396400

Chart of Accounts

Assets
111 Cash
112 Accounts Receivable
114 Prepaid Rent
115 Snow Supplies
121 Office Equipment
122 Accumulated Amortization,
     Office Equipment
123 Snow Equipment
124 Accumulated Amortization,
     Snow Equipment

Liabilities
211 Accounts Payable
212 Salaries Payable

Owner's Equity
311 Pete Mack, Capital
312 Pete Mack, Withdrawals
313 Income Summary

Revenue
411 Plowing Fees

Expenses
511 Salaries Expense
512 Advertising Expense
513 Telephone Expense
514 Rent Expense
515 Snow Supplies Expense
516 Amortization Expense,
     Office Equipment
517 Amortization Expense,
     Snow Equipment

Group B Problems

(The blank forms you need are on pages 5-15 to 5-30 of the *Study Guide with Working Papers.*)

Review of preparing a worksheet and journalizing and closing entries

5B-1.

To:	Matt Kamimsk
From:	Abbey Ellen
Re:	Accounting Needs

Please prepare ASAP from the following information (attached), (1) a worksheet along with (2) journalized adjusting and closing entries.

Check Figure

Net Income $3,530

GERHARD'S ACCOUNTING SERVICE
TRIAL BALANCE
JUNE 30, 2011

	Dr.	Cr.
Cash	10 15 0 00	
Accounts Receivable	5 0 0 0 00	
Prepaid Insurance	7 0 0 00	
Supplies	3 0 0 00	
Equipment	12 9 5 0 00	
Accumulated Amortization, Equipment		4 0 0 0 00
Accounts Payable		5 7 5 0 00
Gerhard Franks, Capital		15 1 5 0 00
Gerhard Franks, Withdrawals	4 0 0 00	
Accounting Fees Earned		5 2 0 0 00
Salaries Expense	4 5 0 00	
Telephone Expense	7 0 00	
Advertising Expense	8 0 00	
	30 1 0 0 00	30 1 0 0 00

CONTINUING PROBLEM

Tony has decided to end the Precision Computer Centre's first year as of September 30, 2010. Below is an updated chart of accounts.

Assets
1000 Cash
1020 Accounts Receivable
1025 Prepaid Rent
1030 Supplies
1080 Computer Shop Equipment
1081 Accumulated Amortization, Computer Shop Equipment
1090 Office Equipment
1091 Accumulated Amortization, Office Equipment

Liabilities
2000 Accounts Payable

Owner's Equity
3000 T. Freedman, Capital
3010 T. Freedman, Withdrawals
3020 Income Summary

Revenue
4000 Service Revenue

Expenses
5010 Advertising Expense
5020 Rent Expense
5030 Utilities Expense
5040 Phone Expense
5050 Supplies Expense
5060 Insurance Expense
5070 Postage Expense
5080 Amortization Expense, Computer Shop Equipment
5090 Amortization Expense, Office Equipment

Assignment

(See pages 5-49 to 5-54 in your *Study Guide with Working Papers*.)

1. Journalize the adjusting entries from Chapter 4.
2. Post the adjusting entries to the ledger.
3. Journalize the closing entries.
4. Post the closing entries to the ledger.
5. Prepare a post-closing trial balance.

Sullivan Realty
Reviewing the Accounting Cycle Twice

This comprehensive review problem requires you to complete the accounting cycle for Sullivan Realty twice. This will allow you to review Chapters 1 to 5 while reinforcing the relationships among all parts of the accounting cycle. By completing two cycles, you will see how the ending June balances in the ledger are used to accumulate data in July. (The blank forms you need are on pages 5-58 to 5-74 of the *Study Guide with Working Papers*.)

On June 1, John Sullivan opened a real estate office in Hamilton called Sullivan Realty. The following transactions were completed for the month of June. Note that facsimile documents have been provided to illustrate these events:

2010

#1, p. ~~214~~ 192 → June 1 John Sullivan invested $17,000 cash in the real estate agency along with $3,000 worth of office equipment.

#2, p. ~~214~~ 192 →   1 Rented office space and paid three months' rent in advance, $2,100, cheque No. 601.

Sullivan Realty
Chart of Accounts

Assets
111   Cash
112   Accounts Receivable
114   Prepaid Rent
115   Office Supplies
121   Office Equipment
122   Accumulated Amortization, Office Equipment
123   Automobile
124   Accumulated Amortization, Automobile

Liabilities
211   Accounts Payable
212   Salaries Payable

Owner's Equity
311   John Sullivan, Capital
312   John Sullivan, Withdrawals
313   Income Summary

Revenue
411   Commissions Earned

Expenses
511   Rent Expense
512   Salaries Expense
513   Gas Expense
514   Repairs Expense
515   Telephone Expense
516   Advertising Expense
517   Office Supplies Expense
518   Amortization Expense, Office Equipment
519   Amortization Expense, Automobile
524   Miscellaneous Expense

1.

CURRENT ACCOUNT
DEPOSIT SLIP

ROYAL BANK

June 1, 2010
DATE

DEPOSITOR'S INITIALS	TELLER'S INITIALS
JS	PRL

CREDIT ACCOUNT OF

SULLIVAN REALTY

PLEASE LIST FOREIGN CHEQUES ON A SEPARATE DEPOSIT SLIP

VISA AND CHEQUES		DETAILS	CASH (INCL COUPONS)
	VISA VOUCHER TOTAL		
Sullivan	17,000.00	X 5	
		X 10	
		X 20	
		X 50	
		X 100	
		X	
		COIN	
		CANADIAN CASH TOTAL	
	17,000.00	VISA & CHQS	17,000.00
U.S. CHQS		RATE	
U.S. CASH		RATE	
	NET DEPOSIT		17,000.00

I: 05337 123'498'6   51

COMPARED WITH ORIGINAL DEPOSIT SLIP AS TO TOTAL ONLY

2.

SULLIVAN REALTY   601
485 KING STREET WEST
HAMILTON, ONTARIO L9H 6W3   June 1 20 10
PHONE (905) 527-1223

PAY TO   Hamilton One Property Management Co. $ 2,100.00
THE ORDER OF
~~~ Two thousand one hundred ~~~~~~~   00/100 DOLLARS

THE ROYAL BANK OF CANADA
MAIN BRANCH
204 KING STREET WEST   SULLIVAN REALTY
HAMILTON, ONTARIO L9H 4Z9

FOR   Rent – June-August 2010   PER   John Sullivan

II"000601 I: 05337   123'498'6

2010

#3a & b, p. 215 193 →	June 3	Bought a company automobile. Cheque No. 602, $12,000.
#4a & b, pp. 215 & 216 →	4	Purchased office supplies. Wrote cheque No. 603, $300.
#5, p. 216 →	4	Purchased additional office supplies on account, $150.
#6a & b, pp. 216 & 217 →	7	Sold a house and collected a $6,000 commission.
#7, p. 217 →	8	Paid gas bill for car, $22. Cheque No. 604.
#8, p. 217 →	15	Paid the salary of the part-time office secretary, $350. Cheque No. 605.
#9, p. 217 →	18	Sold a building lot and earned a commission, $6,500. Payment is to be received on July 9.
#10, p. 218 →	21	John Sullivan withdrew $1,000 from the business to pay personal expenses. Cheque No. 606.
#11a & b, p. 218 →	21	Sold a house and collected a $3,500 commission.
#12, p. 219 →	22	Paid gas bill for car. $25. Cheque No. 607.
#13a & b, p. 219 →	25	Paid $600 to repair automobile. Cheque No. 608.
#14, p. 220 →	30	Paid the salary of the part-time office secretary, $350. Cheque No. 609.
#15a & b, p. 220 →	30	Paid the June telephone bill, $510. Cheque No. 610.
#16, p. 221 →	30	Received advertising bill for June, $1,200. The bill is to be paid on July 5.

3a.

2674 King Street West
Hamilton, Ontario L9H 1A1
Phone (905) 527-9755; Fax (905) 527-9756

INVOICE

INVOICE NO. WEA1097

DATE: June 3/10

TERMS: Cash

To:
Sullivan Realty
485 King Street West
Hamilton, Ontario L9H 6W3

Ship To:

Pickup

QUANTITY	DESCRIPTION	UNIT PRICE	AMOUNT
1	ONLY 2008 Z75 4-Door Automatic	12,000.00	$ 12,000.00

Make all cheques payable to Auto City West	SUBTOTAL	12,000.00
	FREIGHT	
PAYMENT RECEIVED - Cheque #602 - Thank you	TAX	
	TOTAL DUE	$ 12,000.00

THANK YOU FOR YOUR BUSINESS!

3b.

SULLIVAN REALTY   602
485 KING STREET WEST
HAMILTON, ONTARIO L9H 6W3
PHONE (905) 527-1223   *June 3* 20 *10*

PAY TO   *Auto City West* $ 12,000.00
THE ORDER OF
~~~~ *Twelve thousand* ~~~~~~~~~~~   00 /100 DOLLARS

THE ROYAL BANK OF CANADA
MAIN BRANCH
204 KING STREET WEST   SULLIVAN REALTY
HAMILTON, ONTARIO L9H 4Z9

FOR *Automobile - Inv. WEA1097*   PER   *John Sullivan*

⑈000602 ⑆ ⑆05337   123⑆498⑆6

4a.

Office Depot   INVOICE

#53 Niagara Mall   **DATE:**   Jun 4/10
Hamilton, Ontario L9H 1B1   **NUMBER:** D198795
Phone (905) 527-1233, Fax (905) 527-1234   **TERMS:**   Cash

SOLD TO:	**SHIPPED TO:**
Sullivan Realty 485 King Street West Hamilton, Ontario L9H 6W3	Sullivan Realty 485 King Street West

DATE	DESCRIPTION	UNIT PRICE	AMOUNT
Jun 4/10	Office supplies PAYMENT RECEIVED - CHQ #603 - THANK YOU		$300.00
		Subtotal	300.00
		Total	$300.00

Business Number: 115555559

THANK YOU FOR YOUR BUSINESS

PLEASE PAY
THE ABOVE

4b.

SULLIVAN REALTY
485 KING STREET WEST
HAMILTON, ONTARIO L9H 6W3
PHONE (905) 527-1223

603

June 4 20 10

PAY TO THE ORDER OF Office Depot $ 300.00

~~~ Three hundred ~~~ 00 /100 DOLLARS

THE ROYAL BANK OF CANADA
MAIN BRANCH
204 KING STREET WEST
HAMILTON, ONTARIO L9H 4Z9

SULLIVAN REALTY

FOR Office supplies PER John Sullivan

⑈000603 ⑆ 05337 123'498'6

5.

Office Depot

INVOICE

#53 Niagara Mall
Hamilton, Ontario L9H 1B1
Phone (905) 527-1233, Fax (905) 527-1234

DATE: Jun 4/10
NUMBER: D198825
TERMS: net 30

SOLD TO:
Sullivan Realty
485 King Street West
Hamilton, Ontario L9H 6W3

SHIPPED TO:
Sullivan Realty
485 King Street West

DATE	DESCRIPTION	UNIT PRICE	AMOUNT
Jun 4/10	Office supplies		$150.00
		Subtotal	150.00
		Total	$150.00

Business Number: 115555559

PLEASE PAY THE ABOVE

THANK YOU FOR YOUR BUSINESS

6a.

CURRENT ACCOUNT DEPOSIT SLIP
ROYAL BANK

June 7, 2010
DATE

DEPOSITOR'S INITIALS	TELLER'S INITIALS
JS	MG

CREDIT ACCOUNT OF
SULLIVAN REALTY

PLEASE LIST FOREIGN CHEQUES ON A SEPARATE DEPOSIT SLIP

VISA AND CHEQUES		DETAILS	CASH (INCL COUPONS)
	VISA VOUCHER TOTAL		
H. Penchant	6,000 00	X 5	
		X 10	
		X 20	
		X 50	
		X 100	
		X	
		COIN	
		CANADIAN CASH TOTAL	
	6,000 00	VISA & CHQS	6,000 00
U.S. CHQS.		RATE	
U.S. CASH		RATE	
NET DEPOSIT			6,000 00

⑆ 05337 123'498'6 51

COMPARED WITH ORIGINAL DEPOSIT SLIP AS TO TOTAL ONLY
~~~

6b.

SULLIVAN REALTY				
COMMISSION REPORT			*Date*	June 7, 2010

Name:	Mr. and Mrs. Harold Penchant			
Date	*Sales Description*	*Sales No.*	*Commission Amount*	
Jun 7/10	*Home at 44 Brookhaven Crescent*	*A1001*	*$6,000.00*	*Paid in full.*
C001			*Remarks:*	

7.

S	**SULLIVAN REALTY** 485 KING STREET WEST HAMILTON, ONTARIO L9H 6W3 PHONE (905) 527-1223	604
		June 8 20 **10**

PAY TO THE ORDER OF _Anderson Petroleum Ltd._ $ 22.00

~~~~ Twenty-two ~~~~~~~~~~~ 00/100 DOLLARS

THE ROYAL BANK OF CANADA
MAIN BRANCH
204 KING STREET WEST
HAMILTON, ONTARIO L9H 4Z9

SULLIVAN REALTY

FOR _Gas bill – June 6_   PER _John Sullivan_

11"000604 1: 05337   123'498'6

8.

S	**SULLIVAN REALTY** 485 KING STREET WEST HAMILTON, ONTARIO L9H 6W3 PHONE (905) 527-1223	605
		June 15 20 **10**

PAY TO THE ORDER OF _Pamela Dawson_ $ 350.00

~~~~ Three hundred fifty ~~~~~~~~~~~~~~~ 00 /100 DOLLARS

THE ROYAL BANK OF CANADA
MAIN BRANCH
204 KING STREET WEST
HAMILTON, ONTARIO L9H 4Z9

SULLIVAN REALTY

FOR _Salary – June 1-15_   PER _John Sullivan_

11"000605 1: 05337   123'498'6

9.

SULLIVAN REALTY				
COMMISSION REPORT			*Date*	June 18, 2010

Name:	East End Land Developers			
Date	*Sales Description*	*Sales No.*	*Commission Amount*	
Jun 18/10	*Lot at 999 King Street East*	*A1002*	*$6,500.00*	
C002			*Remarks:* Payment due July 9, 2010	

10.

SULLIVAN REALTY 485 KING STREET WEST HAMILTON, ONTARIO L9H 6W3 PHONE (905) 527-1223	**606** _June 21_ 20 **10**

PAY TO
THE ORDER OF _John Sullivan_ $ _1,000.00_

~~~ _One thousand_ ~~~~~~~~~~~~~   _00_ /100 DOLLARS

THE ROYAL BANK OF CANADA
MAIN BRANCH
204 KING STREET WEST
HAMILTON, ONTARIO L9H 4Z9   SULLIVAN REALTY

FOR _Withdrawal_   PER _John Sullivan_

⑈000606 ⑈ ⑆ 05337   123'498'6

11a.

CURRENT ACCOUNT
DEPOSIT SLIP

ROYAL BANK

June 21, 2010
DATE

DEPOSITOR'S INITIALS	TELLER'S INITIALS
PD	AS

CREDIT ACCOUNT OF

SULLIVAN REALTY

PLEASE LIST FOREIGN CHEQUES ON A SEPARATE DEPOSIT SLIP

VISA AND CHEQUES		DETAILS	CASH (INCL COUPONS)
	VISA VOUCHER TOTAL		
L. Harrison	3,500 00	X 5	
		X 10	
		X 20	
		X 50	
		X 100	
		X	
		COIN	
		CANADIAN CASH TOTAL	
	3,500 00	VISA & CHQS	3,500 00
U.S. CHQS.		RATE	
U.S. CASH		RATE	
	NET DEPOSIT		3,500 00

⑆ 05337 123'498'6   51

COMPARED WITH ORIGINAL DEPOSIT
SLIP AS TO TOTAL ONLY

11b.

SULLIVAN REALTY

COMMISSION REPORT   _Date_ June 21, 2010

Name: Ms Laura Harrison

Date	Sales Description	Sales No.	Commission Amount	
Jun 21/10	_Home at 842 Alder Road_	_A1003_	_$3,500.00_	_Paid in full._
C003		_Remarks:_		

12.

SULLIVAN REALTY
485 KING STREET WEST
HAMILTON, ONTARIO L9H 6W3
PHONE (905) 527-1223

607

June 22 20 10

PAY TO THE ORDER OF _Anderson Petroleum Ltd._ $ 25.00

~~~ Twenty-five ~~~~~~~~~ 00/100 DOLLARS

THE ROYAL BANK OF CANADA
MAIN BRANCH
204 KING STREET WEST
HAMILTON, ONTARIO L9H 4Z9

SULLIVAN REALTY

FOR _Gas bill - June 22_   PER _John Sullivan_

⑈000607 ⑆ 05337   123'498'6

13a.

AUTO CITY WEST

2674 King Street West
Hamilton, Ontario L9H 1A1
Phone (905) 527-9755; Fax (905) 527-9756

INVOICE

INVOICE NO. WES3750

DATE: June 25/10

TERMS: Cash

To:
Sullivan Realty
485 King Street West
Hamilton, Ontario L9H 6W3

Ship To:
Pickup

QUANTITY		DESCRIPTION	UNIT PRICE	AMOUNT
1	Only	Z75 Air conditioning repair		$ 600.00

Make all cheques payable to Auto City West

PAYMENT RECEIVED - Cheque #608 - Thank you

THANK YOU FOR YOUR BUSINESS!

SUBTOTAL	600.00
FREIGHT	
TAX	
TOTAL DUE	$ 600.00

13b.

SULLIVAN REALTY
485 KING STREET WEST
HAMILTON, ONTARIO L9H 6W3
PHONE (905) 527-1223

608

June 25 20 10

PAY TO THE ORDER OF _Auto City West_ $ 600.00

~~~ Six hundred ~~~~~~~~~~~ 00 /100 DOLLARS

THE ROYAL BANK OF CANADA
MAIN BRANCH
204 KING STREET WEST
HAMILTON, ONTARIO L9H 4Z9

SULLIVAN REALTY

FOR _Automobile repairs - Inv WES3750_   PER _John Sullivan_

⑈000608 ⑆ 05337   123'498'6

14.

SULLIVAN REALTY
485 KING STREET WEST
HAMILTON, ONTARIO L9H 6W3
PHONE (905) 527-1223

609

June 30 20 **10**

PAY TO THE ORDER OF _Pamela Dawson_ $ 350.00

~~~~ Three hundred fifty ~~~~~~~~~~~~~~~~ 00 /100 DOLLARS

THE ROYAL BANK OF CANADA
MAIN BRANCH
204 KING STREET WEST
HAMILTON, ONTARIO L9H 4Z9

SULLIVAN REALTY

FOR _Salary – June 16-30_   PER _John Sullivan_

II⌐000609 I: 05337   123'498'6

15a.

Phones Ontario

#2110 Steel Place
Hamilton, Ontario L9G 4B4
Phone (905) 529-7190
Fax (905) 529-0063

Your Statement

In Account with

SULLIVAN REALTY
485 KING STREET WEST
HAMILTON ON L9H 6W3

Account #09444 710-190

Payment received July 2, 2010 **Phones Ontario**

Billing Period: June 1 to June 30

Payments/Adjustments/Deposits Details
Opened account June 1, 2010. Thank you. $0.00

Monthly rental and changes to service   510.00

Amount now. due
Payment due after July 10, 2010 $522.75   **Total Due** $510.00

15b.

SULLIVAN REALTY
485 KING STREET WEST
HAMILTON, ONTARIO L9H 6W3
PHONE (905) 527-1223

610

June 30 20 **10**

PAY TO THE ORDER OF _Phones Ontario_ $ 510.00

~~~~ Five hundred ten ~~~~~~~~~~ 00/100 DOLLARS

THE ROYAL BANK OF CANADA
MAIN BRANCH
204 KING STREET WEST
HAMILTON, ONTARIO L9H 4Z9

SULLIVAN REALTY

FOR _June phone bill_   PER _John Sullivan_

II⌐000610 I: 05337   123'498'6

16.

```
                            City News
                  85 Main Street, Hamilton, Ontario L9H 0C0
                  Phone (905) 527-1030        Fax (905) 527-1031
                        I N V O I C E

   SOLD TO:    Sullivan Realty            Invoice No.:   4879
               485 King Street West       Date:          June 25, 2010
               Hamilton ON  L9H 6W3       Due Date:      July 5, 2010
```

DATE	DESCRIPTION		AMOUNT
June 25/10	Advertising in City News during June 2010		$1,200.00
		SUBTOTAL	1,200.00

Business Number 944122338
MAKE ALL CHEQUES PAYABLE TO CITY NEWS.

| | TOTAL | $1,200.00 |

Required Work for June

1. Journalize transactions and post to ledger accounts.
2. Prepare a trial balance in the first two columns of the worksheet and complete the worksheet using the following adjustment data:
   a. One month's rent had expired
   b. An inventory shows $50 worth of office supplies remaining
   c. Amortization on office equipment, $100
   d. Amortization on automobile, $200
3. Prepare a June income statement, statement of owner's equity, and balance sheet.
4. From the worksheet, journalize and post adjusting and closing entries (page 3 of journal).
5. Prepare a post-closing trial balance.
   During July, Sullivan Realty completed these transactions:

2010

#17, p. 222	July	2	Paid for June office supplies purchased on account, $150. Cheque No. 611.
#18, p. 222		2	Purchased additional office supplies on account, $700.
#19, p. 222		2	Paid advertising bill for June. Cheque No. 612.
#20a & b, p. 223		5	Sold a house and collected a commission, $6,600.
#21, p. 223		6	Paid for gas for car, $29. Cheque No. 613.
#22, p. 224		9	Collected commission from sale of building lot on June 18.
#23, p. 224		12	Paid $300 to send employees to realtor's workshop. Cheque No. 614.
#24, p. 224		15	Paid the salary of the part-time office secretary, $350. Cheque No. 615.
#25, p. 225		16	Sold a house and earned a commission of $2,400. Commission to be received on August 11.
#26a & b, p. 225		19	Sold a building lot and collected a commission of $7,000.
#27, p. 226		23	Sent a cheque for $40 to help sponsor a local road race to aid the poor. (This is not to be considered an advertising expense, but it is a business expense.) Cheque No. 616.
#28a & b, p. 226		26	Paid for repairs to automobile, $590. Cheque No. 617.
#29, p. 227		27	John Sullivan withdrew $1,800 from the business to pay personal expenses. Cheque No. 618.

#30, p. 227

30 Paid the salary of the part-time office secretary, $350. Cheque No. 619.

#31a & b, pp. 227 & 228 July 30 Paid the July telephone bill, $236. Cheque No. 620.

#32, p. 228 30 Advertising bill for July was received, $1,400. The bill is to be paid in August.

17.

SULLIVAN REALTY
485 KING STREET WEST
HAMILTON, ONTARIO L9H 6W3
PHONE (905) 527-1223

S

611

July 2 20 **10**

PAY TO THE ORDER OF *Office Depot* $ 150.00

~~~ *One hundred fifty* ~~~~~~~~~~~~ 00 /100 DOLLARS

THE ROYAL BANK OF CANADA
MAIN BRANCH
204 KING STREET WEST
HAMILTON, ONTARIO L9H 4Z9

SULLIVAN REALTY

FOR *Invoice #D198825* PER *John Sullivan*

II⌐000611 I: 05337 123'498'6

18.

Office Depot

#53 Niagara Mall
Hamilton, Ontario L9H 1B1
Phone (905) 527-1233, Fax (905) 527-1234

INVOICE

DATE: July 2/10
NUMBER: D1996035
TERMS: Cash

SOLD TO:	SHIPPED TO:
Sullivan Realty 485 King Street West Hamilton, Ontario L9H 6W3	Sullivan Realty 485 King Street West

DATE	DESCRIPTION	UNIT PRICE	AMOUNT
July 2/10	Office supplies		$700.00
		Subtotal	700.00
		Total	$700.00

Business Number: 115555559

THANK YOU FOR YOUR BUSINESS

PLEASE PAY THE ABOVE

19.

SULLIVAN REALTY
485 KING STREET WEST
HAMILTON, ONTARIO L9H 6W3
PHONE (905) 527-1223

S

612

July 2 20 **10**

PAY TO THE ORDER OF *City News* $ 1,200.00

~~~ *One thousand two hundred* ~~~~~~~~~ 00 /100 DOLLARS

THE ROYAL BANK OF CANADA
MAIN BRANCH
204 KING STREET WEST
HAMILTON, ONTARIO L9H 4Z9

SULLIVAN REALTY

FOR *Invoice #4879* PER *John Sullivan*

II⌐000612 I: 05337 123'498'6

20a.

SULLIVAN REALTY				
COMMISSION REPORT			**Date** July 5, 2010	
Name:	Mr. and Mrs. Andrew Tran			
Date	*Sales Description*	*Sales No.*	*Commission Amount*	
July 5/10	*Home at 1014 Cedar Lane*	*A1004*	*$6,600.00*	*Paid in full.*
C004		*Remarks:*		

20b.

CURRENT ACCOUNT DEPOSIT SLIP **ROYAL BANK**	PLEASE LIST FOREIGN CHEQUES ON A SEPARATE DEPOSIT SLIP			
	VISA AND CHEQUES		DETAILS	CASH (INCL COUPONS)
		VISA VOUCHER TOTAL		
	A. Tran	6,6000 00	X 5	
July 5, 2010			X 10	
DATE			X 20	
			X 50	
DEPOSITOR'S INITIALS / TELLER'S INITIALS			X 100	
PD / MG			X	
CREDIT ACCOUNT OF			COIN	
			CANADIAN CASH TOTAL	
SULLIVAN REALTY		6,600 00	VISA & CHQS	6,600 00
	U.S. CHQS.		RATE	
	U.S. CASH		RATE	
		NET DEPOSIT		6,600 00
I: 05337 123'498'6 51			COMPARED WITH ORIGINAL DEPOSIT SLIP AS TO TOTAL ONLY	

21.

S	**SULLIVAN REALTY** 485 KING STREET WEST HAMILTON, ONTARIO L9H 6W3 PHONE (905) 527-1223	**613**
		July 6 20 **10**
PAY TO THE ORDER OF	*Anderson Petroleum Ltd.*	$ 29.00
	Twenty-nine	00/100 DOLLARS
THE ROYAL BANK OF CANADA MAIN BRANCH 204 KING STREET WEST HAMILTON, ONTARIO L9H 4Z9		SULLIVAN REALTY
FOR *Gas bill – July 6*	PER	*John Sullivan*
II"000613 I: 05337 123'498'6		

22.

CURRENT ACCOUNT DEPOSIT SLIP **ROYAL BANK**	PLEASE LIST FOREIGN CHEQUES ON A SEPARATE DEPOSIT SLIP			
	VISA AND CHEQUES		DETAILS	CASH (INCL COUPONS)
		VISA VOUCHER TOTAL		
	East End		X 5	
	Land		X 10	
July 9, 2010 / DATE	Developers	6,500.00	X 20	
			X 50	
DEPOSITOR'S INITIALS — PD / TELLER'S INITIALS — MG			X 100	
			X	
CREDIT ACCOUNT OF			COIN	
			CANADIAN CASH TOTAL	
SULLIVAN REALTY		6,500 00	VISA & CHQS	6,500 00
	U.S. CHQS.		RATE	
	U.S. CASH		RATE	
			NET DEPOSIT	6,500 00

I: 05337 123'498'6   51

COMPARED WITH ORIGINAL DEPOSIT SLIP AS TO TOTAL ONLY

23.

SULLIVAN REALTY
485 KING STREET WEST
HAMILTON, ONTARIO L9H 6W3
PHONE (905) 527-1223

614

July 12 20 10

PAY TO THE ORDER OF   Hamilton Realtors' Association $ 300.00

~~~ Three hundred ~~~~~~~~~~~~   00 /100 DOLLARS

THE ROYAL BANK OF CANADA
MAIN BRANCH
204 KING STREET WEST
HAMILTON, ONTARIO L9H 4Z9

SULLIVAN REALTY

FOR   Workshop registration   PER   John Sullivan

II"000614 I: 05337   123'498'6

24.

SULLIVAN REALTY
485 KING STREET WEST
HAMILTON, ONTARIO L9H 6W3
PHONE (905) 527-1223

615

July 15 20 10

PAY TO THE ORDER OF   Pamela Dawson $ 350.00

~~~ Three hundred fifty ~~~~~~~~~~   00 /100 DOLLARS

THE ROYAL BANK OF CANADA
MAIN BRANCH
204 KING STREET WEST
HAMILTON, ONTARIO L9H 4Z9

SULLIVAN REALTY

FOR   Salary – July 1-15   PER   John Sullivan

II"000615 I: 05337   123'498'6

25.

SULLIVAN REALTY				
COMMISSION REPORT			**DATE** July 16, 2010	
Name:	Mr. Hans Hollemeyer			
Date	*Sales Description*	*Sales No.*	*Commission Amount*	
July 16/10	Home at RR2, Site 3	A1010	$2,400.00	
C005			*Remarks:* Payment due August 11, 2010	

26a.

CURRENT ACCOUNT
DEPOSIT SLIP

ROYAL BANK

July 19, 2010
DATE

DEPOSITOR'S INITIALS	TELLER'S INITIALS
PD	PRL

CREDIT ACCOUNT OF

SULLIVAN REALTY

PLEASE LIST FOREIGN CHEQUES ON A SEPARATE DEPOSIT SLIP

VISA AND CHEQUES		DETAILS	CASH (INCL COUPONS)
	VISA VOUCHER TOTAL		
B. Game	7,000 00	X 5	
		X 10	
		X 20	
		X 50	
		X 100	
		X	
		COIN	
		CANADIAN CASH TOTAL	
	7,000 00	VISA & CHQS	7,000 00
U.S. CHQS.		RATE	
U.S. CASH		RATE	
NET DEPOSIT			7,000 00

COMPARED WITH ORIGINAL DEPOSIT
SLIP AS TO TOTAL ONLY

I: 05337 123'498'6 51

26b.

SULLIVAN REALTY				
COMMISSION REPORT			*Date* July 19, 2010	
Name:	Mr. and Mrs. Benjamin Game			
Date	*Sales Description*	*Sales No.*	*Commission Amount*	
July 19/10	Building lot at 5004 King St. E	A1005	$7,000.00	*Paid in full.*
C006			*Remarks:*	

27.

S	**SULLIVAN REALTY** 485 KING STREET WEST HAMILTON, ONTARIO L9H 6W3 PHONE (905) 527-1223	**616** *July 23* 20 *10*

PAY TO THE ORDER OF _*Mustard Seed Ministries*_ $ 40.00

~~~ Forty ~~~~~~~~~~~~~~~~~~~~~~   00/100 DOLLARS

THE ROYAL BANK OF CANADA
MAIN BRANCH
204 KING STREET WEST
HAMILTON, ONTARIO L9H 4Z9   SULLIVAN REALTY

FOR _*Aid to the poor*_   PER _*John Sullivan*_

II⊓000616 I: 05337   123'498'6

28a.

AUTO CITY WEST

2674 King Street West
Hamilton, Ontario L9H 1A1
Phone (905) 527-9755; Fax (905) 527-9756

INVOICE

INVOICE NO. WES3945

DATE: July 26/10

TERMS: Cash

To: Ship To:

Sullivan Realty
485 King Street West   Pickup
Hamilton, Ontario L9H 6W3

QUANTITY	DESCRIPTION	UNIT PRICE	AMOUNT
	Z75 75,000 km maintenance		$ 590.00

Make all cheques payable to Auto City West

PAYMENT RECEIVED - Cheque #617 - Thank you

SUBTOTAL	590.00
FREIGHT	
TAX	
TOTAL DUE	$ 590.00

THANK YOU FOR YOUR BUSINESS!

28b.

S	**SULLIVAN REALTY** 485 KING STREET WEST HAMILTON, ONTARIO L9H 6W3 PHONE (905) 527-1223	**617** *July 26* 20 *10*

PAY TO THE ORDER OF _*Auto City West*_ $ 590.00

~~~ Five hundred ninety ~~~~~~~~~~~~   00 /100 DOLLARS

THE ROYAL BANK OF CANADA
MAIN BRANCH
204 KING STREET WEST
HAMILTON, ONTARIO L9H 4Z9   SULLIVAN REALTY

FOR _*Automobile repairs – Inv. WES3945*_   PER _*John Sullivan*_

II⊓000617 I: 05337   123'498'6

29.

SULLIVAN REALTY
485 KING STREET WEST
HAMILTON, ONTARIO L9H 6W3
PHONE (905) 527-1223

618

July 27 20 10

PAY TO THE ORDER OF _John Sullivan_ $ 1,800.00

~~~ One thousand eight hundred ~~~~~~~~~~   00 /100 DOLLARS

THE ROYAL BANK OF CANADA
MAIN BRANCH
204 KING STREET WEST
HAMILTON, ONTARIO L9H 4Z9

SULLIVAN REALTY

FOR _Withdrawal_   PER _John Sullivan_

II'000618 I: 05337   123'498'6

30.

SULLIVAN REALTY
485 KING STREET WEST
HAMILTON, ONTARIO L9H 6W3
PHONE (905) 527-1223

619

July 30 20 10

PAY TO THE ORDER OF _Pamela Dawson_ $ 350.00

~~~ Three hundred fifty ~~~~~~~~~~   00/100 DOLLARS

THE ROYAL BANK OF CANADA
MAIN BRANCH
204 KING STREET WEST
HAMILTON, ONTARIO L9H 4Z9

SULLIVAN REALTY

FOR _Salary – July 16–31_   PER _John Sullivan_

II'000619 I: 05337   123'498'6

31a.

Phones Ontario

#2110 Steel Place
Hamilton, Ontario L9G 4B4
Phone (905) 529-7190
Fax (905) 529-0063

Your Statement

In Account with

SULLIVAN REALTY
485 KING STREET WEST
HAMILTON ON L9H 6W3

Account #09444 710-190

Payment received July 30, 2010
Phones Ontario

Billing Period: July 1 to July 31

Payments/Adjustments/Deposits Details	$510.00
Payment Received July 2. Thank you.	-510.00
Monthly rental and services	236.00
Amount now due	
Payment due after August 9, 2010 $241.90	
Total Due	$236.00

31b.

SULLIVAN REALTY
485 KING STREET WEST
HAMILTON, ONTARIO L9H 6W3
PHONE (905) 527-1223

S

620

July 30 20 *10*

PAY TO
THE ORDER OF *Phones Ontario* $ 236.00

~~~~~ *Two hundred thirty-six* ~~~~~ 00 /100 DOLLARS

THE ROYAL BANK OF CANADA
MAIN BRANCH
204 KING STREET WEST
HAMILTON, ONTARIO L9H 4Z9

SULLIVAN REALTY

FOR *July phone bill* PER *John Sullivan*

II⌐000620 I: 05337 123'498'6

32.

City News

85 Main Street, Hamilton, Ontario L9H 0C0
Phone (905) 527-1030   Fax (905) 527-1031

I N V O I C E

SOLD TO:	Sullivan Realty	Invoice No.:	5400
	485 King Street West	Date:	July 27, 2010
	Hamilton ON L9H 6W3	Due Date:	August 6, 2010

DATE	DESCRIPTION		AMOUNT
July 27/10	Advertising in City News during July 2010		$1,400.00
		SUBTOTAL	1,400.00
Business Number 944122338		TOTAL	$1,400.00

MAKE ALL CHEQUES PAYABLE TO CITY NEWS.

Required Work for July

Ct 1,2,3   Step 1,2,3

Ly's   Step 4,5,6,7

Ct pt

1. Journalize transactions in a general journal (pages 4 and 5) and post to ledger accounts.

2. Prepare a trial balance in the first two columns of the worksheet and complete the worksheet using the following adjustment data:

   a. One month's rent had expired.

   b. An inventory shows $90 worth of office supplies remaining.

   c. Amortization on office equipment, $100

   d. Amortization on automobile, $200

Ct 4   Step 7

3. Prepare a July income statement, statement of owner's equity, and balance sheet.

Ct 5   Ste 8,9

4. From the worksheet, journalize and post adjusting and closing entries (page 6 of journal).

5. Prepare a post-closing trial balance.

Index

Purchases Returns and Allowances, 418, 450

Q

Quebec Pension Plan (QPP), 290, 304
Quebec Pension Plan remittances, 330
QuickBooks®, 285, 291, 642
Q.W. Page Associates, 577

R

rate of pay, 293
ready for use, 603, 604
real accounts, 173, 196
realization/recognition principle, 5
receiving report, 422, 450
recognition. *See* realization/recognition principle
reconciliation, 368
Record of Employment, 297, 297f, 299f, 304
recording transactions
accounting cycle, 84-91
cash payments journal, 430-431
cash receipts journal, 387-388
credit memorandum, 373-374
debits and credits, 46-48
in journal, 84-91
journalizing, 84
payroll, 295-297
synoptic (combined) journal, 476-477, 476f, 481-484
Remers, Gerry, 284
Remittance Form (PD7A), 334-337, 336f, 344
remittance formula, 329, 345
rent paid in advance, 87
Request for a Business Number (Form RC1(E)), 329
residual value, 132, 606, 607, 629
restrictive endorsement, 232
retailer, 363, 395
revenue
defined, 30
described, 14
on income statement, 538
recording of, 14, 16, 89
Unearned Revenue, 509
revenue expenditures, 615
reversing entries, 549-551, 553
Rogers, Jim, 472

S

safekeeping. *See* cheque truncation (safekeeping)
salaries payable account, 134-135
sales
gross sales, 363

net sales, 365, 538
sales discount, 365
Sales Returns and Allowances, 364
sales discount, 365, 373, 395
sales invoice, 369, 380, 395
sales journal
blueprint, 396-397
defined, 395
described, 369
with GST, 381f
posting to general ledger, 370-371
recording to accounts receivable subsidiary ledger, 369-370
sales returns, 373
Sales Returns and Allowances, 364, 372-373, 395
sales tax
Goods and Services Tax. *See* Goods and Services Tax (GST)
Harmonized Sales Tax (HST). *See* Harmonized Sales Tax (HST)
and the Internet, 362
provincial sales tax, 366
sales tax payable, 388
salvage value, 606
see also residual value
Sarbanes-Oxley Act, 2, 30
Sawadsky, Nick, 230
schedule of accounts payable, 430, 440
schedule of accounts receivable, 388, 395
Second Cup, 328
self-constructed capital assets, 624-625
selling expenses, 538, 553
service charges, 237, 239f, 260
service companies
business services, 474
defined, 30
described, 4, 4t
professional services, 474
synoptic (combined) journal, 474-479
shift in assets, 10, 30
shortage, 253-255, 256
signature card, 232, 260
Simply Accounting®, 285, 291, 642
single lines, 58
site restoration costs, 623
skimming, 241
slide, 101, 111
sole proprietorship, 3, 30
special journals
cash payments journal, 427-430, 437-440
cash receipts journal, 385-388, 394, 396-397
defined, 395
described, 367-368

purchases journal, 422
sales journal. *See* sales journal
synoptic (combined) journal. *See* synoptic (combined) journal
spreadsheet software, 129, 482
standard account, 44, 67
Starbucks, 328
Statement of Account, 236
statement of cash flows
blueprint, 654
cash flows from financing activities, 646-647
cash flows from investing activities, 645-646
cash flows from operating activities, 643-645
defined, 653
described, 642
direct method, 647, 648-650, 654
financing activities, 643
indirect method, 642-647, 654
investing activities, 643
noncash investing and financing activities, 643
operating activities, 642
statement of financial position. *See* balance sheet
statement of owner's equity
defined, 30
described, 20-21
ending capital, 144
main elements, 22
merchandising companies, 539
preparation from worksheet, 141
update, 144
stock exchanges, 1
straight-line method, 131, 606, 629
subdivisions of owner's equity, 18
subsidiary ledgers
accounts payable subsidiary ledger, 422, 430-431, 432, 433
accounts receivable subsidiary ledger, 368, 369-370, 375
defined, 395
described, 368-369
Subway, 24-25, 62, 145, 186, 257, 302, 343
sum-of-the-years'-digits method, 608-609, 629
sundry accounts, 385, 395
supplies, 10, 30-31, 87, 140, 474
S.W.I.F.T. codes, 243, 260
synoptic (combined) journal
accrual accounting synoptic journal, 480-481
adjusting journal entries, 481
Art's Wholesale Clothing Company examples, 480-484

chart of accounts, 474-476
closing journal entries, 481
defined, 487
described, 473
electronic spreadsheet, 482
end of month, 481-484
payroll deductions, 477-479
posting, 477, 481-484
purchase of, 474
recording transactions, 476-477, 476f, 481-484
service companies, 474-479
small businesses, 473

T

T account
  and accounting equation, 46-47
  balancing an account, 45
  balancing the equation, 47
  basic parts, 44-45
  credit, 45
  debit, 45
  defined, 67
  described, 44
  ending balance, 45
  footings, 45, 57, 67
  normal balance of an account, 47
T4 slip, 297, 305
T4 Summary, 339, 340f, 345
T4 Supplementary, 297, 305, 345
T4A, 297, 305
take-home pay, 296
tax calendar, 345
taxes
  and bad debts, 587
  capital cost allowance, 131, 609-612
  employer tax remittances. See employer tax remittances
  half-year rule, 610
  income tax. See income tax
  maximum CCA, 611
  sales tax. See sales tax
  undepreciated capital cost (UCC), 611
TD1 forms, 287, 288f, 290, 304
temporary accounts, 173, 185, 196
three-column account, 93, 111

Timothy's, 328
title to goods shipped, 419
TNT International, 503
TONI (Tax on Income), 286, 304-305
trade discounts, 430-431
trade-in allowance, 618, 629
transaction analysis chart, 48-54
transactions
  analysis of, in journal, 84-91
  compound entry, 49, 67
  inside transactions, 129
  recording. See recording transactions
  T account. See T account
transposition, 101, 111
travel industry, 83
trial balance
  adjusted trial balance, 135-138
  common mistakes, 100-102
  correcting the trial balance, 100-102
  corrections after posting, 101
  corrections before posting, 101
  defined, 67, 111
  described, 57-58, 99
  entry posted to wrong account, 102
  financial statements, preparation of, 58, 59f
  incorrect totals, 99
  items not shown, 99-100
  listing order of items, 104
  merchandising company worksheet, 509f
  opening trial balance, 183, 546
  post-closing trial balance, 183, 185, 196, 546
  preparation of, 99-103
  undetected errors, 100
  on worksheet, 129

U

undepreciated capital cost (UCC), 611, 629
Unearned Rent, 506
Unearned Revenue, 509, 518
union agreements, 291
union dues, 291, 305
United Parcel Service, 503

units-of-production method, 607, 629
useful life, 606, 629

V

virtual bank, 240

W

WCB expense, 332, 345
weird jobs, 472
WestJet, 83
wholesalers, 363, 395
Wilson, Chip, 641
withdrawals, 15, 17, 21, 31, 89, 177-178
workers' compensation, 291, 305
Workers' Compensation Board, 332
workers' compensation premium, 341
workers' compensation remittances, 332
worksheet
  accounts on, 128-129
  adjusted trial balance, 135-138
  adjustments section, 129-135
  balance sheet section, 138a
  financial statements, preparation of, 141-143
  function of, 128
  heading, 129
  income statement section, 138
  for merchandising company. See merchandising company worksheet
  net income, placement of, 138
  net loss, placement of, 138
  spreadsheet software, 129
  as tool, 176
  trial balance section, 129
WorldCom, 2
writing down goodwill, 624
writing off uncollectible accounts
  blueprint, 590
  described, 579-580
  direct write-off method, 586-587
  income tax regulations, 587
  using Allowance for Doubtful Accounts, 585-586